Days Out of Doors

DAYS

OUT OF DOORS

BY

CHARLES C. ABBOTT

AUTHOR OF "A NATURALIST'S RAMBLES ABOUT HOME"

NEW YORK
D. APPLETON AND COMPANY
1889

PREFACE.

I AM free to confess that, were our animals as stupid
and machine-like as many observers represent them and
as certain would-be critics assume them to be, I should
not feel tempted to spend my days in a series of more
or less protracted outings continuing through the year,
nor look upon experiment as one whit better than a
pleasing pastime.   But the beasts and birds, reptiles,
fishes, and "such small deer" are nothing of the kind,
and their intelligence still not only offers a wide field
for study, but adds a zest to every contemplative stroll.

Strictly inanimate nature is, for me, far less exhilarating.   "Antres vast and deserts idle" figure better in
poetry than in fact, and the lifeless wastes of the world
offer little that has roused my enthusiasm so promptly
as some familiar field with its scattered sparrows, and
perchance a bluebird on the rude worm fence; and as
yet I have no fear that at last there will be no novelty
and my well-tramped fields will pall.

"To-morrow they will wear another face."

Not only the

> " ragged cliff
> Has thousand faces in a thousand hours,"

but this I find true of the tamest pasture, where not even the clover and buttercups of one side are the twins of the buttercups and clover of the other; and think of the bees, birds, beetles, and butterflies that come and go! These, I know, are not the same, yesterday, to-day, and forever.

Whether it be the crested tit defying the chilliest blast of January; violets mantling the meadow banks in April; thrushes singing their farewell summer songs, or dull and dreary dim December days it matters not—they never repeat themselves, or else I am daily a new creature. Nor sight nor sound but has the freshness of novelty, and one rambler, at least, in his maturer years is still a boy at heart.

If one could take an airy, bird's-eye view of this level country, he would see, more prominently than all other features, save one, a sinuous, leafy serpent, miles in length, with gaping jaws upon the shore of the river, and a delicate, thread-like tail, afar in the outstretched fields. It is the valley of a near-by creek.

One has nowhere more than a few rods to walk back from the stream to find either fields, gardens, or the public road; but such a walk! It is a wilderness that woos the birds; it is a wild wood that protects the beast; it is the haunt of many a creeping thing, squat toad, sleek frog, and slippery salamander. Much as has been written of it, far more remains well worthy of recording. Or, looking northward, one traces from the distant mountains trending toward the sea the more pretentious valley of the river. Here I have found a new country, teeming with delights. Its wreck-strewed shores, its sandy beaches which the tide lays bare, its wild and wasting islands and open reaches of wind-troubled waters, have alike held me as the days rolled by. And so it happens that, after many a ramble in far-off regions, where rocks, lakes, rivers, and boundless pine barrens offered endless novelty, it was ever a pleasure to return to the unpretending creek and modest river, and spend my days with "old familiar faces."

Perhaps,

> "Because I was content with these poor fields,
> Low, open meads, slender and sluggish streams,
> And found a home in haunts which others scorned,
> The partial wood-gods overpaid my love
> And granted me the freedom of their state";

the world seemed more full of meaning here. Therefore I hold that one need not mope because he has to stay at home. Trees grow here as suggestively as in California; and the water of our river is very wet. Remember, too, if trees are not tall enough to suit your whim, to lie down beneath the branches of any one of them, and, as you look up, the topmost twig pierces the sky. There is not an oak but will become a giant sequoia in this way.

One need learn no magic to bring the antipodes home to him.

For permission to reprint portions of several of the following chapters the author is indebted to the publishers of "Harper's Young People," of the "Popular Science Monthly," of "Garden and Forest," and of "The American," of Philadelphia.

C. C. Abbott.

Prospect Hill, Trenton, N. J.,
   March 20, 1889.

CONTENTS.

Jan 1st, 1903.
135 Warren L

DAYS OUT OF DOORS.

CHAPTER I.

JANUARY.

BECAUSE our Indians happened to call January *Anixi gischuch*, or the Squirrel Moon, I do not expect to find these animals at all abundant, even if it is mild at New Year's, or later when we have the thaw said to be characteristic of the month. Why the Indians associated the month with squirrels can not be determined, but, as this people's language far antedates their coming to the Delaware Valley, it had to do, doubtless, with the squirrels of some other region. Certainly, those of the home hill-side have no predilection for the middle of winter, and if it be very cold are as soundly asleep as any typically hibernating mammal. They appear to sleep for much more protracted periods than do the flying squirrels. And now a word about an indoor outing when flying squirrels figured prominently. As the weather was intolerably bad, I compromised matters by spending a half-day in the garret; and this, by the way, is a part of every country house that, even if but a century old, is a hunting-ground not to be despised. Particularly is true when the house has remained from generation to generation in the same family. But it is only with reference to a single zoölogical aspect that I refer to the garret at home, although its fauna is quite extensive. Certainly the environment is favorable for the non-social wasps, and, judged by their effective work, their stings are developed out of all proportion to their bodies, and triply envenomed.

But that January day. It neither rained nor snowed, but both. There was no steady wind from some one point, but stinging blasts that came from every quarter. It was neither warm nor cold, but chilling to a degree that made all wraps unavailable. I stayed at home.

It had been whispered about that strange noises were sometimes heard in the attic, and I proposed now to investigate the matter. Somewhere between the roof and the ceiling, in a long and narrow, densely darkened space, the flying squirrels that have made my house their home for many years were now cozily quartered. Of this I was sure. They could not, it seemed to me, have suspended a nest from the rafters; so their only alternative of resting upon the plastering made it easy for me to locate them. With a little hammer, I tapped upon every square inch of that ceiling, and then listened for some response. If I thought I heard such, I tapped still harder, and so continued, going over the same ground many times, until at last I found the spot. Here every blow of the hammer elicited a growl-like squeak, and I knew that the squirrels were not only there, but awake.

Having advanced thus far in my explorations, I rested from my labors. No, I merely endeavored to do so. It happened that my incessant but, as I thought, gentle hammering excited considerable curiosity, if not fear, in the mind of an interested party on the lower floor, and, as I was about to descend thereto to announce my unqualified success, I heard approaching footsteps, which, without knowing why, I desired to avoid, but was hemmed in, and could but wait and wonder. The expression of my unwelcome visitor, as she gazed at what I too now saw was a damaged ceiling, was very dramatic. While at work I was not aware that I had broken any plaster, but I know it now, and have learned never to mention a syllable about sacrifices in the cause of science. Oh! the unutterable scorn when last I did so!

After the skies had cleared and I dared return to the garret, I failed, to my intense disgust, to remember the precise spot over which the squirrels were found to be resting. The unfortunate hammer-marks were in bewildering proximity, and I dared not repeat percussion as a means of locating the animals. While wondering what to do next, I was startled by a strange, half-musical humming, as of an Æolian harp that was muffled. There was no distinct utterance, but so rapid a succession of quick cries that to distinguish any one was impossible. The volume of sound increased perceptibly, and then very slowly died away. The moment it ceased another squirrel took it up, and so what I believe to have been a half-dozen squirrels sang in rapid succession.

Listening under such disadvantageous circumstances, I can not well be sure of anything I heard, but I feel convinced that in this particular of different individuals taking up and repeating the song I am right. Indeed, it is hard to believe that the same squirrel could have repeated these prolonged sounds six times in such quick succession.

On attempting, later, to dislodge these squirrels, I found them on the alert, and no sooner was their nest overturned than away they scampered in all directions. The nest was a mass of paper and rags, the former torn or nibbled into bits about the size of beech-leaves. Near by were the empty shells of a few hickory-nuts, gathered, not from the meadows, but from the little store which, in October, had been spread upon the garret floor.

The squirrels were evidently not seriously incommoded by their unceremonious eviction, as in a short time after I

retired they returned and reconstructed their nest in the
same spot. From underneath I could hear the patter of
their busy feet and the rustling of the scattered papers,
but not a squeak or sound of any kind; and from that
day until late in April they continued to sleep and sing—
active and noisy when the nights were warm, and still as
death during the winter, whenever the mercury sank low.
But their noise at night was not a vocal one, the singing
I have mentioned being wholly a diurnal phenomenon.
During the day, when the squirrels were evidently not
moving about, they appeared to rouse from their slumbers
and sing, one after the other, and then relapse into
silence.

But enough of indoor outings, even in January.
While it is not so suggestive a month as most of the
others, it is not without certain features that are ever welcome to the rambler; and one feels more content with
extremely cold weather at this time than if it comes earlier or later. The fact is, the season is but ten days old
at New Year's, and speculation is curiously active as to the
weather that is to be. No two of my neighbors agree,
each "goin' by a sure sign," and, of course, a different
one. All prove wrong, yet each swears the next spring,
he "hit it exactly."

As evidence that I am not misrepresenting rural
humanity, let us consider for a moment the view taken by
many of my neighbors of the ever-expected but really uncertain, if not mythical, January thaw. Our winters, as
we well know, are budgets of meteorological uncertainties.
While I write I am listening to warbling bluebirds, and
there are yet green leaves peeping above the sered sod of
the meadows; and beyond, a long train of laden coal-cars
is passing by, each car with its freight of dusky diamonds
capped with a deep covering of glistening snow. The
many warm showers that we have had of late have been

snow-squalls on the mountains. Here, the meadows and uplands alike have been bare for days, save a few thread-like remnants of the deeper drifts; and now we are having that spring-like interim which all know as a " January thaw."

I can find no descriptive reference to this feature of the year's first month, nor can date the origin of the familiar phrase.

Let but a little noonday warmth moisten the tapering tip of an icicle, and the village weather-prophet straight-way predicts a coming thaw; but just what degree of mildness and how much melting of snow and ice is ne-cessary to make the thaw a typical one remains to be de-termined. Certainly, it very seldom happens that all frost disappears if the preceding December has been cold.

That I might gather information on the subject, I re-cently visited two places near by, where the graybeards of the neighborhood most do congregate—the cross-roads smithy and the tavern opposite.

I found Benajah Bush at the former, and fortunately in a communicative mood. " Do we always have a Janu-ary thaw?" I asked.

" Yes," he promptly replied, and then added, " no; not always, but most generally."

" What is the January thaw?" I then asked.

" Why, it's what we're havin' now; a regular break-up, and the snow gone and the river open"; and then, after a pause, he added, " We're pretty sure to have it, as I've noticed for the last sixty years."

" But it often happens," I replied, " that we have no winter until Christmas; and how are we to have a thaw, if there has been no freezing?"

" That's so, and them's the years that we skip the thaw," Benajah remarked, meditatively.

" And it's the case in about one half of our winters, so

I can't count you one of our weather-wise folks," and with this ungracious parting shot I skipped over to the tavern.

In the bar-room of the White Horse I found Asa Thorngate sitting near the stove, and I asked him the same question and got much the same reply that Benajah had given, but he added the one important item that " you can't calc'late on the winters as we used to when I was young."

" Why not ? " I asked.

" Because the snow used to come early; sometimes late in the fall and lie on the ground until well on in March. It was winter steady, and you could put up wheels and travel on runners the whole season."

" And didn't you have any January thaw ? " I asked.

" Oh, yes; pretty regular, and the ground would be clean—"

" You would go sleighing on bare ground then ? " I interrupted.

Garrulous old Asa looked up with a puzzled expression, and was about to explain, but I did not wait; and now, after thinking it over, have concluded that the distinction between a January thaw and a " warm spell " in December or a " break-up " in February is insignificant; and that the one is about as likely to occur as either of the others, and not one whit more so.

A January thaw, to be a prominent feature of the month, is necessarily dependent upon the degree of frost prevailing during December. If the latter month is mild, with little or no snow, then the still milder weather after New Year's will produce no very marked effect. Fortunately, it sometimes happens that there is considerable snow and a firmly frozen river in December, and then the typical thaw terminates with a midwinter freshet, often disastrous, it is true, but sure to open up a charming new world to the outdoor naturalist.

Along the river, and in every pent valley of the smaller creeks, is enacted an exciting drama. Animal life, that long since withdrew into snug quarters to await the coming spring, or had cozy retreats from tempestuous weather and ventured abroad only when the day or night was fair, is alike now turned out of house and home, and put to its wits' ends to find a place of safety.

Occasionally, I have known a hollow, globular nest of closely matted grass, filled with the tightly curled body of a soundly sleeping jumping mouse, to roll from the crumbling bank of a creek, and, as it was borne along toward the river, the occupant to be roused by the encroaching water. One such poor creature was plucky and struggled bravely to reach the shore, but only to find its strength exhausted, and my subsequent careful nursing could not save its life. There is no staying power in these little bodies to withstand so great a change, and I am surprised that they should ever rouse from a torpid condition under such circumstances.

Very different is it, however, with the omnipresent meadow mice. They bob up serenely to the surface when the flood covers their grassy runways, and, swimming with ease, spend their time in voyages of discovery, making every floating object that will sustain their weight a port. When you approach them, they await your coming until nearly within your reach, and then dive abruptly, sinking from sight as though suddenly turned to lead. On the other hand, the poor shrews, although not timid when about the water in summer, and active enough in winter when their coats are dry, find the current too swift and bewildering, and often succumb after swimming a few rods.

The reptile world at this time is represented by the familiar water-snakes, and they, too, are well worthy of a moment's notice. All know, I presume, how sensitive to

cold are serpents generally. This species is one, at least,
that is not helpless when plunged into icy waters, and has
no idea of soaking to death when a January thaw sub-
merges its winter quarters. Why they are disturbed by it
at all I do not know, for they hibernate in mud and not in
dry earth. However, the freshet brings many to the surface, and their activity adds to the attractiveness of the
flooded meadows. They are not so quick-motioned as in
midsummer, but rarely are caught napping, even by the
wary crows, which enjoy harassing them upon every occasion, yet never, or very seldom, kill and devour them.

Insect life likewise is roused from its slumbers and
probably no time is so favorable to gather beetles as when
they are floated to the shore by the rising waters. I have
seen the meadow margin lined with them, and hundreds of
specimens could be gathered of species rarely to be found
at any other time.

All predatory animals that withstand the rigor of winter look upon the January thaw as their annual jubilee.
Minks, musk-rats, hawks, and crows, particularly, are ever
on the alert for the benumbed mice, snakes, turtles, and
insects that are now, if not helpless, at least at a great
disadvantage. All day long they are prowling along the
shores of the new-born lake and congregate on the little
islands that are formed by the knolls. While eager to
prey, they are mindful that their arch-enemy, man, may
prey upon them; so they keep out of sight when danger
threatens, and the naturalist must be cautious indeed as
he rambles over the submerged meadows. But if so, then
every moment will prove precious and no day too long,
and if the day is followed by a moonlit night, then will his
cup of happiness be filled to the very brim.

The last January freshet, while not remarkable for the
depth of the overspreading waters, all the higher meadows remaining uncovered, had the great merit of con-

tinuing several days, and so gave me an opportunity of exploring it at all points, and by night as well as by day. Many a wide tract was too shallow even for a canoe, but here I could wade with safety. This method of rambling proved much more tedious than ordinary walking, but had advantages that well repaid the extra exertion.

I proved a puzzle to every creature I met, when wading through these shallow waters, for, except a few ducks, none seemed positively afraid. I kept my coat wrapped closely about me, having learned from the late Richard Jefferies that nothing so frightens an animal as our swaying arms; and I moved so evenly that the water was but slightly agitated. So, whether I was man or log, was a problem solved by few of the many creatures that I met.

As might be expected, I disturbed many meadow mice that were as active in the water as though strictly aquatic animals, and it was evident that the permanent change of environment would not render this species extinct. Certainly, animals so little incommoded by freshets as are these mice would have great advantages over the other mice that are found here, if radically altered conditions were brought about. As they swam, dived, and crouched at the roots of the bunched weeds and grasses, they looked like and constantly suggested pygmy musk-rats. This is the more interesting because these creatures are by no means confined to the meadows, but are abundant in the highest and driest of upland fields, where even drinking-water, except the dew, must be hard to find.

During my longest stroll I found no larger game than the mice I have mentioned, until in the very middle of a wide meadow, where the water was less than a foot deep, I overtook a musk-rat—one of the largest and blackest that I have ever seen. I thoroughly enjoyed the animal's discomfiture, and I can vividly recall its look of defiance

2

and occasional demoniacal grin. The water was too deep for it to run rapidly upon the ground, and too weedy to allow it to swim with ordinary speed. Its alternated efforts to effect escape in either way were extremely ludicrous. I think it soon saw the utter hopelessness of averting the supposed danger by such means, hence the bold face that it put on from time to time.

In this case, as in many another, despair led to desperation, and reckless bravery became the impelling force. As the timid bird will unhesitatingly attack its most dangerous foe in defense of its mate or young, so mammals like the musk-rat show absolutely no fear at times when their ordinary means of defense or of escaping danger are evidently of no avail. If we study almost any of our higher animals under such conditions, the evidence that their thought-power is really considerable when roused to its extreme of action is very apparent, and often stands them successfully in need. Either this, or, like the stupid opossum, they are overcome with fear, and so through mental weakness fall a victim where more intelligent animals might escape. I have seen a flying squirrel, when surprised by a cat, throw itself into every conceivable position, and change from one to another with such rapidity, uttering sharp cries all the while, that the cat was not only bewildered, but actually so alarmed as to beat a hasty retreat. Here, indeed, fear led the squirrel slightly beyond the bounds of reason, as the violent efforts continued for a few seconds after the danger was over. The effect of this was not, as might be thought, to seriously affect the squirrel's nervous system or result in fatal collapse. After a brief rest the plucky little fellow was able to climb to a high branch of a tree, and from it fly to its nest in another, some distance off.

It may be claimed that this was purely hysterical and meaningless; it appeared to me at the time, and I still re-gard it, as designed for the purpose that it accomplished, namely, the cat's discomfiture.

To return to the musk-rat. I continually headed it off, and did not notice at the time that in spite of my movements it pursued the same general direction. Often I was startled by the mighty leaps it made, not quite clearing the water, but so disturbing it that for the moment I lost sight of it in the commotion. Whenever I approached very near, and stooped as though to touch it, the rat would show its teeth and look more ferociously than ever, but utter no sound. Even when it came to a hassock or thickset growth of weeds it made no attempt to dive, but once, on the contrary, climbed quite above the water, upon a low projecting stump, and squatted upon its hind-legs, as though to see what chance, if any, offered to rid itself of my obnoxious presence. Certainly, the controlling emotion of the animal was intense anger and a determination to frighten me, rather than that of fear, which under such circumstances would have overcome its discretion and rendered it helpless.

Perhaps the cunning rat knew the geography of the meadows better than I, for, as it proved, a deep and wide ditch was soon reached, and when I was quite off my guard the animal gave one desperate plunge and disappeared; an effort on its part so vehement that it may well be described as—explosive.

I must confess to the cruelty of my actions in all this, for the mental suffering of the musk-rat was doubtless intense. "Suppose I had been teased in this manner by a cougar or bear," I said to myself, and, as I walked away, resolved in the future to be more merciful.

But this spring-like mildness and the accompanying freshet is but a transient feature of the month, and often within the same week come bleak winter days. How full of meaning is that short word "bleak"! It suggests every discomfort of a winter day. It means that the world is cloud-wrapped, and sunshine but a memory. It means the relentless north wind buffeting the forest; the face of the upland fields scoured with eddying clouds of sand and snow. The traveler, turning his back to the world, scans the southern sky 'twixt hope and fear; for when winter days are really bleak it indeed needs sharp eyes to spy out each shadowy promise of relief. Such was a recent day, when from my cozy corner the familiar outlook was wholly forbidding. But for hours I had wondered what of the wild life that only yesterday had made merry the same scenes. Was every creature now a victim of despair, crouching soulless and dumb in some safe shelter? or could it be the fields, wood, and meadows were deserted?

Summoning all my courage, I sought the frozen meadows as probably the least dreary spot within reach, for there the winds were stayed by the winding terrace with its towering trees; and while yet on the hill-side, thinking, I know not why, of shrews, I found fresh leaves. Wintergreen, bright as May blossoms, dotted here and there the ground, and above them waved the ranker foliage of sassafras and bay. How weak to impute our own want of courage to all Nature!

> I need but seek some sheltered nook
>   The giant oaks atween,
> And, spite the chilly northern blast,
>   I find some trace of green.
> Some hopeful flower, brave of heart,
>   Makes glad the lonely spot,
> And cheerless Winter's deadly grasp
>   On Nature is forgot.

I had been thinking of shrews, and now, strangely enough, from a narrow snow-drift suddenly a black speck appeared. It immediately became larger, and assumed definite shape. It was a shrew. When fairly upon the surface of the snow, the little creature commenced leaping in different directions, as though desirous only of stretching its limbs. I was several paces off, and, eager to have a closer view, cautiously drew nearer. A single step taken, and the wary creature stood up in a nearly erect position, much as a squirrel might do, then dived into some small opening in the drift. Every movement suggested that the creature was largely guided by the sense of sight; yet, they are held to depend upon hearing almost entirely; and, too, they are nocturnal creatures. However, the day was as gloomy if not as dark as night.

I can make nothing of these animals. It is by mere chance that I ever see them, and yet the cats continually bring them from the hill-side, leaving them on the porches or the garden walk. I recently chased one, as I thought, into the heaped-up leaves that filled an angle of a worm fence, but could not find it, until, on reaching home, it was discovered, dead, in a pocket of my overcoat. How it got there I can only conjecture. However bleak the day, then, there is at least one form of mammalian life astir.

The creaking of the wind-tossed branches overhead was by no means assuring as I passed to the open meadows; but courage revived when I heard the defiant cry of the crested tit. Did the world know this bird better, there would be fewer cowards. At the very outset of my proposed walk my steps were stayed. A prominent feature of the meadows here was a relic of the very recent past. The last January freshet was a very transient phenomenon; it came and went in a day or two, and within a week was forgotten by half the neighborhood; but the beach-mark still remains, and standing afar off, this sinuous, dull gray line, the free-hand autograph of the recent flood, is pretty as a whole and tells a winsome story. Drawing near, I saw with what strange ink had this one been written. Sun-dried mud, dead grass, twigs, stranded bushes, and here and there a drowned animal, were well blended, strange as it may seem, and as a whole were quite in place, as they wound, like a ragged ribbon, along the hill.

If but merely glanced at, nothing could be found more in keeping with a bleak winter day than this relic of the recent flood. Every object you saw—leaf, twig, or animal—was dead. So, too, has seemed the whole world as seen from my study windows. But upon stirring the matted mass it proved to be harboring life in many forms. The sunshine of preceding days had been stored up here, and throughout the maze many creatures of many kinds found all things favorable for active existence. Almost the first leaf that I overturned disturbed a gaunt, grim spider, that mounted a short projecting twig and glared back at me with a torrid rather than a frigid countenance. Deeper in the drifted mass, where the trickling waters of a little spring had formed a shallow pool, were numbers of a long, lithe, yellow salamanders, which I had not found before, and so had held were not to be included in our fauna. I forgot for the time that others might have been more fortunate, as was the case, and so my denial was on a par with that of many critics, for with them denial is about their only stock in trade.

Even insect life was not wanting, and small black beetles that had outlived the summer were abundant, as well as the dried bodies of many that had droned through hot August nights, and hidden themselves away when the early frosts of autumn had chilled them to the core.

My dictionary defines " bleak " as " cold, open, exposed, cheerless, and solitary "; the sum, in short, of all outdoor miseries; and perhaps the meadows will prove to be typically bleak. So I thought, but as I wandered on, as far as the bank of the river, and even over the rough ice that now hides the wide stream from view, I found no spot as terrible as the definition implies. Everywhere it was cold, open, and exposed, but never cheerless and solitary. Scarcely had I crossed the beach-mark than twittering tree-sparrows came floating through the air, each breaking the silence as it reached the earth, as though bearing a dainty sleigh-bell on its breast.

Even the frozen river was not bleak. It proved to be a favorite hunting-ground of the omnipresent crow, and, however funereal in appearance itself, no bird more effectually dispels the gloom. As seen against the dazzling whiteness of the snow-dusted ice, the crows were very prominent objects, and I felt that I had companions while walking over the river, now a new pasture for me, if not for them.

Judging from their constant clamor—for each had unrestricted freedom of speech—these crows were happy as if at the end of a feast; but it is not always so, as I have known the ice to prove very tantalizing, if I mistook not one poor bird's feelings upon a certain occasion. Lately I chanced upon a solitary crow, without being seen by it. I was passing at the time through a little wood, walking upon the frozen creek that divided it. The ice was clear as crystal and every object on the bed of the stream was plainly to be seen. The crow before me was held by some strong influence to a particular spot. At times it gazed solemnly upon or through the ice; then walked round and round, as though looking for some opening therein; then, returning to the fascinating spot, again looked steadfastly down.

I was quickly curious to know what the attraction might be, and approached the troubled bird. It was loath to leave, and flew reluctantly toward the meadows, cawing petulantly as it left the wood. I found beneath the ice, where the crow had lingered, the skinned body of a muskrat, lodged in so appropriate a spot as a bed of mussels. A tempting feast, this, for the hungry crow, which was puzzling its poor brains to determine why such plenty should be left in full view, and yet inaccessible. Every movement of the crow suggested that it was thinking; certainly it was determined to reach that food, if within its power. There are those who insist that birds can not think. I would that all such could have seen this crow. No single act bore special evidence of thought, but the bird's whole manner spoke volumes.

And toward the close of day, when most birds were at rest, from a still open spring-hole started a great blue heron. It flew slowly and sadly, as though it felt the cold, but did not complain. That day is not bleak when I can stand on the lee side of a broad oak and see this stately heron watching the opening waters for unwary frogs. And it is not an uncommon winter sight.

But these cold, sunless days with chilling winds, that seem so bleak to many, are often but the forerunners of other days—days of most marvelous beauty. Since my last outing, an interim of warmth and much rain, filling the hours of a long winter night, was quickly followed by the returning north wind, and at sunrise the whole world was encrystaled. Not even the tiniest twig nor any slender blade of last year's grass but was incased with ice and sparkling as never did fairy cave in our wildest flight of fancy; and with all this was music. The linnets, finding no sure footing in the trees, sang as they drifted in the fitful wind. And later, when the woods resounded with a bell-like shower of falling crystals, the bluebirds caught the spirit of the hour and warbled along the forest's vaulted paths.

In fact, birds were nowhere wanting; and from what strange places they sometimes appeared! Tilted cakes of ice covered the sloping banks of a creek I lately crossed, and from a wide crevice came a winter wren, quick-winged and restless as its summer-tide cousins of my door-yard.

And afar off, hopping amid the stranded rubbish upon the river's bank, are song-sparrows that find our winters passing good, if their daily singing voices their content.

Herein, then, lies the merit of our winter—it does not leave us to grope about in silence; for the rustling of dead leaves, the cracking of great trees or of the ground during intense cold, and the booming of the ice-bound river, alone, are but hollow mockeries, but coupled with the songs of our many winter birds each is a soul-stirring melody.

So seldom do we have a really deep and long-lasting snow that when one comes the familiar fields have all the charm of a new country. I speak advisedly when I say that a deep snow is unusual, and, having the records of a hundred years, fear no damaging contradiction. The geology of the region has something to do with this, for the higher and colder clay soils to the north and west are often deeply covered when there is little or no snow here. Often does it happen that we have a cold and sleety rain when the ground is white scarcely five miles away. Therefore it is that my more distant neighbors have the snow buntings in abundance when not one comes near us; and often across the river, in the dark, rocky woods, the crossbills throng the thickset cedars, while I look for them in vain along the home hill-side. So every petty area has its own attractions to the birds, and where the snow lies longest and the vegetation best recalls their northern homes will our winter visitants most surely be found. In the home fields a really deep snow is so far uncommon that I honestly love it.

I have in mind one such, in January—a very marvel of a midwinter storm. There were no huge drifts and desolate areas of naked ground, but every space and tree and tiny twig was weighted to the utmost: this, in brief, the effect of the storm that continued during the silent

hours of the night; and then, the day following, a flood
of brilliant sunshine.

> " Firm-braced I sought my ancient woods,
> Struggling through the drifted roads;
> The whited desert knew me not;
> Snow-ridges masked each darling spot;
> The summer dells, by genius haunted,
> One arctic moon had disenchanted."

The deathlike stillness of the mantled woods, with
their trackless paths leading from hushed to silent soli-
tudes, repelled at first, but the ever-present feeling that one
is never absolutely alone led me on, and I crept beneath
the bent branches that arched above me; at every step
hoping some companion, however humble, would, after its
fashion, greet me "good morning." But at times my
faith wavered till I could have kissed a snake. Nature
was under a powerful anæsthetic, and I should soon have
felt the same influence had the silence continued. This
was not to be. Pausing at the partly bared roots of an
enormous oak, I thrust my cane into the little cave beyond
them, and disturbed a lazy opossum that had sought its
shelter. I was not surprised, for the creature had been
reported to me. As usual, it made no resistance, nor effort
to escape. Prodding it until it started to move away, I
followed slowly, watching the curious gait it assumed, as
though endeavoring to avoid sinking into the soft snow
and so become helpless. All the while, the whip-like tail
of the animal trailed upon the snow, and left a slightly
tortuous line, as distinctly marked as the creature's foot-
prints.

I was delighted to have the company even of an opossum, although I have always insisted that the animal is
very foolish, if not a downright fool. Nor do I expect to
recant. Naturally, I recalled the musk-rat with which I
had rambled in the meadows, and every comparison was

in favor of the rat. To have gone very far, however, would have proved as monotonous as the silent snow-bound woods, and I was planning how to create some variety when, at a bend in the path, my sedate opossum suddenly rolled itself into a ball, in true armadillo fashion, and went spinning down a steep slope into an (to me) impenetrable thicket of smilax. That it was a sudden thought generated in the animal's brain and thus expeditiously acted upon I do not believe. It is more probable that a misstep frightened it, and the curling up on the brink of a precipice, was a mere coincidence.

If opossums, when surprised in the fields, were accustomed to run for the woods and roll down the nearest slopes into thickets, then I could believe in the forethought of my opossum in the snow; but I have never known these animals to act in such a well-planned manner.

It may be illogical to assert it and yet claim so much intelligence for our other mammals, but the opossum, it has always appeared to me, throve more through good luck than good management.

Practically, it is a step in advance from the stupid marsupial in the thicket to blue jays in the trees above it; for, however it may run counter to the systems, there can be no question of the jay's mental superiority. The world acquired a new interest the moment these birds appeared; for the presence of birds at any time is magical in effect. They are magicians that transform every scene; make of every desolate desert a garden of delights. No other form of life has the same importance to the rambler. I have often seen mammals under the most instructive conditions, and followed in their wake thousands of reptiles, fishes, and insects; but my motive then was always simple curiosity, a desire to learn something of their ways of life, and little chagrin was mine if my labor went for naught. It is different when I meet with birds. Then

my enthusiasm is all aroused, and pleasure or pain pre-
dominates as they venture near me or hold back in fear.
Birds are creatures by themselves, and have little in common with the elaborate laws of those naturalists who know
them only by the structure of their bodies and not by the
exhibition of an advanced intelligence; which, indeed, is
persistently denied them.   The scale of bodily structure is
one thing, that of intelligence quite another; but all this
matters not at present.   The layman can rest assured that
be a bird's brain wrinkled or smooth, large or small, it is
the seat of a quicker wit than many of our wild mammals possess.

These chattering jays were as deeply impressed with
the novelty of the surroundings as I was.   They entered
heartily into the spirit of the white, wintry day, and played
what I may call a game of snow-showering.   Flitting and
fluttering through the laden twigs, these joyous birds were
often lost in a cloud of whirling flakes, from which they
would emerge, screaming wildly their delight.

Perhaps they made a virtue of necessity, and, being
too clumsy to alight without displacing the snow, turned
their awkwardness into sport.   This explanation may be
correct as applied to indefinitely distant generations back,
but I do not think it applicable to the present time.   The
jays along my hill-side evidently love fun as much as do
our children, and if they, furthermore, do not really
laugh, their hearty screams are at least closely akin to
laughter.

It will doubtless be thought by many, if not by most
of my readers, that it is an overbold statement, but I do
not hesitate to say that I have long been convinced that
many of our birds and some of our mammals have a
fairly well developed sense of humor.   Dr. Lindsay, in
his work on "Mind in the Lower Animals," states the
case as follows: "Certain animals, including species and

genera so different as monkeys, apes, orangs, and baboons, the dog, cat, horse, elephant, rabbit and squirrel, the parrot, mocking-bird, starling, magpie, and goose, not only perpetrate practical jokes on each other, or on man, but they enter thoroughly into the spirit of the joke or fun; they enjoy, exult in, their or its success." To this view of the question I heartily subscribe.

But not all of our winter birds are clumsy in the snow, if blue jays really are, and before this merry group of them passed on to deeper recesses of the wood I saw a ruby-crowned kinglet. Perfectly fearless, it came almost within reach of my hand and, leisurely flitting from branch to branch of clustered spice-wood bushes, disturbed nothing that it touched, and, as I found by careful examination, scarcely left its mark, and never a foot-print, as it rested on the delicate ridges of snow. What the bird found to eat I leave the world to conjecture, but if this lone kinglet was hungry, it was not unhappy, and occasionally sang so clearly, sweetly, and with so much earnestness as to be suggestive of June rather than January.

One word more concerning this species of kinglet. I was near enough to identify it beyond question. This is really not an important matter, but I recalled then, as I do now, that it has been stricken off the list of New Jersey birds, or of winter residents—upon what authority, I do not know; but, notwithstanding this, the bird remains with us every winter, and is so happy when clambering about our waste places, or insect-hunting among the evergreens on the lawn, that no one would suspect that it was transgressing any law of migration.

That snowy day I would rather have remained where I then stood, and kept the pretty kinglet near me, but of course could offer him no inducement to remain. Like the jays, he too moved on, and it remained for me to follow their example; this, indeed, was all I could do if

I would see what wild life was astir. At other times a well-chosen stand is better for general observation, creatures of every kind often passing in review before you, but a deep snow changes all this, and one must seek for nearly every object that he is favored to see.

Turning toward the meadows that stretch out for miles from the foot of the hill, I thought of a great oil-cask that years ago was sunk in the ground to collect the waters of a little spring. It is a favorite spot with me at all times, and I was curious to know how its many inhabitants had fared of late; for frogs, snakes, turtles, and salamanders never fail, in winter, to make it their home; and, I may add, many a mouse and tortoise find it their grave.

Before I reached the spot, I was delighted to make out faint foot-prints on the snow as I advanced, and so to learn that some creature had passed that way since the storm ceased. I supposed the spring to have been the goal of the creature's journey, as it was of mine, and I proved correct in this, for the first object that caught my eye when the spot came in view was my late friend the opossum of armadillo-tactics notoriety. His mental caliber began to loom up into respectable proportions in my estimation. Was he such a fool, after all? I wondered much, and was ready to believe a great deal, before it occurred to me that this might really be another opossum; and certainly the tracks it made, and the absence of the mark made by the tail, suggested another individual. What the animal's object was in visiting the spring in the broad daylight must remain unknown, for my abrupt appearance on the scene quite disconcerted him, and he retired with as much haste as the superlatively rough walking permitted. That the opossum sought food rather than drink at the spring is eminently probable; but upon any of the animals living in its waters, I am not aware that it ever preys. Possibly, being omnivorous, opossums are fond of frogs, and yet I doubt their ability to catch them, except by mere chance. But this is all vain speculation. It would not be strange if this particular marsupial differed from his fellows in such matters as that of food. Tastes vary among the lower animals, as among mankind, and one in a thousand opossums might have a fancy for frogs and the cunning necessary to capture them, and the fact escape notice. Fixed habits are few; the whims of individual tastes are countless.

The frogs in the spring were not disconcerted by my presence, and many remained sunning themselves, squatted upon every object that would sustain their weight and which reached above the water. Some were mottled, others of a nearly uniform green or brown. Some were large, and many more were quite small; and all were sleek and plump as you would expect to find them in midsummer. Either fasting had not decreased their bulk or they broke their fast at intervals during the winter. Both suggestions, I think, are true. I stretched forth my hand to take up these frogs, one after the other, but all objected, moving backward into the deep water with a crab-like celerity and grace. Not one of them turned his back on me and dived; but all simply withdrew, and, to my surprise, always to a position quite out of reach, suggesting that they measured the distance while *en route.* I have always held that frogs were witless, so I suppose that it was all mere coincidence. A few of these to-day were not content with deep water, but passed on down into the loose sand. Another possible coincidence, but I think not, was that the deep green aquatic growths waving ceaselessly from the sides of many of the half-rotten staves found no favor with the frogs as a place of concealment. Neither then nor since have I found any of them among them, while they often rested upon the bare wood, and were, of course, quite conspicuous. It would seem as though they trusted wholly to their sight and take the chances of being surprised. When on land their hearing is also largely depended upon.

One patriarchal bull-frog—a giant even among his gigantic race—was far more entertaining, as it proved, than the small fry that shared with him this cozy notch in the hill-side. Perhaps he was asleep all the while, or too lazy to look up; but there he sprawled upon a water-logged chip, down on boiling sands that at times shut him from view. By more uncertain light I might have questioned his identity, and the strange figure he cut when I prodded him with my cane prompted me to exclaim, " Whence and what art thou, execrable shape?" The sound of my voice appeared to rouse him, although beneath the surface of the water, quite as much as my cane had done. There appeared then a knowing glitter in his eyes, and he scanned me closely as might a gem in its matrix, were it conscious. I determined upon that great frog's capture, and after a deal of trouble succeeded. But I was repaid for it all. Taking his frogship up very tenderly, I handled him until quite warm and active, and then placed him very gently upon a ridge of snow, some twenty feet from the spring. The frog was evidently quite bewildered, and the contact of his aldermanic paunch with the snow was not only a novel but painful experience. After some slight alterations of position—as though seeking relief—the troubled creature gave one mighty leap and landed in a little drift that had no sustaining crust. The frog quite disappeared, and, to my great astonishment, when I reached the spot I found that he was burrowing with all his strength, in search evidently of the ground beneath.

Bringing him again to the surface, I expected to see either another leap for life or a repetition of the burrowing; but no, his exposure to the cold was becoming too much for his endurance, and in a most pathetic way he rose upon all fours and commenced walking, as if determined at least to protect his precious stomach to the last. A more ludicrously awkward gait is inconceivable. I can liken it only to the hopeless sprawling of the patent jointed tripod that came with my camera. I laughed long and heartily at the plucky creature, but offered no aid, when, it must be admitted, I should have pitied him. As he was all the while approaching the spring, however, I so far atoned for my cruelty by not again molesting him, and really rejoiced when, with his remaining strength, he plunged into the sparkling waters that are still his home.

The sunshine to-day was unremitting, and every bird that loved a clear sky was finally astir during the afternoon. I could hear them everywhere, yet saw distinctly but very few. Every distant object was to be seen but dimly through the glimmering air—sound alone meeting with no obstruction; and as the notes were sifted through the snow-bound twigs, the familiar song of many a favorite reached my ear.

But there is another phase of winter sunshine worthy of notice. It is when dense, dull gray clouds obscure the sun, except for the briefest intervals. Such times affect our birds in a curious manner. Passing the long smilax thickets, where I expect to see and hear the tree-sparrows at least, there is absolute silence. Even if I force my way into the little openings in the tangle, or throw stones into it, or, standing near, shout long and loudly, it all matters not. There is not a chirp to be heard; no, nor the rustling of a dead leaf; but, waiting until the sunshine breaks through some rift in the clouds, and immediately a score or perhaps a hundred birds mount to the upper branches of the shrubs or mazy tangle of the brier, and music forthwith floats along the hill.

CHAPTER II.

OF nominal winter, February is the beginning of the end. Our Delaware Indians called the month *Tsqualli gischuch*, the Frog Moon, and expected to hear the clammy batrachians croaking before its close. This they were pretty sure to do, as their name of the month implies; and here, by the way, we have evidence that the winters of two centuries ago were not so widely different from those of our own time. Certainly of late years it is the rule that the diminutive hylodes, the smallest of our frogs, will alternately peep and rattle "once in February, thrice in March, and all day long in April." I have this from a nonogenarian who claims to know, and it accords, after a fashion, with my own field-notes; but I do not, like my informant, insist that it is a "rule," for batrachians of every kind, like the higher animals, are loath to obey any other law than that of their own sweet will. Hence the absurdity of making *ex cathedra* statements concerning them. Utter confusion awaits those who anticipate finding our animals creatures devoid of individuality. Surely I do not err when I say that a certain toad that lived in my yard recognized me as its friend during the last twelve years of its life. Examined as dead specimens, individuals of a given species can not, perhaps, be positively distinguished; but studied in their proper belongings, year after year, the reverse is largely true. Even in so low a form of life as the frog there may, I now think, be detected some trace of individuality, though formerly I had grave doubts upon this point.

During a warm, drizzling rain, last October, while the outer doors were open, a bright-red wood-frog hopped upon the porch, then into the hall, and finally found its way into the dining-room, where it was captured. Its beauty proved fatal to its future liberty, and now for some seven months this wandering wood-frog has been the pet of a friend, and that it recognizes its master can not be disputed. When I took the frog to my friend it was wild as a hawk, and struggled to escape whenever approached; but now it is submissive as the most sedate old house-cat. To-day it came from its cozy, fern-clad home when called, and evidently enjoyed having its back stroked. It is ever ready to take a fly, spider, or Croton-bug from my friend's hand, and shows in many ways that it has learned much during its rose-colored captivity. While watching the knowing ways of this one, I put the question: Can a frog be taught as well as merely tamed? and the reply was an emphatic and unqualified affirmative, substantiated by the exhibitions of intelligence on the part of this frog, as mentioned.

To fully realize how much an animal may know, as judged by its actions, it is absolutely necessary to see the creature. Mere words, lamely describing this or that act, go for little. I am always in despair when I attempt such description. It is so now. That wood-frog's countenance was full of meaning. Every movement of the limbs, how-ever slight, every turn of the head, and the short, impa-tient leaps, all gave to those present impressions which it is useless to attempt describing to others. The essence of these impressions is, that the frog's brain was at the time the seat of simple thought, as well as of muscular direc-tion and half-automatic movement. And I am disposed—

nor am I alone in this—to go a little further and express the belief that were any number of unbiassed persons present and watching this wood-frog, as I did to-day, they would agree in this, that the animal not only recognized my friend, but had a semblance of affection for him.

But while all may agree that animals can be taught, it is by no means every man who can be a teacher. I have known those with whom our domestic animals, and especially dogs and cats, became friendly at once, while others could never approach them, the dogs showing their teeth and the cats decamping in fear; yet these unfortunate people honestly desired to be friendly, and were really gentle and kind-hearted.

My friend to whom I have referred has, to perfection, the happy quality of gaining the confidence of animals. Within a few days, an old male night-heron, that had been caught in a steel trap, was brought to him. The bird was not of an amiable disposition, if one might judge from its expression. A day or two of kindness and coaxing were all-sufficient, and now the heron is fairly tame, and no one can question that it recognizes its master from all others, coming promptly when called by him and turning a deaf ear to the entreaties of all others. In my friend's aviary, the same evidence that he exerts an all-powerful influence over the birds is at once plainly noticeable. It is amusing to see, of all birds, a pair of Virginia rails follow him about, keeping close at his heel, like a brace of well-bred spaniels. It was an error on my part to judge too exclusively from my own experiences, and I am convinced now that, like the toad, which I have always championed, the frogs too are teachable.

But let us return to the untaught frogs in the meadows. Strangely, I think, they have never received that consideration from our poets that is their due. Is it because their " music " is not popular with the masses? Yet where in all nature is there a more suggestive sound than the earliest singing of these clammy creatures? They are universally said to croak, as though the eleven species of frog and frog-like batrachians that are found in this neighborhood had but one and the same utterance. Think of it! Toad, spade-foot, hyla, the little peeper, and the true frogs, all condemned to do nothing but dolorously croak! As a matter of fact, we have among them a wide range of sound, from the deep bass of the bull-frog to the piercing treble of Pickering's hyla. We hear it commonly said of the raven that it croaks, but not one of our batrachians has so doleful, despondent, and gloomy a voice as has that strange bird. Certainly, not one of them utters any sound that remotely resembles the weird raven's cry. Then, too, there is the advantage among frogs of thousands singing in concert, and the harshness of each individual's voice is softened so that the volume of sound that sweeps over the meadows has a veritable grandeur. We do not stop to detect the defects of any single song, but acknowledge the success of their united efforts in rejoicing at the victory gentle Spring has gained.

February of 1888 proved an exceptional month. The frogs did not sing. There were days and days of warm sunshine, tempering winds, and all the torpor-dispelling agencies in full force, yet they failed to respond. I found them sunning themselves by many a spring-hole, and squatted with noses above water in the marshy meadows, but not one uttered a word of satisfaction. I lingered for hours about the upland sink-holes, hoping to hear the rattling hylodes, but not one rattled or peeped. Although the ice had disappeared and the water was fairly warm, they remained as silent as when frost-bound in January. Yet they were not inactive. The long continued cold had not chilled them until helpless or stupid. They hopped vigorously from me when I tried to catch them. There was to me no apparent reason why they should not have been as noisy as during several days of February, 1887, when the fields resounded with their cries. What past experience gave me every reason to expect failed me here, and the explanation, I take it, it were vain to seek.

Here is something for those to consider who hold that animal life is essentially machine-like, and repeats each year the acts of the preceding season. And so it is, the wide world over. Animals have abundant power over their own movements, and are influenced by agencies we as yet know nothing of.

There are winter days that, without being at all stormy, seem determined to have the world to themselves. The sky, clouds, and every tangible object from which we hope a welcoming gaze, returns our glance with a let-me-alone look that is very disheartening. Such are many of those in February, or have been of late years, and for general dreariness they throw the best efforts of November in this line quite into the shade. November gloom is chilly and depressing, that of February is often the acme of desolation.

In order to test the power of such a day to its utmost, I sought the loneliest spot within easy access, the drift-strewed beaches of a long island in the river, and picked my way through the flotsam of the recent flood " deposited upon the silent shore." I have said " the silent shore." It is true that the sobbing of the waves filled the air, but this, on such a day, is one of those sounds in nature which merely intensify the silence.

The whole island was spread out before me as a subject under the dissector's knife; not only dead, but disorganized. It mattered not how deeply I probed, how freely I cut, there was no trace of latent life, no shuddering, no protest, however faint, and my bungling work, in all its ragged disjointedness, was not traceable in the landscape.

My overturning of every object that I was able to move made it no less in place than before; the confusion was no worse confounded because of my interference. Verily, for once, I thought, I am absolutely alone. But it was not to be. Even when the elements conspire to drive life into the background—as they seemed bent upon doing to-day—the most that we can hope, if desirous of solitude, is to have our senses dulled to the proximity of our neighbors. I stamped upon the brittle twigs covering the sandy shore, that the sound of their cracking might break the monotony of the river's ripple, and broke the glossy willow sprouts that chanced in my way, to hear their screaming swish as I lashed the dead air; and my desperate efforts to rouse the sleepers startled at last one poor, crouching, timid song-sparrow that thridded the tangled underbrush as might a mouse. I had learned what silence really meant, and realized what absolute deafness must be. It was enough to see a bird and not hear it. Here the despised meadow-mouse becomes the song-bird's superior, for with swifter feet it can find a passage even through flood-tossed driftwood.

But there was at least one sparrow abroad, and I was happier from that moment. Trusting the bird would reconsider its needless flight and return, I waited for some minutes, and not in vain. Back it came, flying now, instead of running, and when very near me clutched a swaying willow branch and sang. I have heard birds' songs under endless conditions, but never such hollow mockery as this. Half the notes were caught and strangled, while such as escaped were shorn of all their sweetness. The sparrow knew that it had sadly blundered, and dropped silently into the grass beneath it. Dead days, such as this, tolerate no music, not even a dolorous dirge.

Let me ask why, if one sparrow be abroad, there may

not be a hundred skulking near and likely to show themselves? The chances are that no more would be found should I search diligently for hours. What has become of them? This is a problem for our learned ornithologists to solve, for the sudden coming and going of our resident birds is a strange feature of bird life, and worthy of consideration. There is no spot for miles around where birds are more abundant than on this island, and yet practically all were hidden to-day, so closely that no eyes, however sharp, could have spied them out. Nor is it sufficient, as has been dogmatically asserted, to say that they have sought the better shelter afforded by the hill-sides across the river. Have they, indeed? These same hill-sides have been searched, and not a bird was to be found. There are two alternatives—they either hide or leave the neighborhood. Both are possible; the latter the more probable; but the mystery of the matter still remains. There are winter days—few in number, I am glad to say—that, as my record runs, are birdless ones; and again, others—like to-day—that are nearly so. At the dawn of such days, weak-winged birds, as sparrows, tits, and kinglets, appear to suddenly take flight and pass beyond the limits of an inclement and depressing area, often miles away; and knowing, while at this distant point, when a change has taken place, return as suddenly as they departed. This seems very absurd, yet it is apparently true; for, on the other hand, to say that new birds take the place of those that were here, is to assume what is certainly untrue, so far as resident species are concerned. There are tits and sparrows and Carolina wrens that have as well-defined ranges as ever did a game-cock, and keep as closely to it. One need but become familiar with the peculiarity of some one sparrow's song to know that the same individual will stay not only for a season, but year after year, in one limited locality.

There are, in a general sense, no birds on the island to-day, and if to-morrow be clear they will be abroad in full force; but, as I can testify from repeated experiences, if you stay until to-morrow, keeping a sharp lookout the night through, you will stand guard in vain. The coming of the birds will be without a sign; swift as the first flash of the morning's sun.

However it may be in other quarters of the globe, seasonal migration along our river valleys is in no way remarkable, and presents nothing of near like interest to many a phase of bird life during either the summer or winter season. This sudden change that I have mentioned, and which occurs at all seasons but when the birds are nesting, is more full of meaning, and throws more light upon bird intelligence.

And now of the few birds that remain. Certainly, during this funereal day that one sparrow gave abundant evidence of being in anything but a joyous state of mind. It acted as though it had forgotten itself for a moment, and so was either frightened or ashamed; like a child when it speaks aloud in church and is answered by a frown.

It will doubtless be said that this is a strained, stilted, exaggerated statement of the effect of peculiarly gloomy days, or even a baseless fancy; but such counter-statements, popularly yclept criticism, do not alter the case, and I wish that some I know would winter in the meadows for one season. Well, as my field notes show, other than bird life was inactive. When I chanced to overturn a broad bit of bark, and so unroof the snug retreat of a meadow-mouse, it did not flee, but crouched in one corner as though expecting me to shrink to its size and share its shelter with it. Of a cold, breezy winter day, with blue sky and yellow sunshine, how quickly this same mouse would have disappeared, perhaps before I could have caught a glimpse of it! Surely there is something that pervades the atmosphere of these dead days that tells upon mice as well as men. I may fairly claim a liking for the outdoor world, yet I thought constantly to-day of the comforts of a shelter, and regretted that I had wandered so far from home. Nor would I have remained until the day closed had not a hollow sycamore offered me a safe if not very commodious quarter, from which I could see the river and a fair sample of the deserted shores. But, as so often happens, I reckoned rashly. It were a different matter whether one walked or sat, and now that I had a house I felt the need of a fire. This, to be sure, was quickly provided, and only to find that with its warmth I must take the smoke, and through the latter the dismal river was a still more doleful sight. Thus, the misfortune of being so dependent drove me from my new-found shelter, and, filled with disgust, I turned my steps homeward.

I had not gone ten paces, however, before a solitary blue heron, fearless of the smoldering fire, settled by the river's edge, and solemnly stalked along the narrow beach, passing by with so much dignity that I could scarcely keep from laughing. It was indulging in vain regrets, I fancied, that it had chosen to winter so far north. But perhaps the poor fellow was rheumatic and dared not venture on a migratorial flight. It is well to fortify this statement with a convenient " perhaps," for the measured flapping of the heron's wings, as it came down the river, and no less measured tread as it paced the lonely shore, hardly warranted such a suggestion.

When I left the heron, it was perched upon an uplifted branch of a ghost-like, stranded tree that for years had been bleaching in the storms and sunshine of the up-river region ; and as I hurried toward my boat at the ford, time after time I looked back to see it still standing with its head resting upon its breast, its wings drooping, the very picture of despair. Would it not have been less mopish and disconsolate had the day been brighter? I think so.

It is strange that when birds are seemingly out of place and apparently laboring under every disadvantage, as in the case of herons in winter, they are invested with greater interest than in those ordinary conditions when they are familiar objects of daily observation. The great blue heron and the "quok," that are occasionally seen on the meadows and along the river during the winter, are sure to command a greater degree of attention than during summer, and add unusual interest to the day's outing. They are so associated with warm weather, with minnows in the shallow brooks and frogs in the spring-holes, that we wonder why they are here now, pity them if necessity required their remaining, and are puzzled to conjecture where they find sufficient food. Such was, at least, the current of my thoughts until I found that there never was so cold a day that some open water could not be found, or water so cold that both frogs and fish did not venture to be abroad. But the supply of food from such sources is an uncertain one at best, and probably the land rather than the water is their principal hunting-ground. In other words, they are hunters rather than fishermen. My attention was recently called to this matter by a taxidermist who found three partly digested meadow-mice in the stomach of a winter-killed great blue heron. Following this clew, my own observations convinced me that the meadows were systematically hunted for the innumerable mice that tunnel the matted dead grass in every direction. What of deep snows? it may be asked; but, fortunately for the herons, lasting snows are unknown to the low-lying tracts I treat of, and so do not enter into the matter at all. I would not be understood to say that mice are their sole dependence in winter, but that a sufficient number are caught to make up the deficiency of frogs and fish.

The day suddenly improved in two respects. As I was crossing the river to the mainland it began to rain, and a kingfisher sprung his rattle directly above my head. I am not superstitious beyond what other men are, but the harsh cry of that hopeful bird was more than music then, assuring me of a welcome change in the immediate future, although the sky was now as gloomy as a funeral pall, and every drop of the pitiless rain was cold as charity.

Even though it be an icy rain, some tangible evidence of energy in nature is far more grateful than death-like inactivity, although we know so well that the latter is not real. When out of doors, one never expects to find the world at rest, and anticipates disaster if the appearances but vaguely suggest it. It is said that an ominous silence precedes an earthquake. Neither the silence of to-day nor the kingfisher's cry suggested so soon a change, but I felt that by nightfall there would be a new order issued, and the halcyon's rattle was the apparent herald.

It would have been foolish indeed to have turned my back upon the cheerful blaze of an open fire, and started out in such rain; but to face it, in leaving the island, was a veritable relief. What under ordinary circumstances would be repelling features of such a time were now pleasing and attractive through contrast, and the dripping of the great round drops upon the still adherent leaves of the sapling beeches and oaks that were yet full-leaved was inspiriting music.

As it was late in the afternoon and stormy too, the prospect was far from cheering as I faced a broad and weedy meadow that must needs be crossed; but I had that confident feeling of being repaid for my trouble which so seldom fails me, however unpromising may seem the outlook to others.

Of this strange confidence I can not give any definite description, but that it is not a pleasant mental condition

I can aver. For years I have noticed that, without the least apparent reason, I have suddenly thought of some one animal and straightway it appears upon the scene. It was so this afternoon. I had neither seen nor heard a crow, either before I reached the island or while upon it, and yet that these birds were to be a prominent feature of my homeward walk I was positive; and so it proved. What does it all mean? Did they really exert, unknowingly, some strange influence upon me, as man appears to do upon man when through the senses of sight or hearing they have no knowledge of each other's whereabout? I have long thought that such common experience could not be mere coincidence, and so the whole matter becomes vexatious, for I hate mystery.

I had not gone far before I fell in with a company of silent crows. Twenty or more sat, without uttering the faintest sound, on the lower branches of a huge black birch. I caught sight of them before I had been seen, and so were joined two rare occurrences in the bird world—surprising a gathering of mute crows. I should have waited where I stood, and so had a chance to determine the cause of their silent meeting; but my spirit of mischief overcame discretion and I shouted loudly. With a united cry of alarm that was almost deafening, they took wing and scattered in every direction, but soon gathered again and flew in one direction, down the river; and now their mingled voices, pitched on a dozen different keys, sounded marvelously like an earnest conversation; and I firmly believe that it was.

A silent and solitary crow may not be phenomenal, but when a dozen or more are associated and all refrain from utterance, then rest assured that something of grave import occupies their minds. I do not know how far down in the scale the remark is applicable, but if we have any warrant for judging animals by their actions and voices,

then from fishes upward they frequently stop to think.
As we so often say of ourselves and of other people, so I
am warranted in saying of the crows, they had stopped to
think.   But of what?   Ah! that is another matter.

Poor, persecuted crows! they have a hard time of it,
and only their excellent wit has saved them from annihila-
tion.   I recently read of the efforts to destroy a newly
formed crow-roost, and that the farmers of the neighborhood were divided into crowites and anti-crowites.   There
is no need of coining a new word.   Those who defend
those birds are wise; those who persecute them, otherwise.

There was nothing directly in my path to explain the
presence of these crows, so far as I could see, but this fact
goes for naught.   They are long-headed birds, and not
disposed to publish their plans by remaining too close to
the scene of proposed operations; and so far as their
suggestive silence is concerned, I long ago learned that a
pair of crows, when nesting, could keep quiet on occasion,
as when raiding upon the nest of a sitting hen during her
absence, or when stealing corn from a crib that was near
the farmer's house; and when a water-melon patch is to
be visited, the same caution is often exercised, although at
this time the nesting is over.   I have knowledge of a pair
of crows that always alighted in an adjoining field, and
walked some distance to the fence and then crept under
it, thus reaching the melons in safety.   A chance remark,
jokingly made, led to the discovery of this astonishing
fact.

A few minutes later, as I reached the brow of the hill,
a cold blast from the north came sweeping through the
woods, and as suddenly the sky became brighter.   Then
the western horizon grew brilliant; a bright band of glowing red rested upon the distant tree-tops, and in the hollows of the wood near by the scanty remnants of sheltered

snow-drifts shone with as soft a light, pink, pearly, and pure, as Paradise. And as I looked back from my door over the wide meadows, the river, and that silent island for the last time that day, I saw those mute, mysterious crows returning to the old birch tree.

There is one marked feature of February that merits not mere mention only, but the skill of a ready writer to do it justice. Often the night gives promise of a balmy day, and I retire in hopes of greeting the welcome traces of a spring-like morning; but, however early I may be abroad, the birds are sure to be astir before me. While darkness still lingers on the wooded hill I reach the meadows, only to find them all mist and music. The wakeful tits call from the towering pines, the sparrows twitter from the dripping shrubs. Through the thick air wing the cawing crows, and restless redbirds whistle through the gloom.

And while I stand listening, there comes, borne upon the soft south wind, a faint, tinkling note that thrills me more than all other sounds. It can not be mistaken for any other, and I know that the redwings are on the way. Whatever the time of year, there are joyful experiences in store for every rambler, but few that are more entrancing than to greet the crimson-shouldered blackbirds when they come in full force to the long-deserted meadows. It is true there have been straggling birds both seen and heard all through the winter, but now through their numbers we have sweet assurance that the season's severity is well-nigh over.

It matters not that seldom, if ever, do these large flocks come to stay. Enough to know that their sharp eyes have detected some sign of spring. The fierce north winds send them hurrying back all too soon, but from now until April, as the wind varies, they drift to and fro.

Just where they linger when the frost-king rages, I do
not know, but it can not be afar off. It is but a few
hours after the south wind comes again that they reappear, and

> "The meadows all bespattered with melody."

The weather, as we have seen, has much to do with
both the frogs and blackbirds, and indeed with nearly all
of active life in February; but the bleakness of January
does not hold everywhere, however arctic the world may
appear to the careless observer. Brushing aside the dead
leaves upon the hill-side, that dainty flower, the pale pink
spring beauty, proved to be in bloom. For long its hopeful buds had been waiting for yet a little warmer sunshine, and now, sheltered by the crisp oak leaves from
every chilling blast, while yet the ice arched the meadow
brooks and snow-drifts lingered in the upland fields, they
stealthily opened to the cheerful outlook, as though listening, as I was, to the songs of many birds.

What then does it matter that the frogs fail us at
times, as they did in the memorable winter of '88? The
birds and blossoms did not, and before the February moon
had waxed and waned we had promise that the reign of
winter was well-nigh over—that the beginning of the end
was here.

CHAPTER III.

MARCH.

By the first of March, and often earlier, the world is all agog concerning signs of spring. The welcome accorded winter during the holidays is no longer extended to the remaining snow-storms, and we meet with a frown the last cold wave of the season.

When the outdoor world is ignored—as is so often the case—and the village newspaper becomes one's only source of information, the impression obtains that veritable signs of spring are thick as the clustered stars of heaven. But

> Hast thou, O Spring! some flawless, quick-read sign,
> Outspeeding thine own steps, to herald thee?

Possibly this belief in signs arises from the fact that taking any average village such as lies at the elbow of every one who lives outside a city's walls, and we shall find that about the middle of February half the adults of, we will say, Crankville become weather prophets, and the rest of the community are willing listeners, if not steadfast believers. Not one of the latter but has been periodically deceived since he first pinned his faith on the prophet's assertions; yet not one of them appears to know this very damaging fact. Indeed, it would never have been discovered had not a diarist gone to their benighted village to live, and he it is who has made the writer acquainted with the facts.

4

Crankville, of course, has another name, or I should never have dared to pen these opening sentences.

After the middle of the month of February not a Crankville frog dare croak nor wasp creep from the barn, sheltered maple bud dare swell or daffodil look upward, but straightway the prophets are moved to look their wisest and proclaim that winter is over, and point to the poor animal or plant as their authority for the statement. The gulled listeners, all hopeful that what they heard is true, dutifully salaam the prophets, and Crankville is happy. Biting frosts, deep snows, howling winter storms follow within a week. The earlier proclamations of the weather prophets are forgotten, and when the skies clear and the warm sun cheers the impatient animals and plants again, the same predictions are again made and trustfully received, and so the farce continues until the spring really comes.

Turning our backs now on these innocent villagers, let us take up the subject more soberly, and see if we can find any flawless, quick-read sign of spring.

Stay! There is one sign of spring, not uncommon to February, and very characteristic of March. I refer to the public sales of those who—from necessity or choice—" are about to relinquish farming," as the posters inform us. April 1 being "moving day," during the previous six weeks these vendues usually come off—*vandoo sales*, as my neighbors call them; and not a farmer but finds it convenient to attend, for he not only meets his friends but secretly cherishes the hope that he may "pick up a bargain." The queer folk of a neighborhood, too, that never appear in public except upon such an occasion and at funerals, are out in full force. A vendue, in fact, is as attractive to cranks as is honey to a fly. Partly to study these odd characters, and more that I might purchase some old furniture, I have been attending sales. But aside

from either purpose, there is occasionally the opportunity
of studying one phase at least of early colonial life well
worthy of attention. When there is a considerable offering of household goods, one gets a glimpse of the past
more vivid than any mere description of the historian.
Some rickety chair, tarnished andirons, battered pewter,
a string of shoe-buckles, warped and worm-eaten books—
the outpourings of a dusty garret and a damp cellar—an
omnium gatherum that has been two centuries in growing.
Think of such a display brought again to the sunlight!
The imagination must indeed be sluggish that can not by
such aid recall the earnest folk who settled in the wilderness.

All such sales as these are worth a day's attendance,
even though you dine on peanuts and that mysterious
compound, a sutler's oyster stew. But be not too eager
to bid. To purchase what you really wish and nothing
else; to get for a dime what is really worth a dollar—this,
I now believe, is one of the fine arts; so far as I am concerned, one of the lost arts.

My last attendance proved so unsatisfactory, if not
worse, that I have declared my intention of ignoring vendues in the future. I was tempted by the wording of the
poster, and, in spite of the bad roads and detestable
weather, gave half a day to colonial furniture and all the
belongings of a well-appointed house of those rare old
days. Other and more enthusiastic lovers of such things
were also there, and I always bid in vain. By dimes and dol-
lars every desired object went just out of reach. I felt a
little sore at my ill luck, and, fool that I was, determined
not to return home empty-handed. I have wondered
since if the auctioneer read my thoughts. Be this as it
may, I stood by the remaining heaps of worthless refuse
cunningly packed in broken basins and sieve-like milk-
pans. I saw no gem that had been inadvertently cast

before swine, and my purchase, if I made any, must be some farming utensil, I thought, and I remained by the rubbish only out of curiosity to see if the scattered cranks would now come to the fore as purchasers. Unfortunate curiosity!

After waiting impatiently for a bid and getting but a penny as a starter, the auctioneer suddenly eyed me so searchingly that my head bobbed in spite of me, and I was announced the buyer of a brown jug for a nickel. Now I have never had need for a brown jug. But I was not to be caught again, I inwardly vowed, and braced my head against a tall chest of drawers, so that if the searching eye of that wicked auctioneer singled me out I could resolutely turn my face toward the ceiling. This scheme availed me nothing, for that upward glance was too pronounced, and taken as legal evidence of assent, and I was saddled with a panful of bladeless knives and tineless forks. Now I was half angry, and turned my back upon the auctioneer. " Don't go," he screamed, and as I turned to declare that I would, I became the bewildered owner of a startling array of globular, capacious, aged, if not antique crockery, yellow, blue, and white. This last decision of the fiendish auctioneer provoked an audible smile throughout the crowd in which I could not join; for had I not come to see cranks, and, by helplessly buying all the rubbish, was crowned the champion crank for so doing! I have no longer a kindly feeling toward vendues.

While a plant or an animal remains, there will doubtless be coupled with it some sign of the season—either the time of its arrival or its general character. Its value need not be discussed. So far as spring plants are concerned, there is a host of them that sleep throughout the winter " with one eye open," and stretch themselves, regardless of the almanac, if chance favors them with sunshine and a shelter from the winds. There lives no country boy so unobservant as not to know this, yet such plants are pointed at with great glee by the victims of the mania for seasonal prophecy. And the unthinking audience shout "Spring is coming," for they have seen with their own eyes the evidence. Have they? In January the same plant life was equally prominent, but then the weather prophets had not been moved to speak, so it all passed for nothing.

In localities of a higher grade of intelligence than Crankville, the observant people, curious in such matters but not bigotedly confident, generally watch the birds more closely than any other form of life, and judge of an early or late spring by their migratory movements. This is not a safe guide by any means. A carefully kept record covering a decade will show that birds are very frequently deceived by premature spring-like weather. Jack Frost is the only boy who has scattered salt on birds' tails and so caught them. He it is who has dashed snow so freely about in April that the summer birds have to admit themselves his prisoners.

I have gathered a host of sayings referring to birds and the weather, and have tested them all. Often they hold good, frequently they do not; and the weather prophet is always cunning enough to see with a blind eye only when the facts contradict him. I well remember pointing to a flock of wild geese as they wended their way northward early in February. "Winter is about over," my companion told me. But we happened to have five weeks of arctic weather after that, and I twitted him about his prediction. "They must have been goin' over without honkin'," he said; "that makes a difference, you know." I did not know it, and do not know it now, and never will know it, for it is not true; but what are we to do? If I tell the average Crankville weather prophet he is a prevaricator (if he knows the meaning of the word), he will resent it forcibly, and that is unpleasant.

The character of the winter is by many assumed to have much to do with the early or tardy coming of spring. This is so reasonable on the face of it that one listens hopefully as it is explained that the average of cold is about the same each year, and if the three months of winter proper are steadily frigid, then March will be spring-like in fact as well as name. Alas! those deadly statistics confront us; and March has often followed so closely in winter's footsteps that the lengthening days are our only hope that spring will ever come.

As is my wont, I let not a day go by without some glimpse of out of doors, and more often I am rambling while the day lasts; and wherever I go I find hopeful plants, brave animals, and mark the skyward route of hardy northward migrants.

These may be called signs of an early spring, if you will. In proportion as we long for that goodly season we are tempted to so look upon them. But is there not a more rational view? After all, are these plants and animals not the same as us in this respect? Like us, they are impatient for the winter to be gone. They lend a willing ear to every murmur of the south wind; they welcome the embrace of every ray of sunshine. This, and nothing more. Were they blessed with memory, do you think they would not accuse the weather of being fickle, and would these plants and animals not resent the charge of passing as " signs "?

Hast thou, O Spring, some flawless, quick-read sign?

We ask of her in vain. She has never deigned to reply, and leaves us to choose between ignorance as to the times of her coming or belittle ourselves by listening to the inanities of the weather prophets of Crankville and elsewhere.

But let us consider the year's third month without reference to the libelous insinuation that it ever intends to be interpreted in a prophetic sense. Probably no month is so distinctly *sui generis.* The Indians called it *Chwáme gischuch,* the Shad Moon, and the name is still applicable. Our swarthy predecessors in this river valley were enthusiastic fish-eaters, and they had better and bigger fish than any but the very best of what are captured now. The shell-heaps tell the story, for nothing so delicate but in these kindly beds of ashes has been faithfully preserved. This, of course, has been denied, and the world assured that fish-bones are perishable. Really! and so the bone implements in our museums are all frauds! But mendacious anonymities can not alter the facts. Shad formerly were larger as a rule than the usual " run " of them to-day, but happily they are still large enough to rejoice the rich, and plenty enough that all may feast.

The river is this month's favorite highway. The upland winds are never so keen as those that rush counter to the incoming tide and make a choppy, white-capped sea. The shivering fishermen hold it bad luck then, for the shad are stayed, and water-hauls, though a common experience of all mankind, are never submitted to with a good grace.

The attractions of the fisheries established years ago by our great-grandfathers have well-nigh disappeared. Now it is a mere matter of business; then it was one equally of pleasure—a combination of play and profit. The labor of the farm was lightened by the anticipation of an hour with the net and a feast at breakfast the day following.

With what excitement the net was gradually drawn to the shore, and how eager was every lad to land the great silvery-sided fish that now leaped in terror above the water! How lustily the men cheered when a successful

haul was made, and with what impatience this exultant
shout was waited for by the anxious housewives who stood
at the open doors, with hands curled back of their ears
that they might be sure to catch the welcome sound that
told of the men's success !

The site of the old fishery remains; a bit of one old
net is preserved; the double door of the old kitchen that
faced the river is still swinging, and above it—where it has
rested for more than seventy years—is a rusty sturgeon
spear; but of the happy folk who lived here, that drew
their nets in these waters and deftly speared the floun-
dering sturgeon, now not one remains. There is not left
one link between the closing years of the last century and
this prosy, artificial year of 1888.

Those of to-day may smile if they will, and prefer to
buy what fish they need; but the world lost something,
however much it may have gained, when many a feature
of more primitive times was swallowed up in the customs
of to-day. And this trivial matter of a shad for tea is one
of them. " Catch your shad at 5 and eat it at 7." This
was the long-established rule of one old farm-house not
far away, and no skill of modern cookery can improve
upon the right royal satisfaction of such a feast.

The mid-river alone retains the wildness of primeval
days, the shores being all too likely to be strewed with the
slops of cities. No growth of splatter-dock so rank as to
hide that ubiquitous horror, a rusty tomato can. Even in
the remotest nooks, where I fancied myself the first man
to enter since Indian days, I have found this relic of some
recent feast.

Unless you are in a substantial bateau, no little skill
is required to baffle the waves when the March winds
blow, for a mile-wide stream gives them full play, and
many a white-cap peeps above the gunwales. But you

have nature without man's interference now, and the gulls, the divers, and fish-hawks are royal company.

Neither the gull nor the fish-hawk seems so active and quick-winged when here, far off from the ocean, as when at or near the sea. The latter does not come until late in the month, and only then if the water is high, herring abundant, and the meadows with at least a remnant of a freshet. It is not until April that they are a fixed feature of the landscape. Like many other of our large birds, fish-hawks are not so abundant now as even half a century ago, although the struggle for existence is something less severe than when their arch-enemy, the bald eagle, was comparatively common. They here have a broad field to all appearances quite to themselves, and why it is so sparsely occupied is determined not readily, if at all. It is hard to believe that the supply of fish has appreciably decreased; and certainly there is no lack of suitable and safe nesting sites. As in all cases of like perplexity, I have gone to the old folks, except such as vegetate in towns, and sought from them an explanation. I have never been turned away unanswered; but, alas! though it be contemptible to admit it, I must say I never returned home enlightened. Vague theory reigns rampant when new subjects are broached to the unobservant.

I have said that fish-hawks were a fixed feature of the landscape here. I limit the plural to a single pair, and perhaps because there are but two in the neighborhood, it is that they differ in many ways from their kind that throng the sea-coast. Often have I watched a single one, as it sailed over the weedy fields, an hour at a time, quartering the ground as closely as any mousing harrier. Is the fish-hawk, at such a time, in search of inland prey? The appearances are certainly against them, and I have known farmers to go so far as to insist that no discrimination should be made between them and the true buzzards and falcons that destroy poultry. Argument is useless in such a case. In fact, I invariably get the worst of it. "Why," the farmer asks, " do they not stay on the river or the meadows?" I can not say. "I can tell you, though," he continues, with emphasis, " that I know when a man's fishing and when he's hunting, and its much the same thing with the birds. They don't go to a field to catch fish, and they're after something, that's certain. Delaware herring may not suit their fancy, but they can't vary their diet with my chickens."

Dr. Brewer states that he never knew an instance of these birds attacking birds or small mammals, and the strange fact that they fancy the upland fields to such an extent as to spend much time upon or over them may have no significance. Toads and frogs may possibly be eaten by them, but both are more abundant in the wet meadows. That they will eat them, however, as well as other animal food, is proved by such as have been held in captivity; and further, as having a slight bearing upon the subject, I may mention the fact that an old fisherman has assured me that he had seen them eat dead herring and chub that had been tossed from the shad-nets and were lying upon the shore near the water's edge. This contradicts all statements of their feeding habits that I find; but I can hardly believe that the man was mistaken.

Although differing so widely in all its habits, the gull is another feature of the river and meadows in March of which I could say much; but let us consider them when on the meadows. Every gull-like trait is often gone, and as two or three stand among the hassocks of the mucky meadow they are sure to be taken for my neighbor's geese. In such a case there can be no doubt, I think; but that something attractive in the way of food draws them hither. They often wander to a considerable distance from open water, and only become noisy when they are frightened, and take wing.

The black-headed gulls have recently visited the meadows during March freshets, and these were much more tame than the other species, which ordinarily stays close by the river. In 1887, they even sailed over the upland fields as though, like fish-hawks, they would at least be glad to find some novelty in the way of food, even if they did not expect it.

It was amusing to see with what vehemence the crows protested against this invasion of their territory. They chased the gulls incessantly, and scolded with a harshness suggestive of the most direful imprecations; but all in vain. The gulls were bent upon making these overland explorations, and make them they did. At times a number of crows came together in the trees and discussed the situation with less noise, but yet in no uncertain manner. It was to me a most suggestive sight to watch a crow as he stepped out to some commanding position and harangued his fellows. This, it is no exaggeration to say, more than one crow did, and that there could be no misinterpretation on my part is evident from the fact that at times, and for a moment only, the audience uttered a single word—shall I call it?—of approval; a hearty " That's so," such as you hear upon the streets among crowds of much less brainy bipeds. Then away, in a body, they would fly and chase the scattered gulls that sailed over the fields. But it all mattered not, and the visitors only left when they saw fit.

I am sure that during one whole week I never saw a gull dip down to the ground and pick up any article of food, and very generally they flew at a much greater elevation above the fields than they usually do above the water. What food they got must have been gathered during brief visits to the river, or at night when they roosted, so I was told, upon the water.

It is a little surprising that the Indians did not call March the windy moon, for the fitful blasts that characterize fully one half of its days could not have passed unheeded, although the country then was heavily forested.

I have lately learned to love these blustering March mornings, particularly when they do not bluster; for the north wind is happily often held in abeyance, and at no time can it sweep the sunny slopes that are already green with expectant buds. After all, it is but a question of standing on this or that side of a tree, whether it is spring or winter. A grand old chestnut hard by has had green grass at its roots since Christmas, and at the same time snow and ice were banked upon the wrinkled north side of its trunk.

But granting all this, why call March mornings matchless? Meet almost whomsoever you may, and he will deride the opinion that they can be mentioned except to condemn them. Nevertheless, I claim that they have features unknown to the other months, and while maligned by the many, are not without merit to the few— that happy few who delight in nature's harmless intoxicant, pure air. Perhaps it is that the atmosphere is doubly charged with that subtle quality, ozone, that now for a whole month stimulates every sense; but whatever it may be, there is an all-pervading influence in the clear air of a wild March morning that stirs us to livelier action; something far more potent than the mere thought that a long winter draws to a close. For years, I admit, I honestly hated; now, as honestly, I love these matchless March mornings.

That emphasis of action which we admire in mankind because indicative of their own faith in their work, characterizes every phenomenon in March, and calls forth my admiration, notwithstanding the marked rudeness of a gusty wind tends somewhat to disgust. But here I am manifestly unfair, for the cutting blasts are not unheralded;

and forewarned we are expected to be forearmed. So stick closely to the sunny side of some stout tree and view the airy battle from afar.

The sky is of a deeper blue than during the winter, but not until to-day have the scattered clouds so constantly chased their shadows across the meadows. Fleecy fragments of some distant storm-cloud, the wind has caught them up and now whirls them swiftly toward the sea. Beyond its reach myself, the impelling power is quite forgotten, and something more than lifeless mist is speeding gleefully through space, ever at their heels, but never capturing their own earth-sweeping shadows.

Such days are sure to rouse to liveliest pitch the energies of all our winter birds, and none hug the sheltered slopes so closely as in months gone by. Even the tireless hawks are moved, and, breaking the circles over which they have sailed for hours, dash, with wild screaming, down the fitful wind.

The bird world's lesser lights are no less active. At last the meadow-larks are moved to sing. For long they have threaded their silent way along tortuous paths in the dead and tangled grass; now they rejoice, with full hearts, in the open secret of spring at hand.

Where the old bridge shudders in the blast, as the winds sweep the troubled waters of the cheerless creek, the confident peewee never loses faith, and morning, noon, and night, repeats his cheery call. He has come to stay, and seldom does the severest weather cause him to repent. I have heard him singing when the creek was ice-bound and the ground covered deeply with snow.

From where I stood to-day, there was clustered a rank growth of seedling beeches, with here and there a more spreading growth of alder. A happy group of foxy finches, flitting through this pygmy forest, for hours made merry; and however dismal the day or desolate the world

may appear, the music of these birds will chase the gloom
away.

Most unfortunately it is only for a short time that we
have these princely sparrows when at their best, for day
after day will often pass when they are either silent or
only most monotonously chirp. So it was when I last saw
them; every bird seemed given to meditation, and flew
with reluctance when I drew too near; but to-day, their
clear, flute-like voices drowned all other songs. Every
note of this bird is a marvel of purity, and their variety
greater than the *repertoire* of any other of their tribe; ex-
celling, in this respect, even the song-sparrow. Nor is
the song of every individual the same. They so far differ
that when several birds are singing at one time it gives
the impression of a concert by various songsters, rather
than the united efforts of a number of the same species.

As April approaches, the songs of these birds are more
continued, especially if it is clear and warm at noon. Indeed, April sunshine is required to ripen the music of
their dainty throats. Then it is well worth one's while to
linger about the brier-hidden angles of some old worm
fence, for then, at such time, the melody is next in merit
to the early June-day efforts of the thrush and grosbeak.

Foxy finches advocate squatter sovereignty and are
impatient of intrusion, where they have power to resist.
The blundering sparrows of humbler grade are given
prompt notice to quit, and usually take a gentle hint without show of protest. I have always wished that these pas-
serine nobles would become permanent settlers, for bird-
ful as are our pleasant places, there would be room for
them. As it is, their sojourn suggests but a jolly hunter's
camp, ringing the day long with so much gayety that the
echo of the songs lingers about the spot long after they
have gone.

Much might be written of the long list of singing

birds that like them make glad the waste places during
March, but let us turn now to another and far from
spring-like phase of this much-maligned month. It is
one of historic storms.

I gathered pink and white blossoms of the spring
beauty on the 10th of the present month, and on the 12th
they were under the drifting snow of what will pass into
history as the great storm of March, 1888.

Where the humble flowers dotted the sprouting grass
there now rests a grand curl-crested drift, twenty feet
in height; and where I at times sought shelter from occasional gusts of chilly wind, that same day, now lies an uprooted chestnut with its storm-tossed branches strewed over
the meadow. Borne by the hurricane, the sand-like snow
has formed itself into one long, tortuous mound over the
smilax thickets; glittering and roseate in the morning
sun, cold and pale as death in the feeble moonlight.
The wondering, unhoused birds flitting over it by day
lessen, in part, the present dreariness of the scene; but
when the faint shadow of a wandering owl passed over it
at night the spot was desolate beyond all power of words
to describe.

Twice I attempted out of doors to watch the progress
of the storm, but soon learned the danger of the attempt.
It is marvelous, now, when all is so calm, to think that it
was unsafe to be but a few rods from the house. The
meager landscape changed with wonderful rapidity, and
snowdrifts that I found a shelter from the wind a moment
before were often moved bodily, or so it seemed, and
threatened to overwhelm me. I can liken the roar of the
wind among the trees to nothing less stupendous than Niagara's cataract, but varying in this, that each tree gave
forth a different sound. Among the tall, mast-like
branches of three enormous beeches, the noise was so
shrill and piercing that it drowned at times the deeper-

toned roaring and moaning among the oaks near by.
Except the larger trees, there was little else to be seen,
the fields and meadows alike being enveloped in a misty
cloud-mass of whirling snow that I fancied the smoke of
an icy fire.

The wild weather gave me no little concern with re-
gard to the old trees near my house. I was curious, too,
to know which species was suffering most from loss of
branches and general mutilation.   The snapping and
crashing heard above the wind's roaring suggested universal destruction. Judging from past wind-storms, I looked
for the leveling of the fourteen pines near the house, or
at least that the trunks alone would remain standing; but
these unaccountably escaped all serious injury, and are
still the same sorry-looking irregularities they have been
for the last twenty years.

It is not a little strange that the long rows of white
pines planted by Joseph Bonaparte in his park near Bor-
dentown, New Jersey, more than sixty years ago, have
escaped serious breakage from wind, incrusting snow, and
ice-incased twigs—the three causes that have, separately
and combinedly, effected the uncrowning and disfiguring
of the pines at home, which are no more exposed and
scarcely three miles away. Do not these trees generally
require planting in clusters, so as to be self-protecting, or
to be intimately associated with other trees? A lone pine
is very pretty and poetical, but hereabout it is as uncertain as the average white man.

But to return to the forest in the storm. Of a hundred
or more large trees—oaks, chestnuts, birches, gums, liquidambars, persimmons, catalpas, beeches, and sassafras—
occupying some three acres of southward sloping hillside,
but one, a large chestnut, was uprooted, and this was lifted
bodily from the ground and carried several feet from
where it had stood. The others were twisted; branches

were interlocked, and several so shaken and wormed about that the closely wrapping poison ivy was detached—an occurrence I should never have dreamed could have taken place. Where branches were broken, they were, as a rule, detached from the trunk of the tree as though seized at their extremities and twisted off. Although the wind remained in one direction, it evidently became a whirlwind among the tree-tops, as shown by the direction of fall of several large limbs. One large branch of an enormous beech was broken off, but still holds by long cables of twisted strips of bark, as though the storm had repented and tried to repair the damage by tying it on again.

Of the several species of trees I have mentioned, no two are of like toughness in the texture of their wood, and in this storm the weaker and more brittle kinds did not suffer as much as the tough old oaks. Nor were the detached branches worm-eaten, and so abnormally weak. I was confronted with contradictions whichever way I turned. Associate these with wind having a velocity of fifty-four miles an hour and air full of sand-like snow, and realize how easily one could become bewildered.

In the more exposed upland fields not a tree suffered, the big sassafras, sixty-two feet in height, not losing even a twig. Stranger still, the scattered beeches and white oaks that have retained their withered leaves all winter hold them still. In short, the home woods suffered very little, and what damage there is, occurred where I least expected to find it. Where the exposure was greatest, there every tree successfully weathered one of the severest storms on record. The shrubbery, seedling oaks and beeches, puny cedars, and trim little junipers were bent to the ground and remained prostrate for three or four days. The snow has now melted, and all are again erect; but when I bent some of them to-day as flatly as did the snow and wind, they cracked and were destroyed. Was it that the gradual pressure of the snow prevented the disaster that my more sudden bending caused?

While I rejoiced at having my woodland still intact, there was one aggravating feature about it all. I anticipated a harvest of dead limbs for my andirons; but they too withstood the tempest. To-day they looked down at me with a tantalizing "no-you-don't" expression that robbed me of half the pleasure of seeing one old black alder still with a few of its crimson berries resting upon a dazzling drift of unstained snow.

I was concerned, too, about the many birds that had sung so suggestively of spring on this same wooded slope two days before the storm. They surely had had no warning of the danger at hand, and now I had occasional glimpses of many as they were borne by me with fearful velocity. They seemed at times struggling to rise above the trees, as though aware of the danger of being dashed against them. Snow-birds, pine-finches, tree-sparrows, bluebirds, robins, song-sparrows, and the crows were the several kinds that I could positively identify; and all were equally unable to find a resting-place.

Once there was a decided lull, lasting perhaps for five minutes, and in that brief time the courage of a few tempest-tossed bluebirds seemed to return. Though the air was still thick with snow, and every branch of every tree in motion, I heard these brave birds sing! Only a few most melancholy notes they uttered, it is true, but full of suggestion. Songsters they that merit a poem in their honor! I first caught a glimpse of them among the sweeping branches of the pines, and then saw them reach, after much effort, the snow-laden cedars, but it was not to find rest and shelter therein. A moment later the wind with redoubled fury struck the trees and they were lost in an avalanche. One enormous snowbank toppled over and buried them beneath it. That the bluebirds should have escaped is strange indeed. The broad trunk of a sturdy oak saved me from the tempest's fury, but I dared stay no longer, and while struggling through the ever-shifting drifts I once more caught sight of these same birds, as they were dashed toward the meadows, and above the roar of the wind I heard, as I believe, the bluebird's song.

I have spoken of foxy sparrows as chiefest of this month's musicians; a word now concerning another of our finches. It has not been long since an ornithologist wrote, " The identity of the grass-finch is doubtful," adding that it had not been determined to be a winter resident in New Jersey. No? Well, I identified it as such twenty years ago, and there is not a farmer in the county that does not know it—the " rut-runner," as he calls it—as a winter bird. My critic adds, too, ornithologists would be grateful if I killed a score of innocents for their benefit. Well, I won't! And, again, another versed in bird lore suggests that my winter birds were Ipswich sparrows, which probably never set foot within a hundred miles of my fields. Really, is it safe to call a crow a crow? There need be no mistaking this species for any other, for all who know our birds at all are familiar with this ever-abundant tenant of our fields. I have called it elsewhere the most " resident " of all our smaller birds; even going so far as to suggest that it spent its whole life in the field in which it was hatched. This may be an exaggeration, but is not very far from the exact truth. In the winter of 1887–'88, I saw them in December and January, and two days after the great storm of March 12–14, 1888, found one that had succumbed to the cold and snow. There was no necessity to refer to the text-books, but I did so out of idle curiosity, and, as I knew would be the case, it proved to be a " true," and not a sham, grass-finch, the same that Burroughs has made famous, the bird by others called bay-winged bunting, and christened by the scientific students of birds *Poöcœtes gramineus.*

So much for the critics; now for the bird itself. A robin, three grass-finches, three bluebirds, and a pair of song-sparrows took refuge in the barn, one large mow of which was empty. Here they escaped the snow and wind, it is true, but the cold was, I thought, even more intense than out of doors. I fully realized, for the first time, the meaning of the familiar expression "as cold as a barn," for I gave some time to watching these tempest-driven birds that had here found shelter. In habit, these nine individuals might be grouped as the singers and the silent, for while six were quite happy in the thought of danger escaped and at times feebly lisped a hymn of thankfulness, the grass-finches were silent even to chirping, as though doubtful if barn-floors were much, if any, preferable to death. The ground-frequenting habits clung to them closely. They sped like mice over the ground floor, and only when hard pressed would they fly to the mow, and then did not long remain.

Heretofore it has been my experience to have the grass and slightly ridged surface of even our smoothest fields obscure the bird as it voluntarily wandered about, and every occasion would prove but a series of rapidly recurring glimpses only; while, on the other hand, the bird's hurried motions when trying to keep just ahead of carriage wheels have really no significance as to its method. The barn-floor, therefore, afforded excellent opportunity for observation, and I was forcibly reminded of the European skylarks in the aviary of a friend.

What struck me as a curious feature of the bird's habits, was that of spreading the tail when moving leisurely across the floor, as well as when forced to fly. In the latter case, there is an explanation of the habit, suggested and well supported by J. E. Todd. It is to the

effect that "when general color is inconspicuous" birds
may have some directive coloration, as "colors upon parts
of the body which may be hidden during rest, but capable of display automatically either during flight, at the
moment of stopping, or during a calling cry." Now the
grass-finch can not fly without showing the white feathers
in his tail. It is a habit beyond his control, and when the
outside white feathers are removed, the tail during flight
spreads just the same. The habit is, of course, valueless
when the bird is on the ground, for there it can not be
seen; hence my surprise when I saw the movement while
the birds stood on the barn-floor. It was in each case accompanied with a little trembling, a slight vibratory movement, suggestive of a desire to shake dust or water from
the feathers, yet they were not soiled by either.

The single night these grass-finches remained in the
building they roosted upon the bare floor, and so closely
were they huddled together that at three paces distant, by
lantern-light, they appeared as one bird.

The other birds were as uninteresting as so many
caged ones, and seemed only anxious to get abroad again.
I felt no sorrow when they quitted the barn, but would
gladly have had the grass-finches remain, for they were
not only instructive but had wit enough to see that I
meant them no harm.

This seemingly trite remark can not be held to go for
nothing. It really means a good deal; namely, that birds
can distinguish individuals among men, and, may I add?
can judge of human character. The former is true beyond question; and if the latter is not, how is it that some
people can never gain the friendship of a caged bird?
With a friend, I recently visited an aviary in town. Upon
the finger of its owner a siskin frequently alighted, but
could not be approached by my friend or myself. The
bird had been taught nothing, but through accumulated

experiences had learned that it was perfectly safe to do so. The Carolina wren that allowed me to stroke it while on its nest was suspicious of every other human being that it saw; yet several tried by every means to accomplish that which I could do.

We must not, however, base too much upon such extreme cases as this. Probably there are in existence an exceedingly small number of birds so constituted mentally that they can acquire such a degree of confidence, and far fewer human beings that can win it. And I am reminded here of a really amiable man who says he dare not walk near the curbstone when in town, as every horse he passes tries to bite him. When confiding birds and men who truly love them do happen to meet, the result is interesting. Think of Bradford Torrey playing with a vireo as it sat upon its nest! And what language can be found adequate to describe the villainy of the ·fiend who stole the nest; for stolen it was!

All things considered, it is fortunate for the wild birds and for the non-collecting naturalist that the birds are wild; but in most cases, with a little tact, one can inspire a lesser but sufficient degree of confidence, and so be enabled to witness much that would otherwise be hidden. I can well recall one instance bearing upon this. On the edge of a hill-side path, a pair of cat-birds had their nest. Twice daily, a long row of cows filed singly by, and then the more dangerous small boy. But the latter proved humane, and while he looked, he never handled either the nest or eggs. The result was that the birds, long before their young were old enough to leave the nest, paid no more attention to the boy than to the cows, and never stirred, although often they were feeding the brood, as he passed by. As he put it: "If I could not have picked them up, I could have put salt on their tails." The interesting feature of this case lies in the fact that neither I nor my cousin, who also tried, could pass by in the same manner, behind the cows, without frightening the birds. I do not see how their actions can be interpreted, except by the suggestion that they distinguished one boy from all other persons.

In the case of the pair of <u>peewees</u> that every season have a nest on one of the pillars of my porch, the birds are somewhat timid while the nest is being constructed, less so when the eggs are laid, and quite indifferent to us all when the young are hatched. In this case, strangers are not distinguished; but when some one comes upon the porch and hammers away with the old brass knocker, then the peewees think it time to leave.

I am free to say this does not often happen, but is so frequent that if the same peewees come year after year, they should by this time have got used to the thunder of the ponderous brass; but they have not, and here is a fact to be scored against my view of permanent mating occurring among these birds.

It is in March, if the wind has died away, that we notice so often after sundown flickering lurid patches of dull red light scattered along the horizon. It excites no comment now. We do not wonder, at this time of year, whose house or barn it is that has caught fire—the farmer is burning brush.

This effectual method of cleaning up the ground is a prominent phase of farm life in March, and is an occurrence in which every lover of out of doors can take delight. The day-time preliminaries are not attractive. Raking dry leaves while the wind blows is simply exasperating; and I have often wondered that the farm-hands had any patience left. At last the piles are ready, and fairly secure by the weighting of branches cut from the old apple trees. The night is still; the word is given; the torch applied.

That fire is fascinating, no one will question; but few people, however, seem aware of the peculiarly attractive feature of a fierce blaze at night, when coupled with the feeling that, furious as it may seem, it is nevertheless under control. Of course, the moment that control is lost, all pleasure vanishes and anxiety, if not terror, overcomes all other emotion. Happily, this seldom happens, when it is but the burning of brush.

I was present recently when a pitchy black night was chosen for the fun. The impenetrable darkness beyond a little space, the fantastic shapes and shadows where the red light fell, the sharp crackling and the angry hiss, held me spell-bound. While I felt no temptation to plunge into the fire, I can imagine, I think, why it is that so many animals, and particularly birds, are overcome by the leaping flames. I continually found myself drawn nearer and nearer to the fire and anxious to explore with my cane every nook and cranny of the glowing mass. Not a blackened twig that bid fair to escape but I delighted to throw into the fiercest flames; my own appetite for witnessing destruction becoming as insatiable as that of the fire itself for fuel. The warmth, too, of the surrounding air was exhilarating, rousing every energy to quicker action, instead of drugging them with the noxious gases of an indoor stove.

Something of this is applicable to birds, or so it has appeared when I have seen them drop helpless into the fire. Once, when a saw-mill burned, it seemed as if the birds of the county collected as a cloud and rained upon the flames. Not one appeared to fly deliberately into them; and so far as I was able, under very favorable circumstances, to determine, no large birds, as hawks or owls, were among the victims.

When a field is suddenly lighted up at night, the small birds in the vicinity are not simply excited by the strange aspect of a flickering fragment of noon-day suddenly appearing in their midst; they are intoxicated by the novelty. The warmth, too, rouses their energies, as it did mine, and curiosity brings them to the fore. Alas! that they have not knowledge of the nature of fire. It is as sunlight and as sun-warmth, and its source as distant as the light of day. They play about it in perfect safety, and only fall when they attempt to pass over it.

At last the flames lose strength; the glowing coals grow dull; black and gray ashes seam the ruddy mass, and darkness, creeping from the outer world, broods over all. The aspect is over, the excitement passed, but the memory of an unalloyed joy is not ours. It saddens one to think that the sparrow that delighted us with music throughout the day may have fallen into the flames.

I have said that by March 1 the world is interested in every supposed sign of spring; and all through the month the discussion of each sign's merit has been kept up, not only in the parlor, but in the kitchen, the tavern bar-room, and the village store. Then, too, there have been hosts of meteorological screedlets in the local papers. Boiling all this wisdom down, the residuum is—ignorance.

If ice, snow, unremitting cold, fewer mild days than February boasts, and every variety of chilling wind, go to make up our winter, then count in March. But in spite of every arctic element, there are occasional crumbs of comfort for the botanist, if none for folk less favored. Over his countenance there occasionally flits a gleam of satisfaction, and the winds are tempered when, with a sprig of arbutus in his button-hole, he returns from an outing.

CHAPTER IV.

APRIL.

HOWEVER desirable it may be to feel that confidence
can be safely placed in many mundane matters, and in
some, if not all humanity, the undoubted fact that we can
not do so in the matter of April days is a condition not without merit. The systematic rambler has not grown gray
before he learns that the blissful uncertainty of April is
really a source of a certain joy; for there is abundant
warrant that every day will be full enough, whether clear
or cloudy; whether dripping with intermittent showers,
or white, even, with the last snow of the season. And
here let me say that April snow-storms are not such novelties as has been intimated. However it may be in adjoining States, or even in adjoining counties, here, where the terrace faces southward and where we have less winter than do
others not beyond the horizon, I have waded knee-deep in
snow, and plucked, while so doing, dogwood blossoms,
white as the drift that formed their unwelcome background.

Such short-lived snows have no ill effect upon vegetation, and leave the ground as green and blossom-starred
as it was before the storm. Indeed, there are dainty April
blossoms that seem to enjoy these belated storms, and prove
no mean rivals, in purity of color, to the snow through
which they peep. At such a time, as the thermometer
will show, the ground at the plant's roots and the air that
bathes its delicate branches, if they reach above the snow,

are not chilled, and the intermediate, encroaching rim of winter produces no ill effect. The buds on every tree continue to swell, as might be expected; but creeping plants, as arbutus, are not blighted, for from beneath the snow I have gathered fully opened blossoms. Such occurrences must not be misinterpreted; they do not indicate that arbutus is a lover of cold weather, but that it has strength to withstand it when it comes. It has always appeared to me that a white frost was more destructive than a black one. A cold, dry atmosphere, even when thin ice forms, has appeared not to affect wild flowers; while many blossoms withered when the sunshine melted from them crystals of frost.

It would be hard to determine, in years, how long has April been the uncertain moon it now is: doubtless for tens of centuries, and the vegetation that has become established through natural agencies is not easily disconcerted. It appears to discount all probable contingencies, and the not infrequent snows that March left as its spiteful legacy to the woods and fields are accepted with better grace than is generally supposed.

I have often wished that good old Zeisberger had been more explicit, and not merely stated that the Delaware Indians called April *Quitauweuhewi gischuch*, the Spring Moon. The word has a far different meaning, a fuller one than that, but just what, I have never learned. To say it is a spring month in New Jersey is as unsatisfactory as to say that April is derived from "*Aperio*—I open." It is true that, by actual count, more buds open then than in March, but so gradual is the difference, and so uncertain, withal, that a better name could readily be found. Perhaps the Indians meant, "moon of preparation." I call it the month of expectation. As a whole, it is a horrid hotch-potch, but seldom is it without days when Nature becomes ecstatic.

But before attempting the history of days that proved worthy of a record, what of that feature of the month with which all are familiar, at least by hearsay—its famous showers? These figure with more or less prominence in the literature of the past five centuries from the time when Chaucer sang

> Whanne that April with his shouers sote,
> The droughte of March hath perced to the rote;

to the mechanical rhymes of village weeklies concerning the pretty lie that April showers bring May flowers. Let us determine, then, in what respect a short-lived rain of this month differs from one in May or June. As in many other matters meteorological, the imagination is allowed a more than scientific sway, and peculiarities claimed to exist are much more fanciful than real. In this case, the rain-drops are no less round or damp than usual, or more so. But the country has an aspect now that is quite its own, and this has much to do, though not all, with typical April showers, which are always accompanied by sunshine; rains of a few minutes' duration, from clouds that fleck but not obscure the sky, and offer opportunity, if not to walk between the drops, at least to dodge their sources, and skip from cloud-capped to clear country. I remember one such shower when the east side of the turnpike was dusty, while the west was channeled with tiny rivulets.

We must not look for April showers too soon; the rigor of March may linger in the air; nor too late, for May is often unreasonably impatient, and jostles the elbow of retiring April. It is during the third week, as my records run, that the month may best be studied—a week when leaves are young, when grass is green, when nature teams with promise.

In the forest, the sunlight softly stealing through the half-grown leaves gilds the dark mosses, warms the cold lichens, kisses the purple orchids, makes glad the gloomiest crannies of the wood. Scarcely a cave so dark, or ravine so deep, but the light reaches to its uttermost bounds, and, unlike the soulless glare of the midwinter sun, is life-inspiring. There is a subtle essence in an April sun that quickens the seeming dead.

And while I have stood wondering at this strange resurrective force, at times almost led to listen to the bursting buds and steadily expanding leaves, a veil is suddenly drawn over the scene and the light shadows fade to nothingness. Falling as gently as did the sunlight that preceded it, come the round, warm rain-drops from a passing cloud. Gathering on the half-clad branches overhead, they find crooked channels down the wrinkled bark, poise upon the unrolled leaves, globes of unrivaled light, or nestle in beds of moss, gems in a marvelous setting. Anon the cloud passes, and every rain-drop drinks its fill of light. There is no longer a flood of mellow sunshine here, but a sparkling light—an all-pervading glitter. And it is thoroughly inspiring. Your enthusiasm prompts you to shout, if you can not sing, and the birds are always quickly moved by it. From out their hidden haunts, in which they have sat silently while it rained, come here and there the robins, and, perching where the world is best in view, extol the merits of the unclouded skies. Earnest Sun-worshipers they, that watch his coming with impatient zeal and are ever first to break the silence of the dawn; and all these April days their varying songs are tuneful records of the changing sky.

Does it mean nothing that the robins always go to some commanding point, if not to the very top of the tree, to sing? Starr King, in one of his admirable lectures, remarks: " You never surprise a dog, deer, or bear gazing with satisfaction at the loveliness of the meadow, the curve of a river, or the grandeur of a mountain. They see all

the facts as an inventory could be taken of them, but not
the charm of color or motion into which the details
blend." I am not quite sure about our mammals, which
certainly have essentially prosaic natures, but as far as our
birds are concerned, I am led to dispute the statement;
and Mr. King intended that it should apply to them.
Does this asserted soul-condition fit with that love of locality that we know birds possess? I think not. And
have we any right, as is done by many, to assume that
haunts are chosen wholly with reference to the food supply? If so, many a birdless area should be thronging with
them throughout the summer. Why, if the beauty that
we recognize goes for naught among birds, does the grass-
finch sing most sweetly during the few moments of a brilliant sunset? Time and again, as I have passed over the
upland fields at the close of the day, the sun has suddenly
broken through the cloud-banks on the horizon and filled
the world with crimson and golden light. In an instant
every grass-finch in the field mounts some low shrub and
sings his sweetest songs. Is this always mere coincidence?
Do they not, rather, feel that same impulse which prompts
us to exclaim, "How beautiful"?

And I can not withhold from the falcons that I have
seen credit for some nobler motive, when gazing from the
top of the tallest tree about, than looking for a mouse.

But the typical April shower is not the only variation
during the month from fair-weather days. There are
other rains than these deliberate, partial, poetical ones;
and I never fail to remember this latter fact, and am disagreeable enough to thrust deadly statistics in the face of
those who quote with evident satisfaction pat phrases
about this strange month's beauties. The month has its
charms, and an abundance of them, and all try to forget
its unpleasant features; but when I hear my friends extol
the beauty of tearful April, as though the month was a

fragment of paradise lost, my perverse disposition asserts itself and I quote from the depressing pages of "Peirce on the Weather." Of one not yet forgotten April, he records: "A cold, boisterous northwester . . . made everything tremble and shiver. . . . The blustering snow-squalls which followed would have been more suitable for January. . . . Ice formed on several nights, half an inch thick, which destroyed all the buds, and almost every green thing." Nothing quite so bad as this, lately, it is true; but what has been may be; and arbutus gatherers that had hung their wraps upon the trees, shivered as I read this and thought it was growing cold again. I must admit that I enjoyed their discomfort; and let me ask what is the origin of that mental condition which prompts one to do these things? There is no known animal ancestor from which it could be derived.

A kindly disposed critic has suggested that I visit "the islands of the Niagara River, or even the fields along its shore," instead of persistently "paddling among bullfrogs on Big Bird Creek." I have been along the shores of the river named, and lingered spell-bound about the falls; but my experience was that of my own insignificance. If at home at all, it is by the unromantic, quiet creeks, beloved of bull-frogs, tenanted by turtles and snakes, decked with unassuming bloom, and graced by the unpretentious songs of the sparrows and the wren. These, my constant companions from my youth up, filled my heart long years ago; and I stand in awe of scenes or creatures more wonderful or mysterious.

Leaving a glorious flood upon the meadows, with its untold wealth of suggestiveness, I took my friendly critic's advice, choosing certain promising days of April, 1887, and sought, with some misgiving, a new pasture. I am free to confess that I long reveled in the heaped-up bounties of the wide wilderness into which I plunged.

Hurrying from town to village, and skirting many a piny wood, oak opening, and dismal swamp, I reached May's Landing late in the evening; due south from my home a small fraction more than a degree, and, by the geologist's map, just sixty feet nearer to the ocean's level.

The unremitting whistle of a caged cardinal roused me at early dawn, and, to solve the all-important question of the weather probabilities, I took my first day-time glance at the village, so far as peeping through the slatted shutter would permit.

I found myself practically in another world. Every tree had a foreign look, although but oaks and pines and gum trees, such as I have at home. In spite of the botanists' assertions, they were not the same in appearance. The soil and environment had wrought a nameless something in them that one could see, yet not describe. Such white and "turkey" oaks as shade the village street and cluster about the churches and court-yard do not grow in my own neighborhood, but recalled rather the towering tulip trees that overtop all other growths upon the wooded hill-sides of my home.

The rambler wisely contents himself with moderate pleasure, and is soothed by the chipper's trill when thrushes fail to sing; but still he ever hopes that his fortune may be bettered and the silence broken by his worshiped favorites. This undercurrent of desire for a climacteric experience holds good with every feature of the outdoor world; and while I find abundant joy in what old trees are near at hand, even if they be not large, my constant hope is that every new direction that I take may lead to others and perfect of their kind. Of many species there are such trees, but scattered so widely that but one can be seen each day; and of these, in numbers, the white oak falls to the bottom of the list, though first in beauty of all our forest trees.

There stands in the yard of the Quaker meeting-house, at Crosswicks, New Jersey, a perfect white oak—a tree that for many miles around is without a rival. At the surface of the ground the body of this tree is nearly twelve feet in diameter, and it tapers upward quite abruptly to its minimum cross measurement of five feet six inches. At fourteen feet from the ground the branches start, of which some twenty go to make a beautifully symmetrical crown, gracefully curved above, and extending more than fifty feet in every direction from the trunk. When in full leaf, the tree casts a huge island of delicious shade, and as the old meeting-house—built in 1690—is not so old as the oak by at least a century, six or seven generations of earnest worshipers have gathered weekly within the shadows cast by it.

There are tongues in trees, and often have I wished that this one would speak out in no uncertain way and tell us of the past; tell us of the Indians that met on these pleasant hills—for Crosswicks was a great council-ground three hundred years ago; and tell us, too, of the earnest folk who settled here when, instead of a few widely scattered oaks, there were boundless forests of gigantic trees.

There are still in existence a few pages of an old day-book wherein is recorded the shipping from a point on the creek near by of thousands of " hogshead staves of white oaks "; and, later, millions of feet of hewed timber were rafted from this same place to Philadelphia. It is difficult, at this time, to realize that within sight of the old meeting-house was felled a considerable portion of the timber that supplied the market of that great city. Lastly, came the days of cord-wood supplies, and this completed the destruction. Now, the builder of a new barn must send hundreds of miles for timber stout enough for its frame.

6

That trees must be felled goes without saying; but it is deplorable that the importance of reforesting our less fertile tracts did not occur to our grandfathers. Could I boast to-day of a few acres of Crosswicks oaks, there is no wealth that could purchase their destruction. It is true that extensive forests and modern civilization are incompatible; but not so civilization and ample groves. As all Crosswicks points with pride to its single oak, so, too, the people of May's Landing may well be proud of their beautiful village so generously shaded by its splendid trees.

As the oaks had done, so, too, the many sour gums or pepperidge trees in the village quickly attracted my attention. In a general way they were familiar enough, but at the same time bore their stamp of an environment widely different from that at home, in holding aloft, among their leafless boughs, great clusters of pale green, clammy mistletoe.

The seeds of this parasitic plant, carried, it is thought, by birds, had found lodgment on the outer branches of these trees, and at once demanded tribute—a drain, as it proves, upon the poor tree's treasury. Slowly, but surely, the limbs become knobbed, gnarly, and knotted; then wither and decay.

That the relentless stranger moves steadily toward the base of the tree, as its afflicting presence works the destruction of its host, was evident from the appearance of many branches, yet it does not appear that a tree is ultimately killed by the plant. There were nineteen of these gum trees—all, save one, close to the water's edge—and one hundred and twenty-five bunches of mistletoe were growing thereon; some of them large enough to fill a bushel-measure.

This was something I had never seen before, and so far of passing interest, but it roused no feeling of admiration—seemed, indeed, a miserable blunder—and I was glad to turn away and gather nodding spikes of white cassandra. These, with the beautiful seed-pods of the stagger bush and needle-like foliage of the pine beauty, made for me a novel nosegay, which I carried until fresh novelties paled their prettiness.

Turning from the glistening sands of a well-worn wood-road, I threaded my way a few rods between scrubby oaks and dwarfed pines, and over a carpet of tufted gray-green reindeer moss, still flecked with the crimson berries and bronzed foliage of wintergreen. What the trees wanted in stateliness and height was more than compensated for by the luxuriant growth of lichens that draped their branches. The bearded giants of Florida were here bearded dwarfs, but no less venerable in aspect.

There were two very distinct species of these drooping lichens, one of which often measured fully two feet in length. The other was but little less vigorous a growth, and, though semi-erect, was equally graceful. This one bore aloft the daintiest of pearl-gray cups—goblets that flies might have sipped at, had they not all been empty; yet many were large enough to have held a drop of dew. Never before had I seen the well-known forms growing so luxuriantly. They gave a misty, cobwebby look to the woods, as though the spiders of the world had held a summer-long convention.

Plunging into this tangle, my first thoughts were of the animal life that it must shelter. I listened for birds to sing; there was no sound. I scanned the nearer branches; there was no moving creature. I shook the tufted lichens; not a bug crawled forth. The cracking of brittle twigs beneath my feet alone broke the silence. I was in a beautiful yet lifeless country.

Then came an abrupt change in my surroundings. Reaching higher ground, the crisp, crackling mosses gave way to fresher growths, and wreath-like patches of glittering, snow-white sand made a fitting background for the delicate pyxie. Straightway, on seeing this plant, I forgave the country for its want of birds. It were too great good fortune to have both, perhaps. Gray says of it, "found in the sandy pine barrens of New Jersey," but call no land barren where the pyxie grows. The sands of an ancient ocean-bed were here; the murmuring pines echoed the long silent surf. The spot seemed less a land than an earthly monument to a forgotten sea, and over it was spread a mantle of richest green, starred with the sparkling pyxie. No other blossoms intruded; no thoughtless growths crowded. There they were left to grow, in a wilderness that now was silent as a tomb, immortelles decking a dead ocean's grave.

Call this a " pine barren " if you choose, wherein plant lovers may peep and botanize, but must never hope to find a fortune; yet may it not after all have capabilities men now wot not of? Surely a cottage with pyxie at the door were a pleasant place to live, attractive as any garden of roses, and more suggestive of content than a lodge in a garden of cucumbers.

I longed for a boat, when I turned my face villageward to explore the tempting shores of the river that hurries by, but, deferring this promised pleasure, gave the remaining hours of a crowded day to "the pines," and a mile or two of the creek that thridded them.

Where bared sands could not boast a blade of grass I gathered curious earth stars; and then pines in front, on either side, and pines that walled the village from my view, muttered and murmured. A home for birds in abundance, yet what a beggarly showing! Not until the open country immediately adjoining the creek was reached did I hear a single chirp. A single pigeon woodpecker had ventured thus far, and twice I heard robins. Later a warbler was seen and heard, but all so indistinctly as to make it unsafe to guess the species. I listened frequently for the scream of the blue jay, yet heard none. They had wandered to fresh fields, but at times are here in force. At least, to them is credited the planting of the acorns that spring up so surely when the pines are felled. The red squirrel, too, probably has a hand in this, as it is one of the few mammals found in this region; where, indeed, bears and deer are still found, yet " small deer," like mice, are almost wanting. It is true I did not see a single squirrel, but the nibbled cones of the pine told clearly of their presence. I saw no mice, and was told there were none. My admiration for pine woods lessened when I heard this. Why it should be, seems indeed strange, and I doubt not they are indeed rare. It was a new impression of wild life that I had not suspected, to find that about my home, not three miles from a large town, were always at least half a hundred birds and a dozen mammals that, for some unknown reason, shunned a forest miles in extent, and far away from any considerable town.

How I longed to mingle the botany of these barrens with the wild life of the fields, hill-side, and meadows at home !

Time permitted of but a passing glance at the creek— a pine-woods stream here, but the drain of a cedar swamp somewhere above. As I stood upon its grassy bank the waters appeared like ink, except where fretted by fallen trees, when they became mantled with a delicate tracery of silvery bead-like bubbles.

I scanned the sunlit shallows for minnows, but could find none; the projecting stumps and logs for basking turtles—there were none; and I remembered that not a frog leaped into the stream as I drew near. Yet, to my ignorant eyes, there is no spot that seems better fitted for all these creatures. Such experiences chill one's enthusiasm through and through.

Still there was no lack of beauty. The beautiful pitcher plant was in full leaf, and many a one was emptied of its water as I hunted for the insects that nourish this curious carnivorous plant. I found none, nor were the flower-like leaves at all sensitive. Perhaps they were keeping Lent just then, and I doubt not will feast heartily when a cloud of mosquitoes settles in the valley of this forest brook.

I shall always covet the hollies growing there. Some were great pyramids of deepest green, still sparkling with myriads of red berries. These trees grow not only with branches so low that the trunk is hidden, but with the main stem bare for several feet in height, gray as a thrifty beech, and quite as smooth. On one such, a curious lichen —the *Grapta insculpta*—had grown until the tree appeared wrapped in inscribed parchment. Every letter of every alphabet was well represented, and cuneiform inscriptions and runes were noticeably abundant.

That this little corner of " the pines " teems with novelties I have no doubt; that animal life is really more abundant than then appeared is certainly true, but no demonstration of this is possible during so brief a visit. Could I spend a year upon the banks of that little creek I should have much to tell, but to tarry for an hour is of no avail.

Better than to do this—my good-natured critic notwithstanding—is to continue unto the end paddling among bull-frogs upon Big Bird Creek. But I hope to return before the summer ends.

And what of April at home? Alas! it is rarely twice the same, and describe it never so cunningly, a typical " Spring Moon " would scarcely be recognized. In 1886, the month was hot; in 1887, a curious mixture of all other seasons; while that of 1888 could boast of snow-drifts, relics of the great storm of the preceding March; and for four long weeks the west wind had miles of snow-clad country over which to pass before it reached us. Even the resident birds grew tired of it at last, and never were the hill-side and the meadows so silent as during the last days, save two, of the month.

A friend had come from Massachusetts to see and hear the many warblers that pass by in April, *en route* for their northern summer haunts; and, too, to hear such song-birds as do not reach New England. What folly on my part to have promised anything of these same birds!

> We threaded many a tangled brake,
>   Then traced the river's shore;
> We lingered where the marshes quake,
>   We tramped the meadows o'er;
> We listened long for some sweet song
>   Of summer's tuneful host;
> But never a note from any throat,
>   Each silent as a ghost.
>
> Through the lone, trackless swamp we strayed;
>   Full many a field we crossed;
> The pathless bog our steps delayed,
>   The ancient landmark lost—
> We stood in vain, some fancied strain
>   To hear; alas! instead,
> Nor sky nor ground gave forth a sound,
>   The very air was dead.
>
> Cloud-wrapped and sad so closed the day,
>   As sullen proved the night;
> The sun shed not his parting ray,
>   The stars withheld their light.
> No bat so bold to quit his hold,
>   Nor owl dared venture forth;
> The swift brook moaned, the tall tree groaned,
>   While breathed the icy north.

Six consecutive outings, each for the greater part of the day, yielded the poor showing of but fifty-five spe-

cies; and many of these—like the crow, grakle, and kingfisher, and, I may add, the bittern, which only gave us
two thirds of a " boom "—scarcely count as birds at all, so
hopelessly prosaic is their every utterance.   But many,
although persistently silent, and several that timidly
broke the silence, were not without interest.   Once, in a
sunny nook, among chestnut sprouts, my companion and
I found not only shelter from the icy wind, but birds
and blossoms in abundance.   Snowy toothwort and budding mandrake—both notable growths—quite covered the
ground; while ruby-crowned wrens thronged the adjoining thickets, active as ever, but warbling only in a half-
hearted way.   Not once did they sing out with that wealth
of energy characteristic of them in their summer haunts,
and as they occasionally venture to do here in New Jersey during mild winter days.   From their golden-crested
cousins—that at this time largely outnumber them—they
can readily be recognized, even when not seen, by their
more varied song, " lively, animated strains of canary-like
sweetness and clearness."

It has recently been denied that this bird winters in
New Jersey.   Probably this impression arose from observations made in the northern hilly section of the State.
One might as well attempt to study the equator by camping on the shores of Baffin's Bay.

Because those birds which we hoped to find were not
here, the days were not lost in sulking.   There was always
sound if not music, and sound is always suggestive.   As
we rested upon the soft cushions of well-matted leaves,
the bee-like Euryomia hummed about us—a beetle of
which I knew nothing, having, if I saw it at all, supposed
it to have come directly from the hives or a hollow tree.
At times the dead leaves rustled where song-sparrows and
chewinks scratched among them for food, and at once

curiosity is roused to see the birds, although their identity
is without question. As we peer into the thickets, a third
ground-loving bird flits up before us, a skulking hermit
thrush, and, mounting a low branch of a tree, it stares
back at us, with drooping wings, jerking tail, and mute as
those monks who are sworn to silence. When we remember that this same thrush is in New England almost
without a rival as a summer songster, it is a standing
mystery why here, for several months, it is so persistently
silent. Indeed, it occasionally nests in the romantic valley
of the Wissahickon, not forty miles away, and I am told,
even then has been seldom heard to sing; and the opinion
has also been expressed that such nesting birds do not
compare at all favorably with our splendid wood thrush.
As we saw them to-day running among the thousands of
nodding toothwort blossoms, they were less attractive
than would have been so many mice. But the flowers I
have mentioned never fail to command attention. Here
everything was suited to their needs, and they overtopped
the violets, spring beauty, bluets, and even crowded to obscure nooks that marvel of azure bloom, grape-hyacinth's
clustered bells.

Hard by, the rank mandrake or May-apple was not only
beautiful but suggestive. Many a plant was a telling instance of indomitable pluck; or, shall we say, like many
a mortal, born to pitiless ill-luck. Before the frost has
lost its hold upon the stout oak leaves that have lain the
winter long upon the ground, the leaf-wrapped stalk of the
May-apple, that can be likened to nothing so much as to
a closed umbrella, pierces the thin crust. Many meet
with a serious obstacle to their upward growth in the
leaves upon the ground, but their progress is never wholly
checked. Apparently unable to push it aside, the May-
apple pierces the dead leaf, and then lifts it up, often half
a foot above the ground. A decided victory seems at first

to have been gained, but the upward-borne leaf has its
revenge. It is merely pierced, not torn asunder, and
retaliates by holding the May-apple firmly bound, and the
glory of its growth, the outspreading of its umbrella-leaf,
is effectually prevented. I think of more than one poor
fellow, as I write, who has an unyielding oak leaf hopelessly binding his powers. Mr. Blank, over the way, is a
closed umbrella.

Later, while strolling by a meadow pond, and my companion searching for warblers among the scattered trees
upon its banks, I was startled by a shrill screaming, and
was astonished to see with what energy an irate swallow
pursued a kingfisher. The cause of the quarrel can only
be conjectured, but revenge was the evident impulse of
the offended bird, and, with a daring and rapidity of movement that would put even a wren to shame, it struck the
fleeing kingfisher again and again, as it darted among the
trees, screeching with terror.

The courage of a bird accomplishes much, and if all
our helpless species had both quicker tempers and yet remained coolly brave, their enemies, the falcons, would
prove less dangerous. A little cunning would often enable the pursued warbler to outwit the hawk, for the latter
depends upon brute force.

We found a few birds at last. Among tall pin-oaks
in a neglected meadow were yellow red-polled warblers;
restless, of course, as is all their tribe, but silent, save to
those who might be anxious to hear their lisping song.
By dint of listening, their few weak notes were recognized
amid the twitter and chirping of swallows and sparrows;
but the result was scarcely worth the effort required of us.
Think of following through bog, through bush, through
brake, through brier, to hear a mere midget in yellow-

brown feathers sing like a "debilitated chipper"! Such was my companion's comparison. I am not sure that I have ever heard a broken-down chipper sing; but given one in good health, and his tremulous twitter, full of vim as it is, is music that charms. Heard first while yet winter lingers, it is full of spring-tide suggestiveness, and shames our want of faith.

Very different were the earnest notes of a pair of dainty blue-gray gnatcatchers that came dashing through the tree-tops, and at once set us all craning our necks that we might follow their quick motions. They uttered not only two clear notes, but followed these with a rapid trill at times, as though, through the scolding, their stock of syllables bubbled over; and there was always an earnestness in their song, if so one may call it, that compelled attention.

I have been familiar with this little bird for years, and it has always been a matter of surprise that Wilson should have spoken of it as chirping feebly as a mouse, or, as has been remarked by a more recent writer, " like a mouse with a toothache." When nesting, this bird sings, but very rarely, in quite an elaborate manner, but probably much less so than in more southern localities. I have found, on comparing notes with observers in other fields, that the song of the same species differs very widely in different localities.

Much depends, I take it, upon all the circumstances attendant upon the study of a particular warbler, whether it proves of special interest or not. Certainly, as yellow red-polls, northward bound, there is nothing particularly attractive about them; as there is, for instance, about the ever abundant summer yellow-bird, whose few simple notes are so full of satisfaction—as though it was insisting upon the debatable point, whether or not life is worth living.

It is ornithological heterodoxy to speak disparagingly

of the North American warblers, I am well aware; but as migratory birds, seen only in transit, they rouse little enthusiasm, and those that remain suffer by association with birds of other families; with the exception, perhaps, of the Maryland yellow-throat.

The sixth outing was an up-river ramble. Leaving the rocks against which the incoming tides fretted in vain, we started at the end of the non-tidal river and commenced an ascent, so gentle here that the ever down-flowing waters are our only evidence that we rise higher and higher above the ocean's level, almost at every furlong of our progress. But it is a different country. No change from the home meadows could be more abrupt and complete. Here we have the often outcropping bed-rock, and to some extent a different flora. Here, hepatica and bloodroot blossom in the woods, flowers that win our love at the first glance; and later smilacina, delicate as lilies of the valley, cover the crevices of many a bared rock near the water's edge.

Nowhere is there uncertain footing—quicksand, mud, or floating weeds; but always smooth, compacted sand, a thickset sod, or smooth pebbles, long since water-worn, but now only overflowed when the river is at a freshet stage. It was at such now, and a single raft glided past— a few score of insignificant sticks, and as nothing in comparison with the mighty pine and hard-wood timber, that a century ago was floated yearly from the mountains above.

Lumbering on the Delaware is now a thing of the past, and to-day the banks of the stream have next to nothing left that the waters can float to market; but still the mountains are beautiful. Saplings and underbrush, like charity, cover a multitude of sins. As we pass by, their green is as rich as that of forest growths, and we are not unhappy if we do not stop to think.

The practically deserted river is more a relic of the past than an important factor of the present; for although its shores have been occupied by man a hundred centuries or more, probably never until now has the stream itself proved of so little use. To be sure, it is the convenient sewer of up-river towns and the sweet-water supply of the larger cities below; but this counts for little, and even the fishing interest is next to nothing. The fond hope of many an angler, that the salmon might be introduced, can never be realized, so unutterably filthy is the tidal portion of the river for fully a hundred miles from the ocean. Such an ordeal is too much for this lordly fish; and we can only wonder that the delicate shad is not like-minded. But our quest concerned the shores, and not the stream, for bushes and small birds have not yet been exterminated. Migrating warblers were the prime object of our all-day tramp; to see and hear them, if Fate willed it so; and, as may be inferred, Fate did not will it. We saw but twenty-one kinds of birds, only three of which were warblers; and not one of the whole series but was, that same day, far more abundant at home than here upon the rocky river shore.

For want of suggestive material, we had to abandon ornithological field-work for more prosaic pastime, and I ventured upon the dangerous ground of pre-eminently ancient man. Very persuasively, as I thought, I discoursed on the palæolithic implement we found on the gravelly shore, but the significance, as I hold it, of such rudely fractured stone was not made apparent. There was ominously little said in reply when I closed my argument, but the immovable countenance and far-off look of my companion's eyes told me that, like the river before us, not by the breadth of a hair had the current of his thoughts been changed.

Twenty-one species of birds only, we felt, were not of

sufficient interest to repay us for our tramp. Is there not something savoring of unwisdom in this? It is true, every one of them had been long familiar; their habits thoroughly known; yet, paradoxical as the statement may seem, not one but has the glamour of mystery about it. It is only necessary to take up American ornithological literature, and we will quickly find that the world is not of one mind, even as to cat-birds or the chipping sparrow. Scores of white-bellied swallows were darting over the water all day, and there is good ground for believing they have a nesting habit that is as yet unrecorded. We saw a single kingfisher, and I am told that a pair of these birds had once nested in a pile of railroad ties near here, after their nest in the bank of an inflowing brook had twice been washed away by sudden showers that gullied the loose earth which they had tunneled. May not such an occurrence be really less remarkable than we suppose, and have occurred time after time and been overlooked? How is it possible to keep such watch upon birds that all their irregularities shall be promptly discovered. I am more and more inclined to give heed to what I hear, considering how often I have myself seen the unexpected and improbable. Purple martins were abundant during the summer of 1887, and we saw many during our up-river ramble. They must have a nesting-place in the neighborhood, yet no boxes are occupied by them, these being tenanted by the English sparrows. Have they not probably returned to hollow trees? They have been known to do so within the present century.

The rose-breasted grosbeak is essentially a bird of the tall trees, and possibly would die if confined to the open fields, yet I have watched them by the hour, associated most familiarly with chewinks, scratching among the dead leaves. I was held all one forenoon, last May, to a single spot, watching a red-headed woodpecker as it sallied from its post in quest of flies, which it caught with all the grace and in perfect imitation of a typical fly-catcher.

The truth is, there is scarcely a habit but is open to marked influence, and the change may be suddenly brought about. Man often abruptly changes the whole face of nature, and the birds must likewise change or forsake their former haunts, and this many species are very loath to do. Where English sparrows have forced their way into the country, the familiar birds of our door-yards and gardens have been forced to quit, and now frequent localities where formerly they were seldom found and never nested.

In spite of the unpromising outlook, we continued our search for possible warblers. Every house we passed had its grove of tall white pines before it, and into these, with leveled field-glass, we persistently stared, hoping, not to the consternation of timid women-folk. Bird-hunting in this fashion is not yet quite a safe pastime, for the world is not so far educated as to realize that any one would walk a mile in hopes of merely seeing a rare warbler, and such curiosity has brought more than one rambler to temporary grief. I am so far fortunate as to have escaped molestation, to date; although I once chased a wounded bird into a stranger's garden when cherries were ripe. Less fortunate was my good uncle, when State Geologist of New York, for he was detained as a lunatic for two whole days in a country village because his saddle-bags were filled with "broken stones," as the fossils he had collected were pronounced to be.

But with all our care we saw no warblers, and stopped at the first tavern we reached, and refreshed. There is an excellent well of sweet water in the back yard. Here, too, we crossed the river and commenced our homeward journey. Still no birds; and probably never before had I taken a walk of the same length and seen so little. Dis-

couragement dogged our steps from the moment of leaving home until, as the day closed, we re-entered the
house.

Such empty days are by no means valueless. They
teach at least the uncertainty of bird migration, and likewise the fickleness of resident species. Why, indeed, the
latter should have forsaken us is a puzzle I have no hopes
of solving. To walk for hours about a favorite haunt
of winter birds and see a solitary chickadee only is not
an experience to recall except with disgust, yet such was
ours one chilly, gusty, yet cloudless April morning. Even
the crested tit, that storm-defying hero that the winter
long had cheered the naked woods, and whose notes are,
of all sounds in early April, the surest to revivify our
drooping hopes—even it forsook the home hill-side for
an entire week. But the world turned over a new leaf
on the twenty-eighth, and summer may be said to date
from that bright morning, for spring as a season is a
baseless myth.

April is not wholly at the mercy of the weather.
Many a plant, as well as bird, flourishes in spite of frost
or snow or ice; and lately we have had all three. The
black and wintry waters of the meadow ponds, that seem
but a little way off to be well-nigh fathomless, are really
shallow, and what little warmth the fitful sun vouchsafes
is carefully husbanded. The host of crowding water weeds
risk the chill nights and scarcely less frosty days, and
unless it be such a memorable year as 1816, when there
was ice every month, they suffer nothing. Yearly the
farmer frowns at April frosts, declaring that he will be
ruined. His sad prognostications always recall the annual
destruction of the rarely destroyed peach crop.

There was little but strictly wintry weather in April,
1888, and the average tree and plant were two weeks later

than in 1887; but in one sheltered nook wherein the drifts of the great March storm lingered until the second week there was found, almost on time, the delicate Dicentra, with its luxuriance of beautiful leaves and exquisite pendent bloom of ivory and gold. To think that such a plant should be called "Dutchman's breeches"! If this abomination were dropped from Gray's manual, perhaps in time a decent substitute would come in use. But why not call the plant Dicentra?

Fortunately, botany is not, like ornithology, cursed with often worse than meaningless names; execrable Latin and worse Greek that has been foisted upon the science by a recent nomenclatorial congress. A name that is meaningless, misleading, or inappropriate has no right to be; yet such are now claimed to be established for all time. But the world at large has no need of such insufferable rot.

During the same cold April days, where the terrace blends with the level meadows at the feet of stately trees the sod was thickly starred with heart's-ease. Confidence was stamped in each brave little face, and however often the breeze pressed them to the ground, straightway it passed they smiled as sweetly as before.

With these, blue violets, pale bluets, and brilliant buttercups, there was surely enough to tempt the birds, and field sparrows on the terrace and hair birds everwhere sang as merrily as they knew.

So far, this icy April held her own, but at times she struggled against fearful odds.

At all times there was life in the waters, if not in the air, and a long procession of restless fishes passed by whenever I sat on the creek bank or stood still a moment as I came to the meadow brooks. Every one except the eels and cat-fish were dressed in holiday suits; and few people would suspect that many a silvery minnow of later

summer is now decked with every color of the rainbow.
There is always a fascination in the still waters of a deep
pool. The improbable appearance of some strange creature from its depths is the subtle thought that holds me
whenever I chance to pass by the great bend of Pœtquissings. Once, on a chill and dull November day, a great
snapping turtle thrust his head above the surface, yawned,
and disappeared. And how vividly I can recall an experience of thirty years ago! While yet some distance off, I
saw what I took to be an otter, and commenced creeping
slowly toward it, in hopes of a better view. Nearer and
nearer I drew, and the unsuspecting otter remained at his
post. Finally, I reached the water's edge, and looked directly into it. My face was within a foot of the surface,
and directly in front was a nest-making sunfish. Did you
ever look one squarely in the face? If so, you have seen
a monster—a stranger shape than fevered fancy ever depicted. The supposed otter was a slimy log.

I often think of that long-distant day, and when the
quiet waters sparkle with long rows of glistening bubbles,
the gas from decomposing vegetation, I think of creatures
that may startle my maturer years as the great red-eared
sunfish frightened an eager boy.

A feature of winter, and even of spring so late as
April, is last year's leaves. As I walked recently along a
wooded hill-side, over tree-margined fields, and skirted a
swamp too wet, as yet, to enter, I noticed many a tree
with last year's leaves still on it. Except one tupelo,
which usually drops its foliage earlier than our other forest
trees, these leaf-bearers were all oaks or beeches. Thoreau
speaks of the white oaks about Concord retaining their
leaves as a rule, and others deny that this is true, or more
than an occasional occurrence.

The conclusions derived from my own memoranda,

covering many years, and of my ramble of yesterday particularly, are that not only the white oak, but several other species, do retain their leaves, or a considerable percentage of them, until early in May of the next year. Take any oak grove in this neighborhood, and I think it will be found, if the trees are not too crowded for healthy growth, that fully three fourths of them retain from one tenth to one half of their leaves. But when we come to consider single trees, this habit of leaf-retention will be found one of many curious features. For instance, I know of many single trees, both oaks and beeches, that have a single limb that will retain its foliage the winter through, while the other branches are bare from November to May. Again, a tree that stands upon the edge of a wood will hold its leaves on the open, light, and airy side, and drop those that grew upon the shaded limbs. Does the greater vigor of the foliage upon the sunny side explain this?

In one of my upland fields there stands a thrifty scarlet oak that is noticeable for the beauty and density of its foliage. In October the deep green becomes a rich maroon, and later, a lighter and brighter red, and not until nearly New Year's has the ruddy tinting given way to brown. Even then the tree remains a prominent object, and is, indeed, even for an oak, one among a thousand. For the past fourteen years this tree has never failed to retain nearly all its leaves, although in that time there has been every variety of summer and winter that even the powers in charge of our capricious climate could invent.

On examination of the oaks near by, it has seemed to me that they all have a tendency to retain their leaves, and the measure of success in each case is due principally to the exposure of the tree and its general vigor. Here I may be wholly at sea, and only too glad to be informed correctly if in error.

What I have said of oaks applies equally to the beech.

Given shelter from the northwest winds and average
vigor, and many a leaf will cling to its parent stem until
the swelling leaf-buds of the new year shall crowd it from
its place.

While yet the drifts of the late great snow-storm still
lingered, it was a pleasant feature of the landscape to see
the sapling beeches still bearing aloft their last year's
leaves, dimly glittering like wrinkled fragments of old
gold, and filling the air with a bell-like tinkle, soothing
and soft as the twitter of a bird.

I offer it as a hint to the landscape gardener, to bring
about by selection—if it can be done—a fully established
habit of leaf-retention; not making evergreen oaks, but
winter-long, bright brown oaks; for such now lessen to a
marked degree the dreariness of many a winter outlook.
Again, when leaf-retaining oaks are mingled with evergreens, there is an added charm to the scene. Think for
a moment of such a cluster as this: A background of
cedar, scattered oaks with dark brown leaves, a beech with
golden foliage, and crimson-fruited black alder mingled
through it all, for the fruit of the alder clings at times to
the stems until winter is well advanced, and the glowing
color of the berries is not dimmed even when the fruit is
shriveled.

Lastly, it matters nothing what the weather may be,
April has yet another feature worthy of record, one that
gives it a glory above all winter months—the coming of
the pioneer thrush. This year, the mild, moonlit midnight of March 31 wooed him hither. We may be sure
of this, for he is no skulker in early spring, and greets the
sunrise with no uncertain song, wherever he may be.
Very appropriately, then, he was first seen and heard as
the glimmering light of dawn disclosed, April 1st, the
naked fields, the faintly greening willows, and wide

reaches of sparkling waters; for the spring-tide freshet covers all the lowlands, and we have no meadows now, but the ragged remnant of a short-lived lake instead.

It is needless to attempt a description of the lone thrush's song; suffice it to say he sang, and the scattered leaves that the winter long have clung to their parent stems, and the trembling twigs of every tree and shrub seemed conscious of his presence and thrilled by his inspiring voice.

CHAPTER V.

MAY.

NOTHING could more neatly and truthfully express the conditions of the outdoor world in early May than the name given to the month by the Delaware Indians— *Tauwinipen gischuch*, the moon of the beginning of summer. And dearest of all the moons should this one be to him who loves an outing, if it be, as has been said, that by its waxing light many a long-absent migratory bird is guided to its haunts of a year ago.

I have often wondered if an Indian ever said to himself, " To-morrow will be the first of May," and retired in blissful expectation of being aroused by a grand chorus of newly arrived songsters. Probably not; nor can I, much as I would love to have it so, for the reason that many a summer bird persists in dropping in upon us before that magic date.

So far as my own observations extend, the moon influences migration, if it does at all, in some such way as this: If it fulls between April 20 and 30, then the birds that are latest to arrive, as a rule, will be earlier by nearly a week than if the nights are dark, as when there is no moon or a waning one. But this may be all a mere coincidence, and of but one fact I can speak positively—that regularity is not so important a factor of the habit as is persistently claimed.

But May is a month to be enjoyed, not coldly discussed,

and enthusiasm should thrill to the very finger-tips of
every one who, on the morning of the month's first day,
hears the thrush, grosbeak, oriole, and a host of warblers
as they greet the rising sun. And rest assured, dear
startled reader, that unless you are astir before the sun
is fairly above the horizon you will never know what
bird-music really is. It is not alone the mingled voices
of a dozen sweet songsters; for the melody needs the
dewy dawn, the half-opened flowers, the odor-laden breeze
that is languid from very sweetness, and a canopy of
misty, rosy-tinted cloud, to blend them to a harmonious
whole, and so faintly foreshadow what a perfected world
may be.

I spent a portion of May, 1887, in a mountainous
region, for I longed to test the truthfulness of the claim
that there only could I hear the choicest songsters at their
best. Forgive me, home woods and native fields, for I
must confess to its truth.

Reaching my destination at night, I gave little heed to
my surroundings then, and can only testify to the power
of the mountain whip-poor-wills to break the slumbers of
the soundest sleeper. A half-score, at least, of these
strange birds seemed to be perched upon my window-sill,
if, indeed, not in the room itself; and not until dawn did
they cease, except to draw breath, their shrill discordant
cry. I certainly had these birds at their best, and it was
an instance where too great familiarity bred contempt. It
is a trite saying that there is no accounting for tastes, but
it is hard to believe that whip-poor-wills really enjoy the
sound of their own voices. Did noise, like light, attract
insects, then, indeed, they would not be as they now are,
mysterious by reason of their song.

Early the next morning I chose the ▮▮ as my best
point for general observation. And such ▮▮y!

Swallows over the water,
Warblers over the land ;
Silvery, tinkling ripples
Along the pebbly strand.
Afar in the upper ether
The eagle floats at rest ;
No wind now frets the forest ;
'Tis Nature at her best.
The golden haze of autumn
Enwraps the bloom of May—
Fate grant me many another
Such perfect summer day.

The difference of elevation between the mountain lake
and my home on the ridge by tide-water meadows—one
nearly of twelve hundred feet—had, I doubt not, much to
do with the distinctness that characterized the songs of
even the small migrating warblers. Many of these restless birds that I have always had at home to seek out, that
I might catch as best I could the short, sweet songs they
whisper to the flowers only, here rang out their melody
in such bold, decisive tones that even their faintest utterance was heard.

The blue yellow-backed warbler was a prominent species of this numerous family, and an excellent one wherewith to test the question of song variation in different localities. Dr. Brewer states that " it has no song properly
so called ; its notes are feeble and few, and can be heard
only a short distance"; and quotes Mr. T. M. Trippe, of
Orange, New Jersey, to the effect that the song, while
" sharp and lisping," is quite varied, and consists of several
notes. This is quite applicable to such as I have heard at
home, where they are found all summer, and, I am informed, true of them in southern Jersey, where, as along
Cohansey Creek, in Cumberland County, they breed in considerable numbers. But about the lake shore, in Morris
County, where they were abundant, the sharpness and lisp

mentioned by Mr. Trippe were not noticeable, and every note, as both my companion and I heard them, was clear, of moderate volume, and sweet. Furthermore, they sang constantly, and, unlike many other warblers, frequently stopped to sing, as though fond of their own music; and did not, as is so common, merely fling out the notes that gathered in their throats, as though they were obstacles to fly-catching.

Another warbler noted particularly was the black-throated green, which at home sings but moderately well, and, I think, never in a manner to make it noticeable to the unobservant. So far, my own impression, at least, and I was recently much surprised to hear a friend announce that before he arose that morning, he had heard one of these birds singing, although the window was but slightly opened. Perhaps an ardent lover of birds blessed with such acute hearing may be inclined to call the green warbler a fine songster; but it is not likely to be classed as such by the less gifted commonalty. For many a summer I had tried most faithfully to hear the " Hear me, St. Theresa ! " so gracefully described by Wilson Flagg. On the shores of Lake Hopatcong, I at last heard it. Whether these birds were at the very tops of the tallest trees or in the tangled thickets that filled every space between the huge rocks, it mattered not. They sang incessantly, morning, noon, and night; and always as sweetly and clearly as the song was continuous. Here, these birds are found all summer; in other words, are at home, and proved new birds to me.

The redeye, among the vireos, too, had a more flute-like song, and, like the warbler, sang at all hours; but never lapsed into the peevish, complaining, muffled utterance, so commonly heard in south Jersey—as though protesting against the humid, enervating heat. And again, upon the summits of the highest surrounding hills, were

many indigo birds, all of which had a more mellow and
less sibilant song, than have those that sing in my
garden.

But above all the others and ever to be remembered
were birds of three widely different kinds that, for abundance, want of fear of man, and constant singing, far excelled the scores of species that were identified.   They
were the Baltimore oriole, the scarlet tanager, and the redstarts.

The songs of the orioles were so soft, yet clear, and
had so often a perfect flute-like trill, that when I first
heard them in the gray dawn I was sorely puzzled, and
disposed to doubt my companion's decision when he announced one as singing in this sweet, wild way while rol-
licking in the misty air.   Unlike the orioles at home,
they did not first alight and then fairly scream their satisfaction that May days had come.   Alas! that words are
well-nigh useless wherewith to attempt the description of
bird-music!   Accept, then, the simple statement, that
these happy orioles sang as I had never heard them before.   Was it the mountain air or their feeling of security,
or both?   I learned that under no consideration was a gun
allowed to be fired or a bird disturbed on any pretext;
and as a result here were orioles nesting in low shade
trees by the hotel porch, and familiar as the plaguey sparrows of city streets.   From what I saw I believe that
many a new chapter might be added to our knowledge
of birds, if everywhere they were protected as they are
here.

The tanagers were less social, but scarcely less tame.
Look where we would, these brilliant birds were there;
not singly, as they haunt the home orchards, but by scores,
and the same magical influence was exerted upon them.
For once they might be rated as song-birds.   Even the
redstarts might be classed as musical.   Perhaps it was

because a dozen might be heard at once, that their efforts proved so pleasing. One whole day was given to gazing at and lingering about a madcap, crystal brook where the redstarts seemed as numberless as the flies they snapped at. The half-leaved twigs of birches, ash, and sapling oaks were threaded like glinting sunbeams by these merry birds, and each one singing without a moment's rest. These flashing, fire-fronted warblers can be likened, for activity, only to the clouds of May-flies that dim the evening air. I would like to give an estimate of their numbers for the benefit of ornithologists, but forbear; resting with the statement that I little thought so many were to be found in all the State.

To put it coldly, the one marked feature in the case of every singing bird I heard, was purity of tone. And, if I may judge by my own feelings, I would declare that the influence was an atmospheric one. Can it be that the birds of south Jersey suffer from a feeling of depression suggestive of malaria?

Before recurring to other features of this region, let me add one word concerning the sprout-land areas through which a stream may pass. Taken all in all, birds are there to be found in greatest numbers. Nowhere else did we find a tithe of the variety; never elsewhere but a meager fraction of their numbers. Impatient as I was to explore the deep-bayed shores of the beautiful lake, I found a long summer day all too short for one little stream that I have recorded in my field-notes as "Redstart Brook," adding beneath the name:

> From the deep caverns of the distant hills,
> Your growing strength, the flow of many rills,
> In fitful haste adown the uplifted rocks,
> Where dancing sunshine many a shadow mocks,
> With ceaseless song your merry way you take,
> To rest at last in fair Hopatcong's lake.

I marvel that you pause not when the bird,
By happy thought to melody is stirred;
When, as a flash of ruddy flame, I see
The summer redbird poised upon the tree,
Or hear the happy redstart warbling where
The lichened rocks are draped with maiden-hair.

Here would I linger while the summer stays,
Here gladly spend brief autumn's shortening days,
Nor ask a fairer friend the winter through
Than I have found, dear mountain brook, in you;
And when strength fails—my weary eyes grow dim—
Be thy sweet rippling song my funeral hymn.

A word as to this lake. Hopatcong has an altitude of about twelve hundred feet, and lies between high hills that completely hem it in. Look where you will, you can see no outlet; nothing but the wide waters and the wooded mountain-side beyond. To a certain extent, it is artificial, but the visitor would not suspect this from the general appearance. More than half a century ago, the Morris Canal was built, and supplied by a feeder from an outlet of the lake. This, of course, increased the area and depth of the lake, as the construction of gates at the outlet was a necessity; and now the waters, thus backed up, have found their "way through cross-gorges into parallel valleys, originally heavily wooded, and the denuded stems and shorter stumps, standing up through the glittering water or resting in the shallows, suggest a prosaic if not a classical appropriateness in the local name of one of them—the 'River Styx.' In this locality, and in the so-called 'Cedar Swamp,' another deep bay in this nine-mile-long pond," continues our author, "on nearly every floating log or fallen tree-top or loosened stump could be found, when they were turned over, shining patches of white or yellowish gemmules, left in groups upon the smooth surface or partly hidden in little crevices of bark or root." This was in October. I confess to have not noticed or, indeed, thought of sponges, although so many of them are beautiful, while about this same " River Styx," in May; nor is it strange. It was then the paradise of the largest water-snakes I ever saw. Bold to a degree, they permitted of a near approach, and I had abundant opportunity to estimate quite accurately their size. One rusty, wrinkled ophidian patriarch was fully six feet in length. Of this, I think, there can be no doubt, although it exceeds any recorded measurements that I have seen. The temper of this creature was positively fearful, and had the species been venomous, I should have shuddered to approach so near. As it was, my companion and I were the attacked, and not the attacking party. The snake threatened to leap into our boat, and struck savagely at the blade of the oar with which I partly dislodged him from his snug bed upon a floating log. Every inch of ground was contested. When in the water, the angry creature swam slowly, and now appeared even larger than before. My companion and I agreed that had we not seen it before, it would have been prudent not to have mentioned our impressions. The slight ripple of the lake's surface and the turnings and twistings between the clusters of aquatic plants had much to do with the snake's apparent length, and it was very evident that many of the snake stories that find place in newspapers might be related in perfectly good faith by the original observer. Once our gigantic specimen moved into an open space in which were congregated many huge sunfish; they immediately darted off as in terror, and did not return for several minutes.

Wherever we looked, we saw these pretty snakes, or rather saw many that were beautifully marked, and others, the larger ones, that were uniformly brown or blackish brown above. All were in the water or upon the stumps or logs, and not a trace of one on the huge rocks that made up the shore.

I climbed one of these to survey the lake, unmindful of possible danger from venomous species, as the common rattler; and, escaping harm, felt well repaid for the scramble. The water below me was brilliant with floating crowfoot, whose golden bloom fairly rivaled the star-studded heavens when the night is clear; and, when the breezes swept across the cove, "River Styx" became a river of molten gold. The innumerable jutting tree-stumps alone gave the spot a desolate look; and this was lessened by the constant use to which they were put as coignes of vantage by birds, turtles, and the many snakes.

A solitary kill-deer plover, seemingly quite out of place, flitted from one stump to another, evidently ill at ease, and wondering, perhaps, how or why he came there. It was quite unmindful of the continual uplifting of savage serpents' heads about it, and pirouetted on the broader stumps as if really happy; yet I knew that it was not, and wished it far away. It proved a veritable annoyance; and we all know how serious petty vexations may become.

About the rocks there were no birds of any kind, and, indeed, nothing to attract them; but, when at times for a moment the wind fell, many familiar songs were floated from the mountains opposite—songs that linked me to the home hill-side, and forced more than once a longing sigh.

The rock whereon I stood was itself beautiful, as were all others that formed islets in the upper reaches of the lake; the mineral, opaque white, of rectangular cleavage, and but slightly veined with stone of other color. In many seams, often too narrow to insert a knife-blade, waxy smilacina grew and flourished; its deep-green leaves and snowy bloom often extending completely across the rock's surface, and down its precipitous sides. The effect was most curious when seen from a distance—when rocks appeared to be split from top to bottom.

Where a little soil vouchsafed a root-hold, the vigorous columbine grew in phenomenal luxuriance, and now in full bloom offered masses of red and yellow that relieved the occasional monotony of too deep green or glaring white.

Why this hardy plant is in such apparent ill-favor among landscape gardeners, I am puzzled to know. Here on these rocks, and everywhere in the deep woods of the mountains, it formed great clusters, one of which I measured, and found to be over three feet in height and of thrice that girth. As a mass of delicate foliage and pendent, nodding, ruddy bloom, it far excelled any display of wild flowers, save one, that I ever saw.

On other rocks over which I climbed the red-berried elder was a most attractive feature. This shrub was now laden with globes of richest red buds, that afterward expand to pyramidal heads of waxy white flowers. I found them in all stages of advancement, and would have loaded my boat had they not been cursed with a penetrating ancient and fish-like smell.

A curious feature of a few of these rocky islets is the fact that although the soil is but the scanty accumulation of dust and mold, filling narrow crevices, yet hemlocks, maples, aspens, sweet birch, and wild cherry, found sufficient for their needs. That flowering plants and some small shrubs should do so, is not strange, but the hemlocks, for instance, were trees thirty feet high and from eight to twelve inches in diameter.

In many cases, the roots extended like great cables carelessly thrown down over a considerable space, and then disappeared as flattened threads in crannies that might offer a hold, perhaps, but never yield any nourishment. All this struck me the more, because when we plant these trees at home it is thought necessary to dig a small-sized cellar, fill it with selected fertilizers, and tend the tree subsequently as though it were an invalid.

Such trees, however, do not have a long lease of life, even if the barren rock and the atmosphere combine to furnish them sufficient food. They are sure—sooner or later—to be in the track of a tornado, or are too heavily weighted with snow, and so are toppled over. I examined the roots of one such tree that had been overturned but the winter before, and could find no evidence of any root having penetrated a foot in depth. They had merely clasped the rock as the ivy does a stone wall, or the poison-vine the shaggy bark of an oak or elm. This prostrate tree was not dead, although the roots were exposed to the air fully as much as the branches. There was sap in the one and bright green buds all over the other. What growth it would make I then wondered, and now long to know if, this 20th of May, just a year later, the tree still lives.

Of invertebrate life, spiders were most numerous upon the rocks, yet I could find no webs. One noble fellow, richly brown and black and quite an inch long, was the fit companion for the savage skinks that tenant the precipitous rocks; of which reptiles, more hereafter. The spider—whose friendship I endeavored to cultivate—proved quite as much at home in the water as upon the rock, and after finding my persistent chasing was tiresome, or likely to prove dangerous, ran down the side of the rock to a slightly projecting ledge, a foot beneath the surface. He glistened like silver as he went, the hair upon his body and legs holding little beads of air, which serve the double purpose of supplying breath and of buoying him. I tried in many ways to dislodge him, and when, with a switch, I pushed him into the deep water, he came to the surface like a cork, and ran like a "skater" to shore. A second dive was successful. He found safe shelter in a submerged cranny to which I could not reach.

Other species—usually smaller—were also seen, and everywhere on the hot, sunny surface of the bare rocks the short, square-headed jumpers were exceedingly abundant. They were not easily caught, having a trick of walking sidewise and backward, as well as giving forward leaps to a considerable distance. Such as I brushed into the water were quite disconcerted, and more than one fell a prey to the great rosy-finned chubs that leaped above the surface as they caught them.

Into one more retired and wild recess than all the others, I found my way early in the morning of May 18th, and the novelties of the spot were too many to give less than the day to its study and exploration, The preliminary row of some five miles, often where the lake was three miles wide, was of itself thoroughly enjoyable, although the wind was dead ahead and the water roughened until angry white-caps flecked its surface. For more than an hour no sound was borne to us save the rippling of the waves against the boat's prow; but who asks for sweeter music at such a time? The air, too, had all the snap and sparkle of the waters, and mere living to breathe it was a luxury.

The wind fell as the boat neared shore, and now the oven-birds—and there seemed a legion of them—rang out their bell-toned emphasis. For the first time, too, to be positive of it, I heard the lisping but sweet song of six or seven notes of the Blackburnian warbler. These exquisite birds were really abundant all that day, in the thicket of dwarfish aspens and the tangled undergrowth beneath that crowded the ravine between two jutting rocks; and, as if to greet me, these birds came to the front row of trees, and scanned me closely while I landed. They were extraordinarily tame, and I noticed that when they sang they dropped their wings and caused them to quiver rapidly; then off each would dart in quest of flies with all the grace and restlessness of redstarts.

The aspens were not in full leaf, and the young foliage was of a pale gray green that made a most fitting background for the deep orange breast and black and yellow head of this rare warbler.

Sheltered from the wind, the water here was absolutely still and treacherously clear. Not a twig of any overhanging tree but was faithfully mirrored, and the dividing line between the upper and lower world could not be traced. It was difficult to realize that the boat rested upon water, and, quite unguarded, I stepped upon a shelf of rock that seemed not more than an inch below the surface; but it proved to be nearly twelve, and I narrowly escaped a ducking in water thirty feet in depth. My ardor was not damped if my feet were, and, while hesitating between birds and botany, a brown skink, with bright red head, darted by me like a flash. Although I had scarcely standing room, I made a break for him, and nearly broke my arms. But my rashness was the needed lesson, and to salve my wounded feelings I gathered purple trilliums, glaucous corydalis, and other unfamiliar and, to me, unknown bloom. Then, rounding a point of rocks in the boat, I found a better chance for freedom of limbs, and set systematically to hunt for skinks. But to hunt successfully, one must wait for these sly lizards to show themselves, and I kept my eyes upon the broad surface of one great wall of rock, while sitting in the boat, from which only a view could be had. Very soon an exclamation from my companion announced that he had seen one, and I, too, soon caught a glimpse of the skulking creature. Very cautiously the boat was brought closely up to the

rock, and, with a lithe switch, I at last made one desperate
effort to brush the skink into the lake, but succeeded
only in sending it into a deep crevice. It was now a
prisoner, but quite inaccessible to its jailer, and I tried
many ways to dislodge it. Finally a cold douche was
employed, which forced the plucky animal to make a leap
for life. It made it, and landed in the lake. Here its
activity was inconsiderable, and I readily caught it with
my hand. How savagely it bit! It forced its little teeth
quite through my skin, and, while thus expending its
strength, my companion made of a handkerchief a safe
cage, and then I landed with the feelings of a triumphant
warrior. Vixen, as I called my prisoner, has something
of a history, to be related in part hereafter. Suffice it now
to say that while I remained at the lake, and for weeks
after returning home, the creature was ill-natured and
intractable beyond description. Of course, in the mountains the bite of the skink is held to be poisonous. Every
native to whom I showed it claimed that I had made a
very narrow escape, and urged the destruction of the animal. I could as easily have annihilated one or two of the
mountaineers.

What birds were seen to-day, other than warblers, did
not appear to be migrating, and it would not be surprising if in this region there will yet be found single pairs
or even small colonies of species now believed not to breed
south of New England or even Canada. There is little
need to discuss the question; the finding of the nests can
alone decide it; but I am very positive upon one point,
that New Jersey, and even the central portion of the State,
has never been credited by ornithologists with its full
complement of breeding birds.

On the mountains' sides, at least where they slope to
the lake, a species of ant of moderate size, black and

brown, was very abundant, and I came upon many nests.
To-day the largest of these were found, and somewhat
carefully examined. Those that I found near Skink
Rock, as I have called the spot, were great dome-shaped
structures, built of sandy earth, with short bits of grass so
uniformly through the mass that their presence was probably not accidental, but had much to do with the stability
of the walls of the innumerable mazy passages. The least
disturbance caused the exterior of the nest to crumble,
and yet the general appearance was such as to suggest
considerable age. One of the two nests found to-day
measured six feet in diameter and two feet six inches
in height. The shape was that of a flattened cone.
The other was even larger but not so regular in outline.
This I cut in two from peak to surface, with an oar-blade,
and so procured a sectional view that showed a curiously
intricate tunneling throughout. These passages were all
empty. I found no trace of larvæ; no evidence that these
ants had slaves, and no soldiers to protest against my out-
rageous conduct. My destructive acts, however, very naturally caused an intense commotion, and the rapid running
to and fro over the dead leaves that carpeted the ground
made a noise as loud as and very similar to the patter of a
summer shower. And twice afterward, when rambling in
the woods on the opposite side of the lake, I stopped,
thinking it had commenced to rain, although the sky was
clear, and found that I had been deceived by the noise
made by thousands of these ants that were running in
every direction, intensely excited without any, to me, apparent cause.

Strangely, I think, during my whole stay, I saw no
mammals, or traces of any, except a solitary red squirrel
and numerous chipmunks; yet reports of minks, musk-
rats, otters, raccoons, and even wild cats were promptly

forthcoming, when the natives were questioned. Not one but could give a glowing account of the strange "varmints" seen in his time, and I noticed that all were mentioned as seen during the winter or at night, and always in the least frequented tracts of forest. I concluded that every animal named was really scarce, unless it be musk-rats; and judging from my own experience, a mouse at midnight is always enormously magnified.

It was nearly useless to look along the lake shore for relics of the red man, as he is called, although men with skins less red never existed. The raising of the level of the water some ten or twelve feet necessarily submerged all village sites. At present the name alone is all that suggests the ancient Delawares, Hopatcong being tortured Indian for *where the wild potato grows.* As this plant does not bloom until August, and is a rather inconspicuous vine early in the summer, it is not strange that I failed to notice it.

Long ago my eye had caught the following in the New Jersey Historical Collections: " On Lake Hopatcong there is a regular causeway of stone running from an island nearly across to the shore, a distance of about a quarter of a mile. It was no doubt made by the Indians, and was a work of great labor, the lake being very deep. The water is now a little above it, occasioned by the raising of the lake for the Morris Canal. On the opposite shore are found great numbers of Indian arrows of beautiful shape, axes, and broken jars; and appearances indicate that it was the site of an Indian village." Nor causeway nor relics are traceable now, and disappointment only awaits the archæologist.

Batrachian life in all its glory filled every available nook of the shores and islands of the lake. Scarcely a

flat stone could be found that did not shelter a toad, and
every mossy pool had its full complement of frogs. They
were all more silent during the day than at home, and
save an occasional wood-frog in the forest, I am not sure
that I heard them at all. But not so at sunset; then every
one came from its damp and dark retreat, and with all
its strength croaked, clucked, and spluttered. Though
the nights were cool, even the toads were out in force,
and filled the valley with a flood-tide of dolefulness. This,
of all sounds in nature, is the most gloomy; but there is
a grain of satisfaction to be got from it—there is no
better evidence that summer is really here. I do not say
it is good evidence—far from it; but of the many signs of
the seasons, no one is better. I am indifferent to the almanac's dictum of June 21 as the proper date. If there is a
general epithalamial rejoicing on the part of the toads,
then frost, if it comes, is not baneful, and the strawberries
are safe.

As was so plainly the case with the birds, I could detect no difference in the voices of the batrachians here,
as compared with those of their meadow-dwelling cousins,
except in one notable instance. The great bull-frog here
at the lake has a more metallic note, and is like those I
have heard in New England, and differs greatly from the
smothered, guttural cry of the same creature in the tide-
water marshes.

As the nights were still cold, I was surprised to find
both toads and frogs so active and vocal, for at home, a
lowering of temperature is pretty sure to silence them,
and very often the croaking entirely ceases. But none of
those upon the western shore of the lake felt equal to
greeting the tardy sunrise; while I have often heard them
so doing in south Jersey, where, indeed, it is one of nature's pleasant sounds, blending admirably with the songs
of the birds.

The spring, I was told, was neither late nor early—a fortunate circumstance always; and the days spent upon the lake were in all respects such as a rambler hopes for in May—the month of preparation, of many promises. The sun shone brightly as I turned my face homeward, and my last glimpse was the flash of leaping waves—the glint of a caldron of molten gold.

My first visit to May's Landing was too brief and too early, and a longing to return constantly possessed me. With the scent of mountain woods and crystal lake still in my nostrils, I returned, and it would be hard to realize that from the one point to the other is but one hundred and five miles as the crow flies. It was from pole to equator in every essential feature.

Of the village street I have already made proper mention. It is a thoroughfare that other country towns might study to advantage. In less than half a mile there stand in or near the sidewalks more than a score of noble oaks, some of them nine feet in girth; while from mine host's portico I counted one hundred and twenty-one of these princely trees. These cast their cool shadows alike over the churches and court-house, thus offering, after their labors, equal comfort to wrangling lawyers and opinionative priests.

These oaks were in full leaf at this time, and I, too, a stranger, found their cool shadows a luxury after long exposure to the glare of the sun's rays where they fall upon glittering sand. So intensely bright is the light that snow-blindness might be produced. But why mention such trivial matters? One might as well complain that water sparkles. In truth, these so-called barren sands were a well-spring of delight. Acres of them were now sparsely covered with golden Hudsonia—as marked a bloom, and almost as beautiful as arbutus or pyxie, yet without a local name! Because it grows before the villagers' doors, instead of in a swamp a mile or two away, it is a nameless weed! Had it been rare and required sharp eyes to detect, the choicest spot of all the garden would be reserved for it.

Whether the world has learned the fact or not, there is no golden bloom more beautiful than this. The slender, almost thread-like branches, bearing dusty, gray-green leaves, shape themselves into stars, circles, and rudely crumpled mats, while over all is showered triply polished gold, so thickly often that the plant itself is hidden, and there rests upon the glittering sand a fragment of the sun.

Wherever the Hudsonia was found, near by were curious vine-like tangles with pretty foliage, often a rich deep purple, more frequently a delicate shade of green. This plant, unlike the preceding, derives its beauty from the snow-white background and from the rich coloring of the stems and leaves—there being no noticeable bloom. A weed, too, is this in the minds of the villagers, having no name, but known elsewhere as "false ipecac," which is little better than no name at all. This fact, however, carries no influence to the mind of the rambler. Not a wayside growth at home, it troubled me nothing to learn that others ignored it. Wandering for my own pleasure, it stood the test of relative merit so far as I was concerned; for it never failed to attract and command my attention, even when within sight of more pretentious growths.

Beneath the pines—a forest of which came within a stone's throw of the village—the sand was not covered with vegetation, beyond patches of reindeer moss and the yearly crop of "needles" shed by the trees, and which appear never to decay. They pleasingly reflect the sunlight that is sifted through the pines' interlocking branches, and fill the long vista with a tinted atmosphere in which every object stands forth with startling distinctness ; and provide, too, the more prosaic but no less important condition of a firm foot-hold, without which no ramble is an unmixed joy.

At such a place, in such a light, I chanced upon purple orchids growing in great profusion. In every case they stood apart, as though each would be judged by its own merit, and borrow nothing from its neighbors. Aristocrats, every one of them, in the true and not disgusting sense of the term.

They appeared to have no choice in the matter of locality, but by digging down a little I found traces of a black mold, and it was evident that here, at least, their nourishment is derived from decaying wood. These flowers were not so large nor so darkly tinted as many I have seen from nearer home, where the surroundings are totally different, and heavy black soil in upland swamps seems alone suited to them. There need be no discussion as to their preferences in the matter of locality. No change could be greater than from the dry evergreen wood here to the cold swamps near home, where grow deciduous trees almost exclusively.

At another point—where the land was swampy and covered with a mixed growth—I found a striking row of thirteen, each in perfect condition, and the plants of a remarkably uniform height. They were growing along the greatly decayed prostrate trunk of a pine tree. They were all quite pale, as if frightened at being thirteen at a table. If so, their fears were realized, for I plucked one as I passed by; why, I can not say, and I am surprised that I did, for such bloom should be exempt from persecution.

The pines here are of two species, the " scrub " and the pitch pine—called locally " two-leaf " or " smooth bark," and the " three-leaf " or " Indian." What is meant by the " bottle pine " I did not determine. The proportion of each is not readily ascertained, and may differ a good deal

in adjoining neighborhoods. About the village there are
probably twice as many three-leaved or pitch pines as of
scrub or two-leaved. But this is immaterial. The trees
that I saw were all small, the third or fourth growth, perhaps, but still large enough to be sheltering trees, and
crowned with murmuring branches.

Unlike most constant sounds, this of the wind in the
pine-tree tops is never tiresome, fitting as it does so well
with the loneliness of unfrequented woods—for these woods
are lonely; in no sense, as compared with forests elsewhere, are they a chosen haunt of any of our familiar
birds, and, as was the case in April, I saw no trace of any
mammal but the chickaree.

This arises almost certainly from the uniformity of the
locality and consequent comparative absence of both animal and vegetable food; and not unimportant is the fact
that the pine tree does not afford much concealment for
the birds themselves, and even less for their nests; but, as
I continually found, the moment you pass the bounds of
a typical " pine barren " and reach the edge of a swamp,
or even dry area—but with deciduous trees and shrubbery—the birds appear.

In the village proper there were fourteen species of
birds in such numbers as one might expect to find in any
country town with shaded streets and ample gardens. In
the "deciduous tree" and swampy portions of the back
woods I noted but eight species, but one of which—the
wood thrush—is included in the village list. In all my
rambles, including a long row down Great Egg Harbor
River, I saw and unmistakably identified but forty-four
species—a considerably smaller number than can be seen
at any time during the same month at home. Of the list,
there was but one not to be found in central New Jersey
—the log cock or pileated woodpecker. The mocking-
bird—of which I saw one specimen—is as rare there as

farther north. A somewhat curious feature of the distribution of the birds I saw will be referred to subsequently.

Although the orchids were fascinating, the earth-stars
curious, and a scarlet-blooming lichen that I found about
the roots of every pine was a mine of pleasure, it was
nevertheless with a feeling of relief that I detected at last
a sunlit opening in the distance. I hastened thither and
found for a considerable space no evergreen was to be
seen save a single cedar, and all was fresh, crisp, and
sparkling. I did not know how thirsty I was until I saw
the water, and suspect that animals of nearly every kind
love the sight of it, even if it is not a necessity. It was a
woodland basin that I had found, with, in part, quite precipitous sides, and a dripping spring at one overhanging
point that kept the ferns "a nid, nid, nodding" where the
bright drops fell. It would have been strange if no birds
had appeared, but here they were, seven different kinds,
and each a song-bird of merit. Nor were they silent. The
oven-birds sang continuously, but not so loudly as I have
heard, while the single indigo finch, the chewinks, and
thrushes sang simply as they always do wherever they
may be.

But birds alone were not sufficient for such a spot, and
I longed for the sight of a frog, a snake, a mouse in the
grass or squirrel among the trees. No, it is not a fancy,
as I have heard it said; these regions, beautiful as they
are, do not team with life as do the tamer regions nearer
large towns.

The pitcher-plants, which without a blossom were
so attractive a feature of all swampy spots during my
earlier visit, added to their beauty now by bearing aloft
on straight, stiff stems a curiously intricate flower, varying
from deep red to purple, the ruddy portion surrounding a yellow umbrella-shaped growth, the short handle of
which is an ivory globe.

In one little pool near the woodland basin, which, too, had an abundance of these plants and lilies, I counted eighteen pitchers and eight of the curious flowers. With them was a single white lily, and these were all reflected in a pool of inky-black water so distinctly that each was duplicated and no water could be seen a few paces off. The spot was surrounded by an impenetrable growth of sapling birches; and quite encircling the water's edge was a narrow fringe of glistening filiform sun-dews.

It is such places as these pools, swamps, and winding creeks that relieve the monotony of these wonderful "barrens," and will ever make them the Meccas of out-door naturalists—or will, until they are so far "improved" as to have lost those features that now attract. This done, an utterly tame, if not actually repulsive spot will remain. A deforested tract is an eye-sore here, and, as farm-land, will be little better.

In the opposite direction from the village, or southward, with the river usually in sight, I found a region that was very attractive, and quite unlike in many repects any meadow or swamp-land of the Delaware Valley.

Here, instead of in the village, as I supposed I should, I heard song-sparrows, cat-birds, and orioles—birds that usually do not seek retired localities; but here they were at home, for all were nesting; and a pair of tree-creeping warblers, the only ones I saw, took my intrusion into a thicket of stunted oaks so much to heart that I know they too had a nest. Here, too, the air was filled with swallows, and the crested tit, the bird of all others that perhaps I love the best, whistled with a vim no other bird attains, *'t sweet here! 't sweet here!* and the wise little chap was right. It was.

The forest growth was of little moment, except the "islands," as the clustered cedars that grow so closely that

one can scarcely pass through them are called. When
these trees occupy but a comparatively little space, and
are surrounded by open country or deciduous growths,
they certainly are as prominent a feature of the landscape
as are the isles of the sea. All such to-day, and there
were several in the course of my walk, were hurriedly
passed by, although deserving of attention; nor were the
afflicted gum trees, weighted with mistletoe, more than
glanced at. There was too great a wealth of bloom
wherever I turned, and to this I gave all my thoughts,
wondering the while if I might not introduce some of
them into the woods and along the waysides at home.

The lupine with sky-colored clusters; yellow rock-rose
— with no rocks within half a hundred miles; snowy
sandwort—little else within that distance; sand myrtle,
a pretty evergreen, with clustered ivory bloom; purple
toad-flax and even scraggly, dwarfed beach plum; these
all, the pretty playthings as I pass through the village,
and thrown aside for greater novelty when I reach the
edge of a wood. There crimson lambkill dulled all other
blooms and stayed my willing footsteps. A by-road,
over which wagons seldom pass, was lined upon one side
with this sweet shrub. It was not strange that folly
gained the upper hand in such a spot, and I had almost
completed an ill-rhymed stanza, when the road itself became more interesting than the flowers attractive, and I
was promptly restored. This road was simply a long ribbon
of white sand, dotted with low bushes; but the ruts were
remarkably distinct. Examining them, I found what at
first sight appeared to be grass, proved to be thread-like
sun-dews, as thickly set as blades in the rankest pastures.
They glittered, too, with the gummy sap that ever bathes
them—a condition that made them the more noticeable,
for it was now high noon, and nowhere was moisture visible. This gummy " dew " proves terribly fatal to insects.

Except for this, the plant is oh! so very innocent in appearance—I have seen human sun-dews—and scarcely more prominent than now, when its dainty pink blossoms appear; but all this is but a part of a deep-laid scheme, for it depends upon animal food for its own existence, and destroys and devours millions of minute flies, and, indeed, many of a larger growth.

I found also, but not just here, another species with broad and almost circular leaves, and it too was carnivorous as a cat.

Still on, deeper into the forest, or rather forest site, and soon the lambkill gave way to another, more stately and scarcely less beautiful growth. The ground was now more damp, the trees more vigorous, and all other undergrowth was replaced by the exquisite Leucothoë. These bushes were. laden with white, waxy balls that charged the air with the odor of vanilla. One cluster that I picked had twenty-two flowers on a single stem, in an unbroken row and just free of actual contact. It measured exactly six inches in length. As I held the stem in a horizontal position, I was not much surprised that locally the plant is known by the terrible name of "false teeth." My only cause for wonderment is, that the more refined element of the community should not have replaced it with something both appropriate and pleasant; especially, as the botanical name has nothing to commend it.

The limit of my ramble was a denuded tract of literally barren sand, where probably not a dozen species of plants grew, and all were inconspicuous but one. For the first time I say in full bloom the— buzzard weed! No, the turkey beard! Is it not strange that more than a century should pass, and these plants familiar the while to intelligent, flower-loving people, and yet they should not have rescued them from the jargon of those outer barbarians, the charcoal-burners? Professional botanists, of course, will tell you it is the *Xerophyllum setifolium*— but something prettier for common use, please, learned gentlemen.

It was indeed strange to see a lily growing in such a barren, utterly forsaken spot as this; for the Xerophyllum is a member of that blue-blooded tribe, and holds its head aloft more haughtily than gaudy Turk's-cap or the spotted tiger.

From a cluster of grass-like leaves, themselves a foot or more in length, and as harsh to the touch as bits of flattened wire, there towers a cylindrical, greenish-white stalk, covered with hair-like leaves, and crowned with a pyramidal raceme. The delicate flowers open at the base at first, and then daily add to their numbers, until the top is expanded, when we have an oval, feathery mass of purely white blossoms, waxy, and golden at their centers.

The scent of roses, alas! does not cling to them. Rather an odor that perhaps has caused them to be without the pale of lilydom.

My visit ended with a long row down the river—Great Egg Harbor River, as it has long been named, " from the fact that, in Indian times, it was near its mouth a great resort for breeding sea-birds," at least so runs the record that I have. I doubt not but that here, too, far from the mouth, there once nested many inland birds, and this is based on the fact that no sooner had I reached the water's edge than I heard familiar birds, not one of which was seen in the woods. But to this I shall return.

The old wharf is not now a scene of busy industry, and the river, at low tide, is little more than a shallow creek, with weedy bottom and tortuous sand-bars. Trade has found new channels, but we proposed a voyage along the old, and embarked in the Iva, a misshapen and ponderous row-boat that, having carried me many miles, should be mentioned with respect; so no more of the Iva.

The vigorous notes of an excited vireo, the noisy white-eye, were propitious, I thought, and my companion, an able bodied oarsman, struck out into the stream, inspired by them; but the initial vigor was not long maintained, thanks to the ponderous—I mean, safe Iva.

Strange waters, even more promptly than fresh woods and pastures new, arouse the rambler's enthusiasm, and the tide-worn banks of the river were closely scanned as we passed down stream.

The birds of home were here abundant, and I was much surprised to find only along the river's shores many species that are common in gardens and orchards gener-ally, even such familiar ones as the song-sparrow and cat-bird, which were not seen in the village, but were common here. The birds, the yellow splatter-dock, and trees of many kinds gave the river, at the outset, a familiar look, and I recalled the terminal mile or more of Crosswicks Creek; but soon a great difference was apparent. The dock gave place to golden club, the rarest of large aquatic growths at home, and greater interest centers in it than the former, which certainly is painfully prosaic. At high tide the leaves are submerged, and as we passed over them they shone through the amber-tinted waters as iridescent bronze, producing a beautiful effect that was the more striking when great shoals of silvery roach, turning their glittering sides to us, passed quickly through the narrow space between the plants and the bottom of the boat.

In one respect, however, this plant had suffered here. The pure ivory-white and untarnished gold of the clubs were sadly marred by a dull-green deposit, such as I had never seen in the meadows at home.

The stream, before we had gone a mile, was quite broad, and the unobstructed breeze rippled the water and brought pleasant sounds from the woods upon the western shore. These drew us nearer to the clean white sands of the little beach. The sapling growths along the water's edge teemed with song-birds, even the tree-creeping warbler lisping with an energy that suggested the stimulating air of the mountains. Finally, a thrush, perched upon the trembling top twig of an oak, invited us ashore with such persuasive eloquence that the Iva was beached, and we left it for a brief upland ramble.

Scarcely had I gone a rod before I noticed a toad, and then another and another. They were all of such pale coloring as to be quite inconspicuous, and had they not voluntarily moved about I should probably not have seen them. The cause of their activity could only be guessed, and as they were so striking in appearance I stopped to watch them. The pale pepper-and-salt mottling of their skins was a beautiful instance of protective coloring, and one which they stood well in need of, for herons and bitterns both abound and pace these shores by night. The result of my brief observation leads me to ask: Does protective coloring ever serve the useful purpose of enabling the animal to approach the more easily within capturing distance of its prey? One of these toads, which I carefully watched for several minutes, often changed its position by very deliberate movements, always keeping closely to the sand and never hopping. The appearances were all suggestive of cautious approach, and yet I saw no insect, minute crustacean, or any living creature upon which they would be likely to prey.

Leaving the toads, I climbed the sandy bluff for a woodland ramble, but was doomed to disappointment. The charcoal fiend had been at work, and a wide tract of denuded country was spread out before me, concealed from us when in the boat by a narrow fringe of trees and rank shrubbery, which we had taken for the edge of a forest.

9

I had now an explanation of the curiously mingled character of the black and white sand that formed both bluff and beach—it was charcoal-dusted white sand.

The "barren" was a paradise of "turkey beards" and prickly pear, the latter growing more thriftily here than in the sand lots near the village. It was not yet in bloom. The two plants gave the spot a semi-tropical look, so different are they from all our other growths.

Nowhere did there seem to be any animal life, vertebrate or invertebrate, except a few spiders. Leaving the belt of trees upon the bluff, it was simply plunging into a little desert, and when you have gone far enough to be beyond the voices of the birds the silence is very impressive. A curious incompleteness marks much of this region. These barren tracts seem fitted for many a lower form of life, yet, as I recalled one after another, it was only to fail to find any trace of them. Even snakes were absent, although I had been assured that the great spotted pine snake was by no means rare. Had there been no scattered shrubbery, the conditions could have been more readily explained, as without vegetation the insect life would be reduced to a minimum, and animals that subsist upon it would be wanting; and these being food for other forms also wanting, the higher vertebrates could not exist. Doubtless, such tracts, being valueless except for timber, unless they are gradually reoccupied by trees, will remain in their present sadly desolate condition.

Taking to our boat again, we rowed to a marshy island toward the opposite shore. There were some eight or ten acres in the tract, which was now out of water, but at high tide is submerged. Golden club, to the exclusion of every other growth, covered it. The plant was in full bloom, and, so far as I could see, unlike that in the river above, in being free of any sedimentary deposit. Every leaf was clean, every club unsoiled.

Such an island as this was an invaluable plantation to the Indians in days gone by. Did they lend a hand in planting this, or was it Nature's unaided handiwork? It is certain that the Indians introduced this plant into spring-ponds far away from running streams, where it has continued to flourish unto this day; and if the mud-flat or marshy island here is some two centuries old or older, which is not improbable, there is nothing very startling in the suggestion that it was originally a " Taw-kee " field.

"The American Indian, at the time of the discovery of the continent and its early settlement, was a savage, living upon the game and fish he captured," etc.; so runs the average statement of our school geographies and outline histories, and a greater error never crept into print.

It will be difficult, if it is possible at this late day, to change the current of opinion; but the statement is absolutely false. Let him who doubts read Carr's history of the Indian as an agriculturist. It was not a mere matter of a melon patch and a little field of maize, but hundreds of well-tilled acres and orchards containing thousands of trees.

A third landing was at one of those garden spots that no one loving a flower can pass by unheeded. The bluff was wooded to the very brink, and everywhere among the scrubby oaks and dwarf pines grew rock-rose, Hudsonia, lambkill, and viburnum; masses of white, yellow, and pink. With it all were birds of many kinds and one great mystery. The familiar song of the marsh wren was frequently heard, yet it was not a locality where an ornithologist would expect to find that bird. This piqued my curiosity, and I searched for the bird most carefully. Presently a gray lizard appeared upon a pine tree before me, and while stooping down to catch it a yellow-breasted

chat flew to an overhanging branch of the same tree and
sang, imitating the wren's song to perfection. It did not
mingle it with the usual series of uncouth cries, but gave
it alone while sitting; and then, after a distinct pause,
commenced the barking, coughing, spluttering, ventrilo-
quial medley characteristic of the chat. Familiar as I
have been for years with this bird, this is the only instance of the kind that has fallen under my observation.

Our final landing was at a beautiful point formed by
the river turning slightly from a straight course. Here
cedars grew in great profusion, and, indeed, to the exclusion
of other trees. It was not only a beautiful but a commanding point, and I was not surprised, directly upon
landing, to find abundant traces of the Indian. Chips of
jasper and bits of pottery, these were all; yet they told
the story of the "wild Indian," as he is called, as fully as
though we had found his weapons, ornaments, and agri-
cultural tools. Here, I think, had been a temporary
camping ground; one periodically visited, and not a permanent village site. I had come here in hopes of finding
it the latter, but the absence of village indications, as I
have found them elsewhere throughout the State, was complete. There was even no considerable accumulation of
clam-shells, so that the spot could not even be classed
under the somewhat indefinite term of kitchen-midden.
But what was found—chips, sherds, and a bit of worked
bone—proved sufficient to spur the imagination, and on
the return trip I pictured this river and its banks as
they once were, and peopled it with our predecessors, who,
as it seems to me, treated it more judiciously than we
have done—extracting its sweets without draining its very
life-blood.

And with this thought, we returned the Iva to her
owner and became landsmen again.

This whole region, I am told, is one great "pine barren." It is so marked upon the official map, and so reported by the State Geologist; but it is well not to be misled by this vaguely descriptive term, for, while there are acres that are the abode of desolation, there are also, and far more frequently, nature-planted gardens, unmatched by any this great continent over.

In '88, I spent the month at home, and every day had its notable adventure. Indeed, does not every hour have its tragedy or comedy?

As we all know, poets have a "corner" in May day, and let them. Do not suppose it is the only merit of the month. Indeed, if it be hot and sunny, it is not a time for unalloyed pleasure. The noon-tide is too like midsummer.

I chose the fourth for my first considerable outing, with its clouds and brief showers; and how far wisely, let others decide. For me, at least, it was a red-letter day.

Bound riverward, we had the tide to baffle with unwilling oars, for rowing is irksome at best, unless one's thought is only for his muscles. Slowly working our way against the swift current that swirled between the pier and abutments of the ancient bridge, we foolishly looked upward as a wagon passed over us, as though by so doing we might escape some danger, or expected to see the horse drop down upon us, and received the just due of our thoughtlessness in a shower of dust that smarted both our eyes and nostrils.

I have passed under this bridge a hundred times or more, and whenever a wagon crosses it at that moment, I always do this worse than childish thing and receive the merited punishment therefor. Experience has taught me nothing; never will. Verily, "what fools these mortals be."

A shallower and wider portion of the stream once reached, we all breathed more freely, and full of anticipation, if not of novelty, at least of cheerful sights, we found ourselves alone with woods and waters and a solitary crow. Its cawing was not unmusical, then and there. We fancied it the prompter's call and warning that the audience was in waiting. Whether the birds that morning saw fit to play us a trick or were beyond the reach of the lone crow's ringing voice, we shall never know; but the music of our dipping oars, the ripple of the tide beneath the prow, and the distant tinkling of a cow-bell in the marsh, were all we heard. Here, then, was ready nature waiting for the unready birds; and with a tinge of disappointment that so much of our course was without song, we reached a narrower winding of the creek, sparsely shaded by the half-leaved trees: here were music and beauty blended. Swallows in mid-air, greenlets in the willows, and afar off the crested redbird warbled and whistled without rest, while the scarlet tanager flashed like a winged flame through the snowy branches of the bitter plum. Rounding a sudden bend, we startled the great blue heron from his perch, which joined his soaring mate high overhead, and for long they circled above us as we hurried by, eager for fresh fields and pastures new.

Not alone were the trees in the flood-tide of their glory; the meadows were starred with brilliant marigold, and the banks of many an inflowing brook were fretted and streaked with the ivory and gold wands of the rank orontium.

Whatever may be thought of the Bonapartes as Frenchmen, he who lingers along the wooded south shore of Crosswicks Creek, from a mile or more above and downward to its junction with the Delaware, will recall with gratitude the amiable Joseph, who once dwelt here, and be duly thankful that he was so skillful a landscape gardener.

I do not know to what extent the tract was a forest when Bonaparte bought it, but it is well known that the illustrious exile was an ardent lover of trees, and planted many a hundred in his park of one thousand acres. But the creek bank always was, as it still is, a natural arboretum, and contains a greater variety of trees than any other tract of the same area within a radius of many miles. But time and circumstance put us in no statistical mood; we cared little then for the romantic history of the spot, and even less for its purely botanical aspect. The mingling of every shade of green, from the gloomy cedars, looking almost black, to the palest of the freshly budding oaks; the lichen-draped branches of the two-leaved pine and trembling blossoms of the feathery June-berry, were here too marked a feature of the landscape to permit our haste, and we merely stemmed the tide while skirting the bluff.

I would not that any word of mine should be construed as unfavorable to strolling overland, but the vague shadow of a doubt vexes me when I compare my upland with my water rambles. It is of evident importance to get a comprehensive view of one's surroundings, and this you can often do when in a boat; from which, too, we catch glimpses of a wilder side of the world than is ever turned to the public road. Few now are the lanes and byways that are paths in a wilderness; but here the creek margined a narrow reach of unmolested nature, where even the sly otter dared to have his slide. We did not see the wary creature to-day. Perhaps—but no, I will confess it, we even could not find his tracks. But local Nimrods—most veracious of men—have hinted of his ottership so often that the story added its charm to the steep and slippery ribbon of faintly furrowed clay leading from one great overhanging tree down to the water's edge. Whether the spot was an otter-slide or not, that the animal could slip from his nest among the beech tree's roots—if he has one there—to the creek, would never be questioned, and I, for one, ignored a bowlder in the water, suspiciously in line with the bared strip of hill-side, for fear some doubting Thomas might throw discredit on the time-honored playground of the unseen otter.

Hoping against hope that this rare creature might show himself, if but to silence doubt, we long looked backward until the bending bushes closed the view. Then recalling stern reality, we regretted the base use to which the once noble park was now largely put, and with a few vigorous strokes of our oars we darted between the close set pilings of a second bridge and sent our craft spinning over the sparkling waters of the river. No change could be more sudden, more complete. We were no longer hemmed in between bluff and meadow, so near that either could be closely scanned, but out upon really open water, for here the river is a full mile in width.

The clouds had thickened before we left the creek and now threatened the mild disaster of our being lost in a fog; but we braved this and all other dangers and skirted either shore as the element of wildness proved in the ascendant, or made a straight course down stream far from either shore. When not in mid-river we had warbler music in excess, for to-day the willows teamed, for the first time, with these beautiful migrating songsters. Perhaps, they were too tired or too hungry to sing their best songs, but I was not alone in thinking that sweeter than any efforts of theirs were the united voices of the teetering sandpipers. Continually, when we were in mid-stream, they crossed our bow, greeting us in a wild, winsome way that lightened the gray-black clouds and made us quite forget that a shower was imminent; and whenever the wind fell, from the distant shores their clear call could still be heard, as they tripped, lightly as the waves, along the pebbly shore.

I have mentioned the willows along shore. The species is a matter of some uncertainty, perhaps, but probably the *Salix nigra*. At all events I can testify that the remark in Gray's botany, " With the branches very brittle at the base," is quite true of those that grow here. It needs but a single effort to climb into one, to be satisfied on this point. These trees were planted at the very outset of the European occupation of the country, to resist the eroding action of the water, and particularly of freshets; and now, in land that has been lost to cultivation, notwithstanding this care, are many of these old willows—broken, cavernous, the very acme of dilapidation, yet vigorous withal. Such trees harbor enormous numbers of insects, both winged and in a larval state, and are naturally at this time of the year the haunts *par excellence* of the migrating warblers. Here are to be found those rare forms known only to professional ornithologists, and not always to them. Here, too, are earliest heard our vireos or greenlets; all songsters, but of different degrees of merit. The most marked, perhaps, is the yellow-throat, that sings with its whole body, as though the notes were shaken from its feathers; and as different as possible from the robin-toned quaver of the restless redeye.

Mile after mile we marked at distant points solitary cabins close to the water's edge. Forsaken the greater part of the year, they are tenanted now, and the shore near by is the scene of busy industry. The fishermen are reaping the single harvest that this long river yields, the shoals of shad and herring. These fish are now bound upward to their spawning-grounds, and strange it is that ever one reaches the desired goal. As we passed by, our sympathy was with the fisher rather than the fish, and we hoped that every sweep of the seine might land a mighty draught of fishes. But the toilers were not in luck; not nearly so much as I, who, taking a short walk by way of change, saw many a pretty bird, heard others sing, and found a fish-crow lying upon the sand. This is to me an interesting bird; the more so, because so generally confounded with the common one.

In March or April, as the weather proves, fish-crows appear in scanty numbers along the river, following, I think, the spring migration of the shad and herring; and about each fisherman's cabin a pair is very likely to be found. Although so much smaller than the common crow, with a very different cry, and given to hawk-like soaring over the river, these differences have not generally been noticed, and the strange impression has arisen that a fish diet had the effect of making crows foolish, for so the fishermen think these much less wary birds must be—dolts, as it were, from the common crowd of crows.

I have known them to become, at times, almost as familiar, but never as impudent, as magpies; and, waiting until the boat is manned and the shore deserted, they walk to the very cabin door, hunting for scraps, and always searching the *débris* left at the water's edge where the seine is drawn ashore. Were these birds protected and encouraged, they would become, I doubt not, useful scavengers; but unfortunately the unmerited curse of being a crow rests upon them, and the average fisherman is unteachable.

The prominent incident of the day occurred when I reached a bend in the river where stands the bleached trunk of a tall, dead tree. In its present forlorn condition it has doubtless withstood the storms of many a winter; but, though trembling in every breeze, and threatening to fall whenever the wind freshens, the well-anchored roots, grasping the drifted rocks, have strength yet to prevent its overthrow, and, notwithstanding its apparent insecurity, it is trusted by the birds.

As I reached the tree, coveting its outlook far up and down the river, a sparrow-hawk flew from a hollow in the trunk, and then turning hovered above me in an anxious manner. I knew at once that the bird was nesting there. The opening to the nest was small and no projection offered a foot-hold to the bird when entering, but this did not seem to disconcert it.

I presently withdrew a short distance, and the bird re-entered the tree with the same rapidity and command of movement characteristic of the bank-swallows. It was a beautiful sight. I then returned to the tree and slapped the trunk smartly with my hand, when the hawk promptly re-appeared and also, to my surprise, from a hole but three or four feet lower down, a flicker came bouncing out. Again I withdrew, when both the hawk and woodpecker returned. Here, then, were two birds of very different habits, save that of nesting in hollow trees, and one of them a bird of prey, living in the same tree in perfect harmony.

It may be no uncommon occurrence, but I have not in my own wanderings met with another instance, nor recall any record of one.

The day, like all such, proved too full; there was more well worthy of study that we hurried by than I have mentioned in my rambling way. And now, a few retrospective words as I return. Three truly spring-like days had wrought a wondrous change. The wealth of life along the river's shores to-day had largely reached this valley in that time, for April, '88, will long be remembered as a strictly winter month.

CHAPTER VI.

An uninvited townsman followed me to the woods recently, and when I sat down at the foot of a favorite tree, asked, "What have we here?" "Heaven for one," I replied, which he construed as meaning the opposite for two. He was right. What a comfort it is to be correctly interpreted !

Nature speaks freely to the individual, but seldom harangues a crowd; and never is she so communicative as in June. It is desirable, therefore, above all other time, to ramble alone, for actual solitude, which I dread, shadows our path only when the chatter of men drowns the weightier croaking of the frogs.

As May teemed with the noise and bustle of preparation, so June—the preparative work being over—rests and offers for contemplation nature finished. The foliage of to-day will not be denser or of deeper tints to-morrow, and whether in upland or in meadow you will find no new birds. Those that came to stay are now busy with their nests; those that tarried for a while, *en route* for more northern homes, have long since left us. June is a month of fixed facts, but they are none the less interesting because of this. What transpired a year ago, this day or week or month, or even half a century ago, is now being or will be re-enacted. But all was not reported then, and much has been slighted since, so that the danger is slight indeed that the record of any June day out of doors will be a twice-told tale.

One great advantage of observations made at this time is this: Hitherto, we have had, for instance, to content ourselves, as a rule, with casual glimpses of every bird we saw, and could seldom be sure that we saw the same individual twice; but now, not only the same bird, but, better yet, a mated pair can be confidently followed from day to day, for they have a comparatively restricted range, and every movement is more or less with reference to their nest and young. The advantage is obvious. At no other time are the characteristic features of bird life so pronounced, and the one opportunity of each season is offered to determine how far individuals vary as to their intelligence, their tastes, and mode of living.

I have been much interested in watching a brood of Virginia rails that were hatched somewhere in the impenetrable mucky meadow, of which I have so often spoken. No tropical jungle could be more hopelessly tangled than this bit of marsh, and, I may add, few probably shelter a greater variety of life-forms. Here I have found—and can always find—mammals, birds, reptiles, batrachians, and fishes, besides insects and other invertebrate life in the greatest profusion; and here it is that with the regularity of the seasons three notable forms of aquatic birds repair to breed—the king rail, the Virginia rail, and the least bittern. Of these, during the summer of 1888, the smaller rails were the prominent feature.

I occasionally heard them during the month of May, but never caught a glimpse of one until late in June, when a commotion of some sort brought at least two broods and their parents to the edge of the marsh. Occasionally they ran out for a short distance upon the open meadow. The young at this time were not fully grown nor able to fly, I thought, but their activity as runners was really re-

markable. They "peeped" incessantly, their voice being
clear and fife-like, while the parent birds uttered, with few
intermissions, a pig-like note that has been well described
as sounding like *kēēk-kēēk-kék*. I discovered these birds—
but not the cause of their distress—early in the afternoon,
and remained for several hours at the edge of the marsh,
watching their strange antics. As the reeds, rushes, calamus, and dock were all too dense to enable me to see the
birds constantly, I naturally fell to conjecturing what
might have caused the commotion. Of course the probabilities were that some animal had attacked the young
birds. But the speed with which the young could run
rendered it improbable that they were really in any danger, unless surprised. In a fair race they could outrun a
black-snake. While I waited and wondered, several times
the birds moved apparently to the opposite side of the
meadow, judging by their voices, and then in a body came
back to very near the spot where I was lying in wait.
This strange movement materially increased my curiosity,
but I was helpless in the matter. By no known means
could I see more than the birds chose to permit, and that
was provokingly little. But at last—as is usually the case
—I was somewhat rewarded for my patience, for suddenly
the rushes began to tremble violently, and with a quick
bound a large mink made his appearance. He hesitated a
moment as if to recover from fatigue, and then, with that
easy gait characteristic of all the weasel tribe, bounded
across the meadow. It is fair to suppose that this murder-
ous creature had caused the disturbance, from the fact
that directly after its departure silence reigned.

We are apt to consider as instinctive every action of a
very young animal—such as the spitting of blind kittens and
the barking of newly born puppies—but the acts of young
rail birds, that are both strong upon the feet and have excellent vision as soon as hatched, are suggestive of a higher

degree of mentality. Those who have watched young
rail birds when confined will vouch for their cunning,
and those who have seen them in their own homes are
equally ready to aver how knowing they are. Although
watched over by their parents, and constantly warned by
various cluckings of different tone, and so, presumably, of
different meaning, the young take in the character of
their little world very promptly, and act under the guid-
ance of their own considerable intelligence. When deprived of their parents this is, of course, the more evident.
Then, they band together for mutual aid, and roost in the
thickest tangles, at a distance from open water and where
an enemy would only by mere chance be likely to come. I
have, by accident, twice come upon them toward the close
of day, when the young birds—some half-dozen of them—
were resting in tangled cat-tail, at a distance of a foot at
least above the water. To the broad leaves of the plant
they clung tenaciously, and were at first quite indisposed
to run; but on endeavoring to take off one, they all pre-
cipitately fled. Soon after, I heard a faint, quail-like
"peeping," and believe that by this signal they were
again coming together. I know that when I disturbed
them, they fled in different directions. These broods were
both very young, and were evidently orphaned.

When parents and young are kept together in a room,
they remain upon friendly terms long after the latter have
become fully fledged. In fact, the rails in a friend's aviary
went a step further, and one young male married his
mother.

Although these birds grow rapidly and soon become
feathered, the idea of using their wings as a means of
escape seems never to occur to them until the summer is
well-nigh spent; and even in September I have seen
young rail birds that would only run in spite of very close
pursuit by a spaniel. Later, when nightly white frosts

admonish them of the destruction of their close cover, they find the necessity for migration before them, and suddenly, in a night, they depart. Flight must seem a strange faculty to them as they journey for many miles; and when they return one would naturally expect to find them flying rather than running from their foes; but this is seldom the case. Those that year after year summer in the mucky meadow are practically wingless as apteryges. Would, if the necessity of migration no longer continued, the rail birds lose their flight power? It is not improbable. So admirably adapted are they for living in their wet and weedy haunts, and so averse are they now to leaving them, that, through disuse, it is quite natural that one or more powers should be lost. I do not think that in the short journeys peculiarities of the season may render necessary these birds always fly. When a sudden rise in the river has occurred in summer, the rail birds have been found running about the meadows adjoining the marshes from which they have been driven; and a high freshet has sometimes forced them to the upland fields. They seem never to wander farther than is necessary from their chosen haunts, and return to them as soon as the receding waters will permit. Such facts I have interpreted as indicating a great indisposition to wander, and particularly to fly to distant and more pleasant quarters.

A June landscape is incomplete without water. Best of all, the river; but if not this, then a creek, a brook, or even the quiet mill-pond. However pleasant the day may be, the breeze cool, the blossoms bright, the shade dense, the sunshine tempered, there still is something wanting. The world has an unfinished look when there is no water in view, and wild life is largely of the same opinion. I have often found many an upland field almost deserted when the meadows and the river bank were crowded.

Even the solitary bluebird that far overhead was hurrying toward the river valley, warbled in most melancholy tones as it crossed my neighbor's clover, and I, too, saw nothing to stay my steps, and yet it was a perfect June morning. Wayside weeds, clover blossoms, and a long vine-clad worm fence were as nothing; yet had they been by sparkling waters, how readily I should have lingered there! As it was, I felt drawn toward open water, and passed every object in the fields without a glance at any. My eyes thirsted for a watery landscape, and I hurried, without a fear of disappointment and in high hopes of novelty, toward the near-by mill-pond.

The high banks, themselves shut in by the crowded growth of vigorous young trees, hid the pond until I was at its very edge, and then, to my chagrin, I found no sparkling waters between the shores, no floating isles of lilies, no forest of splatter-docks, but instead a wide reach of sun-cracked mud and the trivial forest brook of Indian times. I had come too far not to make the most of a bad matter, and for water I must content myself with mud. The outlook was at first unpromising.

If I mistake not, it had been many years since the mill-pond was so nearly empty as now. As I looked up and down the little stream, the whole region appeared deserted. Desolation brooded over the valley and cast a shadow even upon the adjoining woods. But was this not a condition born of my own feeling of disappointment, and so a false interpretation? Would I have seen more, or heard more, had I found the expected sheet of water instead of a mud-flat? There is no reason to think it. As the animal life that long ago adapted itself to other conditions had proved equal to the emergency of a sudden change, so must I. Whatever had been my plans mattered nothing; what could now be done?

Besides the narrow cracks in the mud there were other

10

depressions, both wider and deeper than these, and all
leading directly from the shore line of the pond toward
the brook. One that I followed from end to end was
deeply impressed with the tracks of a musk-rat that two
nights before had walked instead of swam to the middle
of the pond. I thought of mussels and looked for their
shells, for I always associate the mollusk with this animal,
but found no trace of them. This led me to wondering
what the musk-rats here did eat, and I found the bones of
frogs and a bird at the opening of another burrow on the
opposite side of the pond. The bird was a small heron, and
I will not presume that the musk-rat caught it; that it
found the bird is far more likely. One feature of the
mammal's habits was evident—a meat diet is preferred, if
not essential. In the tidal creeks a mixed one is the rule,
for many tender roots of water-plants are devoured.

A word here about the mussels that in most places
constitute a large proportion of the musk-rat's food. The
shells that accumulate about the burrows and feeding-
grounds of the rat are not without scarification always,
as has been so persistently claimed. Directly below the
cliff, in Adams County, Ohio, whereon rests the Serpent
Mound, Brush Creek meanders over a rough and troubled
course, and is almost stayed at certain points by the huge
rock masses that have fallen into the channel. Here
musk-rats abound, and mussels are abundant. Upon
several projecting rocks I found scattered shells that
clearly exhibited tooth-marks, and several that were
broken about the edges, as teeth and toe-nails tugging at
them would be likely to break them. As a whole, my
gatherings would never lead one to suppose that valves
were ever parted without injury. Such, however, is the
case, and I have heard but a single explanation, although
I have asked many observers—meaning by the latter
trappers and others who had had abundant opportunities

to observe musk-rats under favorable circumstances. They all expressed the opinion that the mussels were carried out of the water and placed in heaps to sicken, if not to die. I can not prove this, nor could my informants, but the details of their observations as narrated certainly warranted them in coming to the conclusion to which they reached; and an accomplished naturalist of Indiana, who has very carefully studied the habits of the musk-rat for years, assures me that he believes the "open-air" theory to be correct, as he had seen in these heaps of mussels many that had been overlooked, and dying; the valves had parted, but the soft parts, the animal proper, had not been extracted.

Mr. A. M. Brayton, in his report on the "Mammals of Ohio," states: "The summer food (of the musk-rat) consists of leaves of various aquatic plants and different species of river-mussels. Every one at all familiar with the shallows of our streams will recall the immense heaps of mussel-shells—often a bushel or more—by the side of some large stone or log, midway, perhaps, of the river, and furnishing easy collecting grounds for the conchologist. These are the 'oyster restaurants' of the musk-rat. Collecting the mussels from the river bottom, the musk-rat mounts the log or stone, sits up on its haunches like a squirrel, and opens the shell with its strong incisor teeth, as neatly as a squirrel opens a nut. Most of the shells are left with the ligament intact. Mr. Kennicott has found massive shells, like those of *Unio plicatus*, left unopened, or with the valves gnawed apart at the back."

To return to the mill-pond. The changed conditions had been comprehended as with a glance, and I doubt if a creature dwelling upon the banks of the one-time millpond was not wholly at home. Curiosity led me to an enormous stump that was now some three feet above the mud. The tree, an oak, had evidently been felled just before the construction of the pond—which was eighty-five years ago—and was not at all decayed. Here the musk-rats had already found a convenient resting-place, and even thus early had left traces of their feasts. The broken shells of crayfish were very abundant.

These ever-abundant crustaceans had resented the sudden outgoing of the waters, and seeking refuge in every nook had withstood the current, and were now crowded into the shallow brook and the little shallows that dimpled the wide expanse of mud. Their efforts to escape were wildly frantic as I drew near, but I could not induce them ever to leave the water. This surprised me, as the pools were but an inch or two in depth, so I tried to force them out upon the mud by placing my cane before me and slowly advancing. Back they darted, and then again and again receded, until they were half out upon the mud; but no further would they retreat. Many burrowed until nearly out of sight, and all might have done so had the mud been less compact, and a few gave a forward leap over my cane and sought refuge in the water behind me. I say a "forward leap," for so it seemed, but the movement was too rapid for me to be positive. This matters little, for I had gained my point; even the crayfish has a modicum of cunning, or, more properly, common sense.

As the child casts away one toy for another, so I turned from the crayfish at last, and they, like the musk-rats, were quickly forgotten. From point to point I wandered, and at last, finding no novelty, wondered at the absence of birds. Here, certainly, was a generous feeding-ground, and yet I neither saw nor heard any, save the chirping sparrows of the thickets. I forgot that in so exposed a position I was acting the part of a scarecrow and kept away the very creatures that I wished to see. Remembering this, I withdrew to a shady nook, commanding a good view both up and down the pond, and there awaited developments; nor had I long to wait. The crows were soon upon the ground, and how I longed for a field-glass! They evidently were in search of food, and doubtless attacked the little crayfish; but the larger ones appeared to give them trouble. At least, I can imagine no other animal in the pools that would defy them. Amid the most vociferous cawing they pranced about the edges of the pools, and thrusting their heads into the water they withdrew with a ludicrously quick jump that appeared to excite or amuse the bystanders. It was a curious sight but did not last. Either the crows were quickly surfeited or discomfited, and left the spot in a body. As soon as they rose into the air I went to the spot, but failed to detect any diminution in the number of crayfish.

Wandering to where the pond was wider and deeper— or had been, when there was a pond—I found the mud in places covered with curious tracks, running in every direction and ending apparently nowhere. These puzzled me at first, but when I recognized them as the footprints of turtles, all seemed clear enough. The bewildered creatures had evidently wandered in a very aimless way, looking for the water that had left their haunts without warning. Where were the turtles now? To solve this problem I assumed to be a very easy task, and walked with confidence to various pools and probed the mud industriously, but not a turtle was to be found. It seemed improbable that they should have been swept down the creek, and yet they were not in the likely spots upon the mud-flat where they had so recently been crawling. On re-examination of the tracks, I found that some led toward the shore, and following these, I was delighted to find one little basin of a bubbling spring filled with quite young snappers. There were seven; none more than three inches long, and each as ill-tempered as the most patriarchal of their race has ever been found to be.

This discovery opened up a greater mystery: what of the many other species known to inhabit the pond? That they were hiding in the woods waiting the return of the waters was scarcely probable, but I commenced to search for them forthwith. By accident, I found a spotted turtle beneath a cluster of dwarf laurel, and then probed wherever the ground was damp. At last I got a clew to their whereabout. My probing attracted the attention of a farmer living near, and he assured me that I would not find the turtles where I supposed, for they had " wobbled over the hill to the ditches in his meadow." This I found to be true. Fully five hundred yards away, in a low-lying meadow, separated from the mill-pond by a high ridge or hill, I found scores of turtles of five species, but not a snapper among them. I can not believe that under ordinary circumstances turtles are ever as abundant as I found them in this meadow, and accept the farmer's statement that they had " wobbled over the hill " from the mill-pond. And now we are confronted with two puzzling problems: Why did not the snappers go? How did those which crossed over to the meadow know of its existence?

They certainly did not look very happy. Some of them gazed wistfully at me, as though expecting the announcement that the mill-pond was again full to the brim and ready to receive them. I picked up four—one at a time—and placed them in the woods midway between the meadow and the pond, and found when I set the last upon the ground the others had not moved. Then I rearranged them, tail to tail, with their heads pointing toward the four cardinal points of the compass, and left them to their meditations. Fully ten minutes elapsed before any one saw fit to move, and then they all seemed influenced alike and set out upon their journeys. The one that faced the pond turned neither to the right nor left, and I followed as best I could, but soon lost it in the underbrush and weeds. Retracing my steps, I searched for the others, but without success.

Did these turtles start out with the idea of searching for water? Had they formulated any plan? Recalling those that I had seen in the ditch as I walked away, I felt the hopelessness of the attempt to unravel the tangle of what chelonian or any other "lower" form of life really is, and particularly how far it is akin to our own. When a dwelling-house is burned, the inmates take refuge in the nearest shelter. The current of a person's thoughts at such a time is readily traced. Even if such an unwelcome experience has not been our own, we are sure as to what we would do and think under such circumstances, and naturally ascribe the same to our neighbors. Are we warranted in following a like plan in judging of turtles? The breaking of an embankment drains a mill-pond, and a score of unhoused turtles seek shelter in the nearest adjoining pools of water. Was the mental process similar to, or identical with that of the supposed case of mankind when a dwelling was burned? If so, to some extent our task is simplified; but "if so" ever stands guard over all such suppositions, and I sometimes fear it ever will.

Since the above was written, I have had the pleasure of reading Lubbock's recent work on "Animal Intelligence," and the following throws a new light upon the subject:

"The general aspect of nature must present to animals a very different appearance from what it does to us.

"These considerations can not but raise the reflection how different the world may—I was going to say must—appear to other animals from what it does to us. Sound is the sensation produced on us when the vibrations of the air strike on the drum of our ear. When they are

few, the sound is deep; as they increase in number, it becomes shriller and shriller; but when they reach forty
thousand in a second they cease to be audible. Light is
the effect produced on us when waves of light strike on
the eye. When four hundred millions of millions of vibrations of ether strike the retina in a second, they produce red, and as the number increases the color passes
into orange, then yellow, green, blue, and violet. But between forty thousand vibrations in a second and four hundred millions of millions we have no organ of sense capable of receiving the impression. Yet between these limits any number of sensations may exist. We have five
senses, and sometimes fancy that no others are possible.
But it is obvious that we can not measure the infinite by
our own narrow limitations.

"Moreover, looking at the question from the other side,
we find in animals complex organs of sense, richly supplied with nerves, but the function of which we are as
yet powerless to explain. There may be fifty other senses
as different from ours as sound is from sight; and even
within the boundaries of our own senses, there may be
endless sounds which we can not hear, and colors, as different as red from green, of which we have no conception.
These and a thousand other questions remain for solution.
The familiar world which surrounds us may be a totally
different place to other animals. To them it may be full
of music which we can not hear, of color which we can
not see, of sensations which we can not conceive. To
place stuffed birds and beasts in glass cages, to arrange
insects in cabinets, and dried plants in drawers, is merely
the drudgery and preliminary of study; to watch their
habits, to understand their relations to one another, to
study their instincts and intelligence, to ascertain their
adaptations and their relations to the forces of nature, to
realize what the world appears to them—these constitute,

as it seems to me at least, the true interest of natural history, and may even give us the clew to senses and perceptions of which at present we have no conception."

But show that a turtle's sense of smell is sufficiently acute to smell water that is a hundred rods distant or hear the trickling stream that is as far away, and it becomes mere machine, as it were, led by these exquisitely developed senses, and need possess no trace of intelligence. Still, I am not willing to set all turtles down as fools. The cornered snapper shows he is not in more ways than one, and I have knowledge of a box-tortoise that certainly recognized its keeper, and would come when he called it.

I returned to the mill-pond as the day was closing, and gave the remaining hours to the few small fishes that found the little brook that remained sufficient for their needs. Little minnows only, and I could not expect much entertainment from them, but they seemed quick-witted enough when I tried to capture a few for identification. Every individual darted into some inaccessible nook when my shadow fell upon the water, and only reappeared when I had stood back for several minutes.

The last time I did so, and while watching their somewhat curious antics in the shallower spots where the smooth areas of dark-brown mud made it practicable to observe them distinctly, I was interrupted by a number of cows that crossed the bed of the pond in a direct line with where I was standing. To my astonishment, these timid minnows did not appear to notice the animals, and continued their sports. This induced me to approach somewhat nearer, and I walked as unconcernedly and cow-like as possible, but all to no purpose. The moment I came within view they darted off. Of course it can not be proved, but the circumstantial evidence is very strong that these minnows, which, I may say, probably never saw a human being before, recognized a difference, and saw in

the cows animals harmless to them, and also saw, or
thought they did, an enemy in me.

I had had a very different experience recently, with an
old sunfish and her brood, and so wondered the more at
the exceeding wildness of the little minnows in the pond.
While gathering snail-like shells from the leaf-stalks of
the lotus, this troubled mother fish was much exercised
because her brood had no fear, and were in danger of
being trampled upon, as I waded in the shallow water.
Then, prompted by an innate love of teasing, I put my
hand into the water, and the young, instead of darting
away, clustered about it and nibbled at my fingers. The
poor old mother became frantic. Fear limited her daring,
and she remained just out of reach. I waited for some
time in an uncomfortable, stooping position, hoping to see
evidence of a power on the parent fish's part to signal to
her young, but discovered nothing that could be looked
upon in that light; or, if the young fish were aware of
any such signaling, they were quite indifferent to it.
After a few minutes had elapsed, I commenced moving
my hand to and fro, and opening and closing my fingers
at the same time. These motions were too like those of
an animal in the act of eating the brood, and the limit of
the parent's endurance was reached. Without warning,
she rushed at my hand with such force that I was fairly
startled, and, withdrawing it suddenly, nearly lost my bal-
ance.

Shortly after this incident the question arose in my
mind, whether this brood of very young fish could distinguish their mother from other adult sunfish. Of course,
the converse of this is always true. To test the matter, I
scooped in a near-by ditch until I caught a fish of about
the size of the parent of the brood, and then separating
the young from their mother and keeping them well apart,
set my captive free among the former. Instantly there

was dire confusion. The released fish was either recognized as a stranger, or as their parent gone mad. The poor things scattered, and showed every evidence of genuine fear. I repeated this, from day to day, for a week, and with practically the same results; but, after all, I am not sure that they have much significance. I failed altogether to determine the main point, and have had to content myself with the feeling that my inference of some intellectual power in very young fishes is correct. I believe this brood of sunfish recognized the strangers as such, rather than supposed them to be their parent in a dangerous frame of mind; this being indicated, too, by the fact that when the parent fish was removed and returned to the pond, the young immediately clustered about her and no evidence of fear was apparent.

To observe to the best advantage the majority of the fishes in our little creeks, it is necessary to study them when associated, as well as during the spawning season, and this is practicable in midwinter. In fact, the absence of vegetation, both along the banks of the streams and in their beds, renders such study a far easier task than in summer; and one has the advantage, too, of often finding several species collected in the spring-holes where the water is appreciably warmer than elsewhere in the bed of the stream. To watch such congregated fishes from day to day, yourself remaining concealed the while, is to become satisfied that, however small the fish, it is never a fool, but really has a modicum of common sense. And let me add, I have never been convinced that a friendly critic was right when he insisted that batrachians were more intelligent than fishes, as a rule. I admit that my more recent field-work has often been contradictory in its results, the observations of one day negativing those of the next, but I find, on careful collation of memoranda covering all the year, that the impression has been further strengthened that fishes as a class are more intelligent than batrachians, and here it may be well to add that the strictly carnivorous fishes are without exception more cunning than herbivorous or even omnivorous species.

I tarried for half an hour after sunset at one very prominent feature of the empty pond, an enormous <u>white-oak stump</u>. Since the pond was built it has been deeply submerged, but as yet has lost nothing of its bulk, save the bark. The tree when felled, in 1803, was one of the land-marks of the neighborhood, and the largest oak, save one, for many miles around, and probably one of the largest in existence.

My grandfather, who was familiar with the tree for more than twenty years, told me that it stood in the middle of the original highway that passed here, and the wagon tracks on each side of the tree were thirty feet apart, the ground being so wrinkled with projecting roots that this wide offing was necessary. Of these great roots nothing now remained, or if not decayed they were deeply covered with silt. Having other oaks in mind, one in the Crosswicks meeting-house yard in particular, it was not difficult to reconstruct the ancient tree and restore the surroundings to their earlier and wilder condition. The little valley must have been a charming spot, and I wonder not that to the few remaining Indians it was a favorite one. Here, during the closing years of the last century, they encamped annually in autumn, making and peddling baskets and bead-work during their stay. The oak tree, if not the surroundings, appeared to be sacred to them, so my grandfather thought, or at least to be associated with certain memorable events in their history.

And at last, when the shadows lengthened until the pond was almost lost to view, I turned toward home, filled with romantic feelings born of the surroundings and of my scanty knowledge of their past history. It is a confession of weakness, perhaps, but tales of long ago, the fireside stories that my grandparents knew so well, are of greater interest to me than all else; so, while I walked, the roadside and beyond were restored to those marvelous conditions of colonial times that forever haunt my fancy.

The delightful uncertainty of threatening days is something for which to be thankful. It is no drawback at the threshold of a June morning to have some gray-beard scan the wrapped sky and assure you with an air of wisdom that " it looks kind o' threatenin'."

What if it does? Must we crawl back to bed, or, like the ground-hog, because he sees his shadow in February, anticipate foul weather and resume our seclusion? It is exhilarating to take the chances. We have the excitement of gambling without its moral degradation. If after all it proves a clear day, as it is very likely to do—for the country folk's predictions, like dreams, often go by contraries— one feels like the fool he really is, if he stayed at home. If the rambler ventures abroad notwithstanding the prediction and the day proves stormy, the chances are many in his favor that he will have the world to himself, which always overbalances the discomfort caused by rain. And herein lies the reason : Looking over page after page of June field-notes, covering many years, I find that a gentle rain has no depressing effect upon animal life, and it occasionally produces the opposite effect. Let me particularize. Not long since, heavy banks of cold, gray clouds rested upon the distant tree-tops, a chilling mist obscured the meadows, and the east wind petulantly dashing against the tide, alike foretold the coming storm. Notwithstanding the forbidding outlook, I pushed my

boat boldly over the intervening strip of mud and rowed
across the river. Scarcely had her keel grated upon the
pebbly beach, than I heard the cheery whistle of the piping plover. There were dozens of these pretty birds, or so
it seemed.   In and out among the coarse pebbles they ran
without fear, and sang their sweet songs at every pause in
their erratic courses. Often they chased each other and
took short flights over the water, always keeping in line
and each piping his very shrillest notes. As I sat quite still
several came very near, so near that I could see their every
movement distinctly, and was delighted when three perched
upon a large and prominent bowlder, sitting as close together as ever huddled three swallows on a telegraph wire.
The long threatening rain now commenced to fall in earnest and evidently interfered with the plovers so far as their
feeding was concerned.   In a few moments they had
gathered in little knots along the pebbly strand, usually
in spots that were somewhat sheltered from the gusty
wind. But they were not silent. Their clear, piping notes
were heard above the 'moan in the bending pines, above
the dash of the petty surf upon the rocks. Group answered
group in such quick succession there were no marked intervals of silence; the patter of the rain was lost in the
bell-like music of the merry birds.

How long the plovers would have remained I can not
tell, but it was not practicable for me to spend the whole
day sitting in the boat; I must be moving, having other
ends in view. As I stepped upon shore each little company took wing one after another, and uniting far out
over the river they bore away down stream. In the driv-
ing rain and mist I soon lost them, and the wind brought
no tidings of their journey.

Here, then, at the very outset of a rainy day, I had
been well repaid;. but how much I should have lost had I
merely retraced my course! Walking up the river shore

to where the birds had been, I found a huge water-snake
that had recently been killed. Not one of these timid
plovers had recognized it, apparently. Many had even
stepped upon it, and yet it lay upon the pebbles in full
view and in a very life-like position. This brings up the
unsolved problem of how far a bird's sense of sight is akin
to our own ; how far all their senses. Lubbock's remarks
that the world may be a totally different place to other
animals must be remembered.

That plovers, like all of our small birds, are afraid of
living snakes will not be disputed. I doubt, indeed, if any
of our largest birds of prey would have dared to attack
this dead snake when alive, for a serpent five feet in length
and stout in proportion is enormously strong. By what
means did this flock of piping plovers recognize that it
was harmless? I only determined the fact by a close examination. There was, of course, no motion ; and as the
snake had been very recently killed, no odor of decomposition. I could not at the time, nor can I now imagine by
what method the plovers had ascertained the harmless
condition of the snake, and it can not be doubted that
they did not fear it, unless it is claimed that they did not
distinguish it from the pebbles upon which it was stretched.
I do not believe this. Whenever I have placed a dead snake
in the poultry yard, the chickens gathered about it immediately and made a great noise, but were slow in attacking
it. They always acted upon the supposition that it was still
alive, and were very slow to be convinced to the contrary.
Have plovers a less acute vision? It was suggested at
the time that the absence of motion assured them that the
snake was dead ; but, if so, then they would never be safe
against serpents that might lie in wait; and I have noticed
that our land birds generally detect such cunning snakes
and give their fellows prompt warning. Again, it has
been said that living snakes give out an odor that attracts

the bird's attention before it sees the animal. This certainly tallies with some results of my experiments with pictures of animals.

When I related some years ago the incident of a bird being terribly frightened at a chromo of a cat, the question was asked, Might not the fright have been due to some other cause? It certainly was not then; but I have since repeated my experiments of this character, and with such results as to leave the whole matter still an open question, for the evidence, however strongly it pointed in one direction, was after all, circumstantial. An anticipated effect was, often produced, it is true, but how far correctly were the actions of the animal interpreted? This, I fear, we shall never be able to ascertain.

Some time after I had made the first series of experiments with life-like chromos which resulted in showing that certain birds mistook the pictures for living animals, I happened to recall what I had read of the peculiar condition of certain low races of mankind, who are unable, as a rule, " to realize the most vivid artistic representations," and it seemed very strange that birds should have a realizing power in any direction greater than that of certain species of men; the more so, when it is so often said that human and animal intelligence differs in degree rather than in kind. But this appears not always to hold good. It is on record that " on being shown a large colored engraving of an aboriginal New Hollander, one declared it to be a ship, another a kangaroo, and so on; not one of a dozen identifying the portrait as having any connection with himself." Few birds would be as stupid as this implies. If a picture is recognized at all, it is correctly recognized.

The chromo of a cat that was so effective was not a square bit of card-board upon which the animal was depicted, but the accurately outlined figure only, and so without any confusing fore or back ground to dim the

vividness of the image. Such an imitation of an animal
was certainly well calculated to deceive.

To prove that outlined pictures, such as I have mentioned, were recognized when those with landscape surroundings were not, I exposed a large portion of a menag-
erie poster that was vividly colored and not inaccurately
drawn in a thicket filled with birds. It was passed by
unnoticed. Cutting away all portions but that repre-
senting an Angora cat, and placing it in a position where
its outline could be seen distinctly against the sky, it produced much consternation at first, and then the birds began to marvel why it did not move, and so suspected its
true nature, or that it was dead; but none were brave
enough to cross the danger-line as, in their discretion, they
had drawn it.

Removing it from its elevated position and placing it
on the ground, it was not noticed. Chewinks and Maryland yellow-throats passed it by without stopping a moment, and a frightened chipmunk went directly over it,
and was only disturbed by the rustling of the paper. I restored it as best I could, and varnished the eyes until they
glistened; then I replaced it in the bushes not far from a
robin's nest. It was believed, I am sure, to be really a
cat, and the birds at once were greatly disturbed at its
presence. Of course, it might be argued that any unusual
object would excite a nesting bird's suspicion, but plain
paper of the same size and having a similar outline had
no effect whatever. On the contrary, a pair of vireos tore
off bits of it for their nest, but never would they have
dared to offer a like indignity to the chromo of a crouching cat.

Of groups of animals, however accurately drawn and
colored, neither birds nor mammals seem to have any
power to recognize. The enormous posters scattered over
the country by Barnum and Forepaugh frighten neither

11

horses, cattle, nor poultry; and the pestiferous street sparrow plucks at their fluttering edges for nesting materials.
Removed bodily or piecemeal to the woods or meadows,
they produce no effect; but single animals scizzored from
them usually do. But not if they are very large. A paper
lion never excites even the curiosity of a cow, so I infer
that the sense of smell has much to do with the matter.
Horses have frequently been frightened by animals which
they could not see at the time, and had probably never
seen, their sense of smell alone telling them of the proximity of a dangerous foe.

Representations of men, although quite life-like and of
life size, are ignored by all birds, unless it be the crows,
which are more cautious but never stand off for any
length of time. The enterprising farmer who bought a
tobacconist's wooden Indian to use as a scare-crow was
sadly disappointed. Every morning at sunrise he saw a
crow perched upon the Indian's crown, keeping watch
that his fellows in the field might not suffer a surprise.
Later it was tied near the top of a cherry tree to protect
the fruit, but not a bird feared it. I should like a wooden
figure of a man, dressed as we dress, and fairly represent-
ing man, as the wild birds are accustomed to seeing him,
to be tested as this fanciful Indian figure was. Possibly
we might have other results; and yet the most life-like
dummies I have ever seen fail very soon to protect our
fields from the crows.

Even fish are more ready to recognize portraits than
are some birds, but the object depicted must be free from
all association with other objects or with landscape. I
varnished a drawing of a pike, and placed it in a commanding position in a brook. The minnows immediately
fled from the spot, and for some time did not come near;
but when the water had removed the varnish in part and
the fierce pike became a limp and rumpled bit of paste-

board, the courage of the minnows returned. I do not think that this case was a mere coincidence, notwithstanding the fact that when I have introduced pike into aquaria where there were small fishes, the latter never appeared to show any fear.

The only conclusion I am willing to express at this time in the matter of recognition of pictorial representations of animals by animals is, that among our birds there is a wide difference as to their intelligence, the more knowing species being those most familiar with man; and in proportion as birds are thus familiar (their intelligence being due to the familiarity), they are likely to recognize, first, the similarity of a portrait to the object itself; and, second, to determine soon after its true character. This is within the capability of a wren or a cat-bird, but beyond that of a warbler or a whip-poor-will.

I recently spent a steamy-hot June night in a neighbor's house, and where I least expected to find birds there they proved to be most abundant. I was desperately tired, and it was not without some misgivings that I climbed a dark box staircase, made scarcely visible by the flickering home-made candle carried before me. As I feared, the temperature was unbearable, and worse than this, mosquitoes hummed ominously before I had set down the light, wasps beat upon the window panes and gently rasped the ceiling, and, as though this were not enough, the chimney roared with the ceaseless stream of swifts that were nesting in it. It needed not a glance at the huge feather bed to know that my only object in entering the room was an impossibility. I had no choice but to slip off when all was quiet down-stairs, or to suffer torment until morning. While debating the matter it occurred to me that I might forget the surroundings by studying the swifts in the chimney, and, more than partially disrobing, proceeded, not to burn midnight oil, but utilize tallow and moonlight in ornithological pursuits.

The house was an early colonial one, with chimneys of massive proportions; but at some time in the past a stovepipe hole had been cut that the room I occupied could be heated. This opening, that had been closed by paper, muslin, and paper, in alternate layers, thick with mouldy paste, I opened, and at once uplifted flood-gates I was powerless to replace. Three screeching, helpless, half-naked birds tumbled in upon the floor, and a parent bird, deceived by the dim glare of the candle, which it might have mistaken for a distant star, rushed after them. At once it commenced darting dangerously near the candle, and before I could place it beyond the bird's reach, the fluttering wings extinguished the sickly flame. I was rapidly getting into a miserable snarl, and, with greater speed, becoming angry. Quite unable to catch the one obnoxious visitor, which declined to rest above my chamber door, or anywhere else, I hastened to prevent others from joining it by the same entrance. But adverse fate was grinning over my left shoulder all the while, and three others had entered while my back was turned. Had it suddenly become cold as Greenland I could not now have slept. The moonlight was too dim to attract the birds toward the window—a mere slit in the thick stone wall that six small panes were sufficient to cover. The bit of gauze that covered the space of two panes was drawn aside, and I tried to drive them out. More fool I! Then I tried the pillow warfare, not indulged in since early youth; it, too, was a failure. Then —but hark! It had never occurred to me that I had been making any noise, and now a motherly voice came ringing up the box staircase: "Charles, is thee sick; shall I bring thee some hot tea?"

How the latter query of the kind old lady still rings

in my ears! Bring me some hot tea! There I was, not
writhing with choleraic pain, as she supposed, but oh! so
hot! Drenched with scalding perspiration, tormented by
the shrill chirping of the young swifts, and exhausted by
my frantic efforts to down the old ones. Visions of a
bubbling spring on the hill-side and the morning breezes
had been faintly floating before my eyes whenever I
paused for a moment's rest, and at such a time and when
in such a mood to be asked, " Shall I bring thee some hot
tea?"

My reply shall forever remain unrecorded. No one
knows it, for my hostess did not catch the words; but I
was sobered by the interruption, and passed the remaining
hours until dawn regardless of the fluttering swifts or
their chirping young. Instead, as I crouched by the
little window, hoping for cooler air, I considered the
swifts in the chimney. There seemed to be a hundred
of them, and each as active now as in broad daylight.
As I interpreted the sounds, they came and went in just
such an intermittent stream as characterizes their diurnal
flights. Is this true? Dr. Brewer remarks: " The chimney swallow is crepuscular, rather than nocturnal, in its
habits. . . . When they have young, they often continue
to feed them until quite late at night. They are not,
however, to be regarded as nocturnal, as they are only
known to do this during a brief period." This did not
hold good this memorable June night. There was positively no difference between 9 P. M. and 3 A. M. The birds
left and returned with the same frequency at the later as
at the earlier hour. Nor have I found that this evidence
of activity at night occurs only when there are young
birds. It appears rather to be a common habit from
April to November, but more pronounced during May
and June. But then the demands of the young are not
confined to these two months. Several times I have

found nests of young swifts as late as September. Dr. Brewer says that in Pennsylvania the swift is reported as double-brooded. I do not know about this, but the appearances indicate that they are even triple-brooded, and often quite ignore the lateness of the season. It is nothing uncommon for them to leave young birds to starve when they finally decide upon their autumnal migration.

The anatomy of the chimney swift does not suggest a nocturnal bird, and the thought that only when there is a bright moon are they active at night, arises. Continuous observations do not bear this out. Be it ever so dark, or even stormy, it matters little. Indeed, I have not been able to detect any difference, and so the bird has remained to me a mystery.

But June has many another mystery than this. It is the month that overflows—the month when all nature presses to the fore, and the student rambler is apt to do the least, though now the days are longest, bewildered by the ever-present confusion that surrounds him.

CHAPTER VII.

JULY.

WITHIN a stone's throw of my house there stands a beech tree that dates back to the days of the Indian. At least, I know that it was called by every one in the neighborhood " the big beech " in 1770, and so it is safe to claim for it a century prior to the date named; and the probability is that it has rounded three full centuries. Near it stand two others, each about half the size of *the* beech, and their interlacing branches give the impression of one enormous tree, at a little distance. Practically, they are one, and in their broad shadow throughout July's sunny days it is more than a comfort to linger—it is a luxury.

This "brotherhood of venerable trees" stand on, or rather cling to, the face of a steep terrace; the largest of the three in front. It is a mere step to leap from the ground into the tree, but when you look outward you look also downward, and there are a thicket and forest of small trees fifty feet below, while beyond all are the wide meadow and winding river. It makes one shudder to think of such a tree losing its hold, for the crash would be terrific; but there is no danger. Trees such as this have roots to correspond with their skyward growth.

A word as to the tree's dimensions. It is eleven feet in circumference, six feet from the ground, and at about this distance start upward the primary divisions, six enormous branches; these again divide many feet above, and finally all terminate in a labyrinth of leaf-bearing twigs that effectually shut out the sun. This leafy roof is sixty feet above me when I stand at the base of the main branches.

One does not always care to ramble at mid-day, at least in July, so I frequently find myself terminating the day's stroll at a convenient twist of certain of the beech's largest limbs, that collectively afford an incomparable resting-place, with a sloping back and arms of equal comfort and greater security than most modern furniture affords. There is no creaking of loose joints nor danger of collision with other chairs. Hercules himself could not have rocked over in this easy chair, and even the blizzard of last March did nothing more than make it tremble. A few bits of coarse bagging nailed from limb to limb smooth away all asperities, and luxury in its truest sense is here, if anywhere, at hand.

But what is gained by sitting in a tree? So much that my allotted space would not suffice to catalogue it. Rather, what is not gained? Cozily seated among beechen boughs—are not those five words tantalizing to the toil-worn folks of the cities, even in early July? Here is a gain not given to him who happens to be on the ground, even though sitting in the shade of some old tree. I find that I am far less an object of suspicion, and the birds ignore me while I take note of their pretty ways.

The casual observer might think that the July woods are entirely deserted, and that little transpired in comparison to the hum and bustle of boisterous May. But this is a sad mistake. May is much like a crowded street; July more like the quiet centers where the great business transactions of the world are quietly effected. What birds we now have are here for the summer, and are nesting too, just now, so whatever transpires is bird life at its best.

The truth is, July woods are never absolutely quiet. I was astir recently at 3.40 A. M., and the festival of welcoming the dawn had already commenced. The wood-peewees were the first to sing; then the robins; these were followed by house-wrens; the song-thrush coming to time a tuneful fourth, and not until broad daylight did the dozen or more songsters that frequent my yard join in the concert. But when they did, the volume of sound was wonderful; and I fancied that it steadily increased until the sun was fairly above the horizon, and then gradually died away. By 5 A. M. the woods were comparatively silent, and two hours later, still, to a marked degree. What then is heard is an almost ceaseless chirping, and the business of the day—feeding and warning young birds—has commenced. Sounds like insect-humming, that scarcely break the silence, of course continue and increase in volume as the noontide approaches; but, however shrill these may be, all other sounds are heard through them. Even the harvest-flies—be they ever so noisy—do not drown the plaintive song of the wood-pewee.

With the birds busy, and the temperature ninety degrees in the shade, one should not expect a continual concert, nor feel surprised if there happened an occasional quiet hour. But I am giving now my own opinion, and not that of certain birds; for here in the beech is a pair of nesting red-eyed vireos, and never the day too hot for them. Thoreau has written:

> Upon the lofty elm-tree sprays
> The vireo rings the changes meet,
> During these trivial summer days,
> Striving to lift our thoughts above the street.

Here the days are too full to be trivial, and the lively birds lift my thoughts to the branch whereon hangs their pretty nest that sways in every passing breeze, yet never fails to hold its contents safely.   From my seat among the larger branches I can see the sitting bird plainly, and it often—so I think—eyes me with a deal of curiosity in its countenance.   A week ago it was timidity that filled its breast, but not so now.   To-day no sooner had the bird left its nest than it hopped to within three feet of me, and while preening its feathers looked at me with an inquiring gaze.   Whether satisfied or not, I do not know, but soon it fell to singing and fly-catching, threading the maze of branches high overhead, and often coming back to its perch just in front of me.   Perhaps it thought so long as I remained where I was, the nest and its contents were safe.   I have little doubt but that this was the impelling motive, yet it needed no active imagination to interpret the bird's actions as evidence that it desired a closer acquaintance, and I almost expected at times to be politely offered a worm.   All went well for several days, and I anticipated much ; but suddenly a change came over the poor redeye's dreams.   In a desolate, absent manner it haunted the tree but avoided the nest, and its mate was nowhere to be seen.   I ventured to examine the nest, and found the eggs gone and a single one of a cow-bird in their place.   For once this fraud in feathers had not deceived the redeye.   It knew it had been villainously imposed upon, and would not be comforted.   I threw out the egg with much vehemence, and just then the troubled redeye chirped loudly.   I took it as commendatory of my act.

I miss these birds, but they have cousins that have been more fortunate.   The warbling vireos sing incessantly.   When at noon even robins are in doubt and the indigo finch stops to consider, they loudly laugh at the idea of discomfort, and do not even seek the shade. A pair of these have a nest near by, but I can not find it. It is so near that its position is unsuspected, and next autumn, when the trees are bare, I shall find it and wonder how it was possible that it escaped detection before. The warbling vireos carry worms to a certain tree, and then like lightning-flashes disappear. It is provoking, but at ninety degrees in the shade, what can I do? I can sit in the beeches and wonder, but never a day's nesting for me in the middle of July.

Another pair kept closely to the corner of the house, but I found them out at last. Search for a long time had proved futile, but, as has so often happened, what I had in vain hunted for was discovered by accident. A large nocturnal moth, such as one seldom sees during the day, was flying about the upper branches of a tall old locust tree, and had attracted the attention of a cat-bird. I saw them both, the moment the latter made an attack, and was watching the absurd antics of the cat-bird, bewildered as it was by the flapping of the moth's huge wings. The commotion was all too near the vireo's young for that bird's fancy, and its distress led to the discovery of the nest—a pretty structure, leaf-hidden and far out of reach.

Another bird that visits me while in the beeches is the less well known black and white tree-creeping warbler. A long name for a little bird, but nothing else has ever been suggested. It is a warbler, but can scarcely be said to warble; it creeps all day long among the trees, but in one sense is not a creeper. A nice muddle in the matter of names, but unavoidable. This bird contents itself with a monotonous *tzeez—tzeez—tsis*, uttered at irregular intervals, and all the while it is intent upon insect hunting. Recently I saw one with a worm wriggling in its beak. It seemed somewhat ill at ease—the bird no less than the worm—and chirped in a peculiar manner. I happened to be seated upon the ground at the time, and remained motionless, to see what direction the bird would go, for I knew it had a nest. But it would not go, and it dawned upon me I might be very near the nest where I sat, and so was the cause of the bird's discomfort. This proved to be true. I had one foot dangerously near the structure, which filled a little cave that I think the bird must have dug. Perhaps not; but it was a happy find, if of other origin. A more unlikely place could not well be imagined. I quickly withdrew, but kept my eye on the spot, and soon the bird flew to it and then came away, chirping in a very satisfied manner. It evidently thought that all danger was passed; and so it was, so far as I was concerned. The young were nearly ready to leave their nest, and two days after, when I again visited the spot, I found the brood had dispersed. It was not a voluntary nest-leaving, however, and soon I found one of the young birds perched in a low shrub. The antics of the parent bird were very amusing and at times pathetic. By every means it endeavored to draw me away by feigning every degree of helplessness. . Its strangest action was to raise one wing straight up and trail the other, as though it was broken, and then run along the ground with a ludicrous halt gait. Finding this of no avail, it came very near me and chirped vigorously, and induced the timid young bird to leave its perch and hide in the grass near by.

The other young were some distance off and not together; so the parent bird had a hard time of it feeding them. I saw but one parent, and this is true of the one other nest I have found. Does the male bird leave his mate after incubation commences? I have found many a nesting bird, particularly vireos and fly-catchers, where but the one parent was to be seen; and I am as yet unable to determine the cause. These pretty creeping warblers have no end of pretty ways, and often are surprisingly unsuspecting. I wandered into a weedy meadow recently, having no special object then in view. Do not think because a meadow is weedy, it is necessarily repulsive. This one was pink with pale erigeron, golden with buttercups, purple with flags, and afar off a tardy cockspur thorn recalled the memorable snow-drifts of March, so dense and purely white were its clustered blossoms. Above all, towered a splendid shellbark hickory, and here I sat down. Inquisitive sparrows quickly found me out, and I had company from that moment. Other birds came; then a snake, and finally a waddling tortoise. To all appearance I was certainly in luck, and yet, strange to say, I soon wearied of my friends, and, not only this, but ere long fell asleep. For a considerable time, leaning against the shellbark's shaggy trunk, I slept soundly, and was roused by the rattling thrill of the loose ribbons of bark that hang from these trees when fully grown. One of these curled strips was still trembling, almost in contact with my ear, as I opened my eyes. I saw no cause for this, and just as I raised my hand to rub my filmy eyes, a little bird, with a shrill chirp, flew from my side.

As is so seldom the case, I had my wits about me at the right moment, and, trusting for a solution of the matter, remained perfectly still. Presently a faint rattling was heard that quickly became louder, and a black and white tree-creeping warbler came around the tree just in a line with my face. It came so near me that I could not see it, for I dared not move a muscle, and then halted, as though not quite satisfied that I was a part of the tree. I waited for perhaps a minute and then heard the bird move from me when I ventured to turn my face toward it. Our eyes met, or at least I saw its plainly, and with a frightened chirp it darted away.

I shall never know but always shall believe that this bird once ran directly over me. I can give no reason, save the paltry one that I thought I could feel the tingle of its claws across my face.

I am not, on second thought, disposed to stamp this

as absurd. I have often been astonished at the boldness
of many a timid creature when it believed the dreaded
foe before it was either asleep or dead. Nor can it be
shown that bravery or fear depends upon the presence or
absence of motion. Certainly both birds and mammals
have discriminative powers largely developed, and recognize even slight differences. We all know, too, how indifferent birds become to locomotives, even when the
whistle screams and the smoke-stack belches forth its
sooty clouds.

I have noticed, while lounging in the beech tree's
branches, for how long the young of many birds follow
their parents. This feature of bird-life necessarily varies
a great deal, but is more prolonged with many species than
is recorded. Many a young bird is practically helpless for
days after it has learned to fly. What an awkward little
ragamuffin, for instance, is the young nuthatch when acquiring his scrambling powers! I watched one of a late
brood recently imitating its parent, and it was pure imitation. Not a morsel did it find, or expect to, I take it,
for it never ceased a most doleful chirping which touched
the heart of the lithe parent, which fed it continually
with white, waxy grubs delved from hidden crannies in
the bark. When the old bird flew, the youngster followed,
and the call of the former was always echoed by the
querulous cry of the fledgling. If other birds came near,
it flew to the branch whereon its parent happened to be at
the moment, and begged protection with trailing, trembling wings.

The flicker—or pigeon woodpecker—often feeds its
young when the latter are fully grown and strong upon
the wing; the rose-breasted grosbeak does the same, and
last summer a brood of pewees was fed at times, by their
parents, after a second brood was hatched and constantly
clamoring for food. Busier birds than these poor parents

I never saw, yet they accepted the situation with apparent cheerfulness.

Nor is it unusual, I may add, to see young birds following their parents in this half-helpless way, even as late as the first week in October. I refer to migratory birds—species said not to nest nearer than northern New England. If so, then young birds capable of a long migratorial journey accompanied their parents, and were often fed by them. But another possibility suggests itself. May there not be overlooked areas in northern New Jersey—hemlock forests, rhododendron ravines, spots that are cool as autumn the summer long—where straggling pairs lurk unseen and rear their young? It is nonsense to say that this or that report of the occurrence of a bird is a case of "faulty identification of the species." Our birds are not so very similar in appearance, as a rule, to make this probable, and I have record upon record of early appearance in autumn (September), or even earlier, of northern species which I believe had not been so extremely far away; and this matter of young but wing-strong birds still following their parents, bears out the impression gained from other sources, that our home mountains are not yet sufficiently well studied. Then, too, there are occasional instances of birds breaking the rigid rule of their kind, which may not be repeated for years. The wood-tattler—or <u>solitary sandpiper</u>—has nested in central New Jersey. Here is a case where faulty identification is simply impossible.

I recently sought a cool retreat of which I had heard the day before, hoping there to escape the terrors of a torrid day. I hopefully trudged for more than a mile down a sunny highway where the shrill creaking of crickets was the only sound I heard. Every weed was wilted; not a daisy but was brown with gritty sand, and the one-time starry St. John's-wort was dulled with dust. Still I plodded on, hoping the cedars, each in its angle of an old worm fence, would offer a cool shade for a moment's rest, but the comfort I fancied proved a fancy only. Then the road turned abruptly and a hedge of nature's planting cast a long shadow; here I tarried, doubtful if anything better could be found. The panting sparrow from the fields beyond gathered here, and squirrels, snakes, and turtles found it a pleasant refuge. But for me the spot proved a relief merely by contrast, and I foresaw the coming noon-tide. It would surely prove but a fool's paradise, and the cool retreat for which I had started loomed up as a garden of delights. I turned without regret from the birds in the hedge, though they sang cheerily, and the wild roses that brightened the shady nooks, and again hurried on until the old mill was reached.

There is something sweetly seductive in those words, " the old mill." How vividly the broad pond with its deeply indented shores and floating isles of lilies comes to mind! And the tumbling waters at the dam; the mill itself, dusty with the grists of ages; and the sparkling race, where the freed waters rejoice as though conscious of valued labors well performed. Not a feature here but suggests escape from tropical July; still I pass all by unheeded, and, with careful steps and slow, seek that mysterious depth beneath the mill where steadily, for nearly a century, a dripping wheel has turned. Not a ray of the outer world's bright sunshine could reach me here, and glittering moss replaced the parched grasses of the roadside.

But my friend had hoaxed me. Of course it was a cool retreat, but the hygrometric conditions were not to be ignored. Cool, but oh, so wondrous damp! The very air was dripping with tangible mist. I had been victimized, but my thoughtlessness deserved the punishment. Still, a few minutes spent in such a place could work no ill, and I ventured, as a zoölogist, upon its exploration before re-entering the tropics overhead. It was a lucky thought.

Peering into the wide cracks between the huge stones of the mill's foundation walls, I found many a one was tenanted. Lithe salamanders, spotted frogs, a mouse, and huge gray spiders innumerable were brought to light, and either darted into inaccessible crevices or boldly plunged into the waters beneath the wheel. One frog was a philosopher. He leaped upon the descending face of the wheel and sat there, the picture of content and defiance, until the water was reached, when he dived into its sparkling depths.

What these frogs found to eat can only be conjectured; for, indifferent as they appeared to be in the matter of food, I doubt if one would dare to pounce upon the ferocious-looking spiders which alone represented invertebrate life in this semi-aquatic spot. Possibly these frogs were cannibals. This is not unusual. I have at present in a Wardian case a specimen of the rare green tree-toad, or Anderson's hyla, captured in " the pines " of southern New Jersey. While feeding it with flies a few days ago— which it takes from my fingers—I was startled by the sudden on-rush of a little wood-frog, which, impatient for its own dinner, seriously attempted to swallow both the tree-toad and my fingers at one mighty gulp. Being prepared by the initial attempt, I coaxed the frog into repeating the effort. A mighty effort it was, too! With widely gaping jaws, which were distended before the leap was made, the frog attempted to scoop up the toad and swallow it, or get such a hold as would make subsequent swallowing an easy task; and yet the difference in size of the two creatures was very little. As for the tree-toad, it took the whole proceeding as a matter of course, not moving a muscle, even when such great danger was apparently imminent. The whole tribe of tailless batra-

12

chians are much alike in this respect, seemingly taking it for granted that they were born to be eaten, and stuff themselves until fate wills it that they go to stuff others. There is an exception to this that deserves mention—all these creatures have a wholesome dread of snakes—but the common hop-toad is the greatest coward. Frogs hop away as fast as they can go; but the toad will squeal as he hurries off, and cries most piteously the moment the snake's teeth pierce his wrinkled skin. But I am scarcely wrong so far as frogs are concerned. I have seen little fellows, just from the tadpole state, in dangerous proximity to patriarchal bull-frogs, which were then only waiting for their appetites to return to swallow a half-dozen of their own grandchildren. It is strange that infantile frogs should have an instinctive fear of snakes, and yet none of their greater enemies, the adults of their own race.

As I disturbed the frogs, all took refuge in the water beneath the wheel, and then worked their way down stream toward the outer world. I followed, but without creeping under the wheel, and found where I little expected it a positively cool and yet not superlatively damp retreat. The sparkling water ran over a pebbly channel, shut in from the direct sunlight by a swinging gate, a half-circle in shape, which nearly closed the great stone arch in the mill's foundation wall. Here I sat down to watch, not only the frogs, but a whole host of little fishes, and soon found that my discovery of this truly pleasant place was an old story with the birds. This sheltered, hidden, half-dark mill-race was their favorate bathing-place.

A fearless wren was the first to appear; then a song-sparrow; then several barn-swallows; and finally a cat-bird. Except the swallows—which, perhaps, did not actually bathe, although they dipped into the ripple—these birds, as bathers, are very much alike, the wren, strangely enough,

being more timid than the others. The song-sparrow appeared to dive, but really did not, and neither it nor
the cat-bird waded into water more than an inch deep.
Perhaps this was due to the swiftness of the current, as
every movement suggested that the birds feared to loose
their foot-hold. How I wanted to give them a good push
from the rear, just as I have treated timid small boys!

It is somewhat surprising that many, if not all strictly
land birds, do not voluntarily take to swimming, considering that they all, when wounded, can paddle over the
water at a lively rate. Many a chase have I had for crippled birds in the old barbarous collecting days. It is
true, these wing-tipped birds could not rise unaided from
the water; but such an accomplishment could readily be
acquired, if these same birds would but practice. This
remark may possibly provoke a smile, but it is not foolish,
nevertheless. I have known birds to practice much more
difficult feats, and persevere, too, until they were masters of
the art. But there is one land bird that can float as buoy-
antly as a duck, and take wing again when it desires—the
familiar crow blackbird or purple grakle. An excellent
observer informs me that he has often seen the blackbirds
settle upon the river in the wake of a passing boat and
gather the floating morsels that had been thrown overboard; that he had thrown bits of bread from his skiff,
and seen the birds alight upon the waters and swim
up to them, eating the smaller pieces and carrying off one
of the larger masses. My informant described the birds'
movements as painfully awkward in appearance, if they
were not so in fact, but never were they unsuccessful.
The tail and wings were kept in an upraised position and,
constantly in motion, as if to keep a buoyant current of
air constantly beneath them, upon which they depended
when flight was resumed. What these purple grakles do
is within the capabilities of our thrushes and finches, and,

could food be got in no other manner, few, I imagine, would starve before they learned to swim.

To return to the bathers. It was a pretty sight to watch the sparrow and cat-bird preening their feathers, each perched upon a projecting pebble, from which they could see themselves reflected in the water, albeit a quivering and distorted image. Did they recognize it? At least, the wren did not, as it sat on the opposite side of the stream, scanning the stone wall in hopes of a lunch. Think of a house-wren contemplating a stone wall in silence! Yet this one did; but it soon proved too great a task, and as it darted through a knot-hole into the outer world, I heard its fault-finding chatter, even above the drip and rattle of the ponderous water-wheel.

Before they left, the swallows went through a series of bewildering antics in front of, above, and almost beneath the wheel. In and out the rolling cloud of mist and through every thin sheet of water pouring from the wheel's broad front, these birds pursued some phantom through the trackless air. Not for a second did they check their course, nor cease to chatter as they threaded like lightning the cramped quarter of the wheel-house. What was their object? Do not ask. Although there may be many who assume to know, it were, in truth, as idle to question the Sphinx as to attempt to unravel the mystery of bird ways. Again and again, as the year rolls by, the rambler must be content to merely witness, not to unfathom the whys and wherefores of a bird's doing; but still this unpleasant experience does not go for naught. It very soon teaches him that birds are something beyond what those who should know better have asserted them to be. To learn this is a great gain. It is well to give heed to him or her who carries a spy-glass; but as to him who merely carries a shot-gun, and robs birds' nests *in the name of science*, faugh!

So, sitting here, within sight and hearing of the mist-enveloped wheel, I spent the long torrid summer afternoon. Perhaps he who thought to play a joke upon me became frightened at my non-appearance and imagined me dead or helpless in the gloomy depth, as he pictured it. I have not yet had sufficient curiosity to ask him what he thought; but when I met him on my way home in the cool of the evening, his astonishment rendered him speechless as I descanted upon the wheel-room's merits and thanked him for his suggestion.

It was one of the unpleasant features of a recent outing to see a bird and not be sure of its identity. Perhaps it was a mocking-bird, a partially albino cat-bird, or a Southern shrike. I incline now to the latter opinion. They are much like their Northern cousins, the butcher-birds, in every habit, and not very dissimilar in appearance. The bird I saw came from over a wide reach of meadows and flew directly to the nearest woods. There it alighted upon an exposed branch of an oak, and from where I sat I could see it, but not so distinctly as to determine its colors. The shrike, if this it was, seemed restless and uncertain as to its movements, and impatiently jerked its tail, as though it would shake it off. Presently it dived into the thicket beneath, and at once there was a commotion among the small fry. Sparrows, warblers, and tits appeared in numbers, chattering vehemently. This, more than all else, makes me think that the bird was a Southern shrike.

The great Northern butcher-bird is also more likely to be seen about the creeks than in any point of the uplands. The character of the winter does not affect its movements, but in December, if not earlier, it comes, be the weather moderate or cold, and in April it departs.

I remember one, demure as a scheming crow, with eyes half shut and with not a trace of treachery or cunning in his face. His blue and white plumage, tastefully trimmed with black, made him conspicuous, but he lessened the ill effects of this fact by the manner he assumed. No bird, however timid, would step aside for such as he. Indeed, they perched upon the same branch of the tree he was on, almost upon the same twig, and—where was he? Like a flash the shrike had disappeared, and now, fifty paces distant, he is perched upon another tree, plucking feathers from a kinglet's head and regaling himself with his victim's brains.

This incident recalls one of these birds I called my " garden " shrike, for in that inclosure he remained nearly three months. It is now ten years ago, but there is no change except the absence of this cunning bird. I first saw him on the morning of November 30. It was a cool, pleasant autumn day, with a veil of thin clouds overhead that allowed only semi-sunshine to sift through, affording a light that casts no shadow and is the most grateful to the eyes. Northern sparrows were abundant, and the winter sojourners generally had arrived, among them many kinglets. My garden shrike may have followed them ; at all events, a moment after I saw him for the first time, he had a kinglet in his beak.

My indignation at the killing of this bird caused me to drive the murderer away, and for a week I saw no more of him. The tall weeds in the garden did not, I think, conceal him, and a host of small birds were apparently free from all molestation. But shrikes are never abundant, and I soon regretted my attack. Had I, indeed, permanently frightened him? Should he come back, he might have a bird a day, without my interference, provided he went to the highway for English sparrows. I certainly could spare no kinglets from my door-yard, even that I might study a shrike. It mattered nothing what I wished, thought, or promised concerning him. That shrike was in the garden all the while, and but for close inspection of every bush for cocoons, I might never have seen him. As it was, he proved unlike others of his tribe, and all day long sat mopish as an owl—except upon occasion.

In past years when I have met with these birds, they have been as active as thrushes, and in their movements so like them that, when known at all, they are thought to be birds of that family. They have a few harsh utterances peculiar to themselves, and a knack of mimicking other birds to a limited extent. This also adds to their thrush-like features, and has led to their being called "mocking-birds." Not altogether a misnomer, either, for they have a direful way of mocking at the protests small birds make when their true characters are recognized; and conclude their mockery by killing another and another of the fault-finders.

I do not know how far it holds good elsewhere, but shrikes in winter, as I have found them, prefer the banks of creeks, and particularly such as are overgrown with evergreens. In other words, they skulk among the cedars rather than roam about the fields, and seldom take a protracted flight. In the limited area they choose for their winter haunts, they are content to remain, provided the food supply is kept up; but they are not content to remain idle. They are, rather, constantly on the go, but only from one tree to another, and at intervals rushing with closed wings from the dense cedars to some thicket near by, from which they promptly reappear, with their victims held hopelessly in their powerful beaks.

One of several mysteries connected with the flight of birds is this of protracted, swift progression with closed wings. I have seen a shrike leave a tree by giving two or three vigorous strokes of the wings, and then, with these held closely to the body, swiftly pass into a thicket

or another tree.   To be sure, it was a downward progression in every case, but the angle of declination was but
slight, and the alighting point evidently predetermined,
and the body's motion was under control of the bird's will
as much as though the wings were in use.   That two or
three, or even half a dozen strokes of the wings should
impart to the bird's body sufficient impetus to progress
fully one hundred feet is incredible; yet there appears to
be no other explanation of the fact.   I believe no other
bird, except the falcons, can exercise this power to the
same degree; and even with them it is always a steeply
sloping course, and not one, as with the shrike, but a few
degrees from a horizontal line.

As the winter wore away the shrike became weaker
and quite tame.   I offered him bits of raw beef, which he
gladly devoured, but would never permit of my near approach.   At first I placed these bits of beef on sharpened
twigs, just as the bird is accustomed to impale small
birds and insects, but those that I so placed the shrike
would not eat.   He did not even notice them, apparently.
When, on the other hand, I laid the food on dead leaves
in exposed positions, he would fly down and dart at each
piece as though it was alive, and then and there devour it;
or, seizing it in his beak fly back, to his perch in the quince
bush, and swallow the morsel after having held it for
several minutes.

His efforts to fly when upon the ground were very
curious.   Having almost no use of his injured legs, the
shrike would throw himself backward until his body was
nearly perpendicular, and then, by a quick vibration of the
wings and an impetuous forward movement of the body,
it would be uplifted sufficiently to enable the bird to fly
as usual.   Occasionally the first and even the second attempt would prove failures, and the bird would become
so exhausted that a rest for several minutes was necessary.

Taking advantage of the bird's absence, I pointed a number of twigs of the quince bush, and offered many more bits of beef than the bird could eat, but none were gathered and impaled, as this bird when in health gathers and impales much of its prey. This was not because the disabled bird was unable to do so, as care was taken to have a series of available thorn-like points within easy reach of his accustomed resting-place. It is a little peculiar that although there are one or more shrikes on the hill-side, and others along the creek, every winter, yet almost never do they indulge in this habit of impaling their prey. Is it because food is always abundant?

The monotonous life of my garden shrike came to a tragical ending. It was a beautifully cool, crisp February morning, with every weed in the garden sparkling with feathery frost. All our winter birds were astir and singing merrily. Up from the hill-side came a pair of cardinals, and they, too, whistled their best tunes in the garden. While seed-hunting, suddenly these restless redbirds came upon the half-hidden shrike. With a loud chirping that brought a robin and several grakles to the spot, they commenced an attack upon the unfortunate creature. Get out of the quince bush he must, whistled the redbirds, yet no one dared to make a direct assault. Finally the robin madly dashed at him, and started the persecuted shrike from his perch. A little half-helpless tumble, and he was on his wings, and, regardless of all the others, pursued one of the officious cardinals. Away it flew, screaming, over the hill-side, into a thicket of smilax, followed closely by the shrike. Whether the latter was actually in pursuit or not could not be determined, although I followed as best I could. In the thicket I lost the birds, and quiet reigned in the garden, as well as on the hill-side; so the birds had apparently gone far off over the meadows. But it proved otherwise; as, later in the day, at the foot of a tall cedar, I found a few red feathers and near them the body of the shrike.

This plucky bird was greatly emaciated, and the legs showed they had been injured months before. Crippled as he was, he had wandered from his distant home, and, under enormous disadvantage managed to provide for himself almost to the time of returning to his summer haunts in the North, or, at least, to the cooler mountains.

There are other carnivorous birds than hawks and shrikes. Among the gentle songsters of our gardens we see little, if any, evidence of their blood-thirsty propensities, and yet they all possess them to a greater or less degree. Evidence of this can be had, particularly during the nesting season, by watching patiently a single individual or a pair of birds. When our small birds fight among themselves or with other species death seldom results. Never does a sparrow, for instance, attack another that it may feed upon it; but are not all birds, however gentle they may appear to us, nest-robbers at times? Occasion offering, will not the great majority of even seed-eating birds kill and at least attempt to devour newly hatched birds? This is a broad question—a sweeping inference; but I make it after years of endeavor to persuade myself that it is not true. What bird can be less suggestive of cruelty than the turtle-dove!—yet I have seen a pair of these birds attack and kill a whole brood of redstarts that, leaving their nest too soon, rested upon a branch close to the dove's nest. We all know how ready are chickens to eat raw meat as well as young mice, birds, or fish; and quails, in early summer, will devour the eggs and young of song-sparrows and bay-winged buntings. Of this I have positive knowledge; and even the nests of larger birds are not safe. The late T. A. Conrad, the geologist, informed me that he once witnessed a long combat between a quail and a brown thrush, the former having raided the nest of the latter. Mr. Conrad said that the quail endeavored to avoid the attacks of the thrush by dodging among the thick weeds, but was not always successful, as the thrush made downward swoops, as a hawk would, and appeared to use both beak and claws to advantage. The quail was ultimately forced to retreat.

How well I remember a long-drawn battle between a pair of great-crested fly-catchers and of bluebirds. By chance they had chosen hollows in adjacent apple trees for their nests, and so were brought daily into more or less close association. So far as I could see, all went well. The fly-catchers hawked for insects among the tree-tops; the bluebirds were content with worms from near the ground. But by and by the eggs of the bluebirds were hatched— at least, I assume that they were—and at that time the young of the fly-catchers were well-nigh grown. Before sunrise, one morning, when the bluebirds were happier than usual, there arose a clatter in the lane, such as I have seldom heard among birds.

Every robin stopped singing, the wrens forgot their broods, orioles screeched, and every cat-bird bawled Murder! without knowing what the trouble was. Even the poultry took it up, and for many minutes that quiet, shady lane, ordinarily the very picture of peace, was an actual Pandemonium. It did not take many minutes to fathom the mystery. While every bird present was thoroughly excited, there were four upon which my attention was at once centered. Brave as lions, the bluebirds, little furies now, hurled themselves against the fly-catchers, which, although stronger, could not withstand them. Vainly they attempted to dodge their pursuers, but the bluebirds were too quick. They had acquired new powers, and with strength, courage, and endurance I never supposed them to possess, they drove the fly-catchers far a-field and kept them there.

The bluebirds had been robbed and, of course, had caught the fly-catchers in the act. The event narrated proves this; and while I saw no trace of the murdered in the young nest of the latter, the bluebirds' home was empty.

Even in the seemingly gentle song-bird world, every community is made up of saints and sinners.

July 1-1913
July 1-1914

CHAPTER VIII.

AUGUST.

EXCEPT in magnificent floral displays, August is not a favorite month with the naturalist. The characteristic features of summer are well-nigh over, and when we linger in the shade of the old oaks, our thoughts are more apt to revert to what has been, than to become centered upon what is. And yet how prone we are to forget the character of the seasons, once they are passed! Probably the remarkable rainfall and excessive humidity of the summer of 1887 were forgotten as soon as the dusty days of September came with their blinding clouds of grit and whirling pillars of new-fallen leaves. As compared with other summers in the last decade, it was one, however, that a naturalist is likely to remember.

Our total annual rainfall varies exceedingly. It has been as little as 23·35 inches, and as much as 67 inches. Comparing 1886 and 1887, there was a difference of 8·49 inches for the first ten months of the year, and this was largely confined to May and the three summer months. Of course, an additional rainfall of two inches effects great changes.

Let us consider the birds, as the most prominent form of animal life in ordinary country neighborhoods. Late in April and early in May the usual host of thrushes, warblers, and finches appeared in their accustomed haunts. They came, they sang, they nested; and the middle of

June found most of them with nothing to do but gather in the damp nooks and corners, and eat. Time hung heavily upon their wings. The season had proved favorable in all respects, no nest-destroying storms occurring; so, by June 20, the songs at dawn had largely dwindled to twitterings of robins and plaint of fretful pewees. There was not that absolutely songless condition that might be inferred from the writings of many ornithologists as common to summer after nesting was practically over—a condition that never occurs—but the vigor of the May-day concerts was wanting. Then, late in June, came the rains, the fogs, the phenomenal temperature. The upland fields became meadows; the meadows, marshes; the marshes, weedy ponds. A tropical luxuriance characterized all vegetation. Insect life responded to these conditions, and besides mosquitoes, forms available as food for birds were abundant and widely spread. Instead of the limited range that a drought causes, the birds were as well off in one spot as another, and soon their spring-time vigor reappeared. First, the songs at day-break were renewed; then the old nesting-sites were revisited, and many species that ordinarily nest but once, nested a second time; this being true, I think, of all such birds as place their nests in comparatively sheltered places. The orioles, on the contrary, made no such attempt, and, more strangely still, the grakles, that colonized the pines about my house as usual, did not relish the constant winds, rain, and electrical storms, and sought the sheltered meadows after the first brood were strong upon the wing. This I never knew them to do before.

The change in habits among mammals was not noticeable, except in the case of the musk-rat, which wandered into the upland fields and ensconced himself in little hollows, ordinarily dry but now miniature lakes. The marsh turtles shared the fields with the box-tortoise; the marsh frogs associated with the upland toads; and these often looked hopelessly at sea, with puddles replacing all their sandy haunts and rank grass growing where seldom a blade of grass had grown before. Even the water snakes ventured from the creek and summered in the highlands, finding many a pool that sufficed them when they yearned for a comfortable swim.

Many of the forest trees budded again and grew a new series of leaves, and early flowers reopened their blossoms and gave the botanist an excellent opportunity to compare fresh specimens of such as bloom in April with those that blossom late. Some of the early autumn blossoms, on the other hand, were hastened to maturity, and particularly about our water courses September flowers were prominent in early August. This may not have been due to the season, however, for these plants vary every year, according to locality, and often single plants bloom much in advance of their proper time. But, more strangely still, some species that were abundant a year ago are now not to be found. They have totally disappeared. Whether this has been brought about by the weather, or causes in operation last winter, as ice, is difficult to determine; but such sudden appearances and disappearances are not uncommon. In the case of the summer of 1887 the excessive rainfall might well be a cause of a plant's disappearance, inasmuch as the ground was so thoroughly soaked that the roots must have been injured, if not destroyed; while the year before, for months the same spot was comparatively dry, and then the plant flourished admirably. But plants also appeared where they had not grown before. Some instances of this kind were very marked. Upon a knoll in one of the higher meadows, which usually supports no other plant life than dwarfish mosses and lichens, there suddenly appeared many patches of bluets and scattered clusters of pent-

stemon, the flower blooming late in August as freely as
ever in June.   Equally marked, but with less apparent
reason, was the second flowering of marsh marigolds,
which gilded a long strip of marsh during the last
weeks of August as brilliantly as they had done four
months before.   Stress should not be laid, however, upon
plants blooming " out of season."   Here on the meadows,
protected by the high terrace that surrounds them from
the north winds, plants know no seasons, or respect none,
as they do upon the upland fields.   Dandelions, bluets,
and violets, of the better known flowers, have been found
in bloom every month in the year.

   There is an important lesson to be learned from such
a summer as the one now waning—a lesson that has not
been taught by those who lecture upon zoölogy; a lesson
not laid down in the text-books—the want of fixity of
habit.   Usually, in our natural histories, after a description
of an animal is given, there is a paragraph, perhaps a
dozen, on the habits of the animal, and these are detailed
in such a way that one gets the idea that the creature
referred to is a sort of machine.   That it comes and goes,
eats, drinks, and sleeps, in precisely the same manner, day
in and day out, and once you have seen it you have seen
it forever.

   This mathematical regularity is often dwelt upon as
characteristic of bird migration, but it does not hold
good; and again of nesting habits, but the past summer
contradicts it; and so through every phase of bird life; it
can be shown that while any given species will prove
much the same bird, year after year, if the seasons are
similar, it needs but little change to bring about all the
differences, especially in nesting habits, such as I have
described as observed during the close of the summer.

   Another phase of the subject may be touched upon—
the close relationship between various forms of animal life,

of plant life, and the weather. There can be no doubt but that the birds were stirred to renewed activity by the unusual abundance of insects available for food, and these again had scarcely any struggle for existence, because of undiminished vigor of plant life due to the unusual rainfall. The interrelationship was clearly evident to any thoughtful observer, and yet it would be impossible to follow the chain link by link. One feature of the conditions described was unmistakable—every form of life common to a given locality was exceedingly abundant, and I well remember how, late in the evening, as I noted down the occurrences of the day, the noise of the katydids, the crickets, and nocturnal insect-life generally, far exceeded that of any preceding summer that I remembered; but while our birds very generally sing long after their nesting labors are over, nevertheless, it was something of a novelty as August closed to hear the rose-breasted grosbeak singing at sunset, with the full measure of his springtide ardor; to hear the thrushes in the lane recall the evenings when the apple blossoms made my yard a garden of roses; to hear, mingled with the crickets' autumn cries, the many voices that mark early May mornings as red-letter days.

The summer of 1887, as we have seen, was a remarkable one in many ways, and in nothing more pronouncedly so than in its influence upon animal life. It showed us the most familiar forms in new *rôles*, and demonstrated beyond all question that no bird, and probably no animal of any class, is so fixed in its habits that sudden and radical changes may not occur.

A word in conclusion. I have spoken of the excessive rainfall in the Middle States; perhaps it was not uniform, and in the valley of the Delaware more excessive than east or west of it; and I would have my readers bear in

13

mind that I am treating of a limited locality that has been
daily under my observation. Because of the assumption
that what is true of one locality must be true of all—at
least, I can think of no other explanation—I have time
and again had my attention called to conditions noticed
by others which conflicted with my observations as described by me, and the question asked if I was not probably mistaken. It never occurs to a critic that possibly he
may have been misled or misinformed. The explanation
lies in the fact that even meteorological phenomena are not
always wide-spread. My correspondence, on the whole,
has proved instructive to me, if not wholly satisfactory to
those to whom I have sent replies, for it has led to determining, in many cases, that even but a few miles away, an
animal or a plant may have quite different habits and
habitats from what obtains near where I live. Let no
one be surprised, then, when comparing notes with his
neighbor, to find how widely asunder are their impressions of the same creatures, plants, and, I may add, phenomena.

I heard a katydid last night, the first of these tiresome
singers, and, I am told, there will be frost in six weeks.
It is certainly appropriate that the frost should occur on
so suggestive a date as September 21—the day when summer really ends. But August suggests the close of the
season in other ways; the gathering of the reed birds in
the marshes, the flocking of the blackbirds, the evening
roostward flight of the crows, to say nothing of early
asters and golden-rod, among flowers that are now blooming along the dingy, dusty roads. I have noticed all
these, and some at a much earlier date than the first faint
lisping of a timid katydid; and all such sights and sounds
are similarly suggestive—the summer is drawing to its
close.

To determine what shall be the objective point of an August ramble is seldom an easy task. Occasionally there is a bewildering profusion of attractive features; frequently, there is a dearth of them.

Recently, when neither upland nor meadow appeared specially attractive in the glare of August sunshine, I plunged into a pathless marsh, led on solely by a hope of novelty.

Except you have had experience in such tramps, there is little to attract one, however rank the vegetation, gorgeous the bloom, brilliant the butterflies, or abundant the manifold forms of life; for the charm of a ramble is lost when too prominent a feeling of uncertainty as to your own safety surrounds you—when we lack the assurance of a firm footing. How often I hesitated to leave the trembling tussock upon which I stood, not knowing but a treacherous quicksand spread out before me! Still, I ventured on, hidden from all the world at times by the tall reeds or sword-like foliage of the stately typha. The testy marsh wrens scolded as I passed; the lisping swamp sparrow stared and stammered from his perch, and great blue herons cast ominous shadows as they fled. Without a vestige of reason for so doing, beyond a forlorn hope of novelty, I still struggled forward, to find at last a bush-clad island of firm earth. Here was a happy combination, as it proved, of novelty—an evidence of summer's close and an opportunity to rest.

It was plainly evident that what was now a marsh had at some distant time been a broad and shallow stream. There was yet to be traced a narrow, tortuous channel, through which flowed the waters that gathered here from a hundred hill-foot springs near by; and now this unsuspected remnant of a prehistoric creek was indeed beautiful—gorgeous with its wealth of pink rose-mallow, not pink alone, but mingled with flowers white as driven

snow, others that were deep rose-purple, and many with
a brilliant crimson eye that glowed like coals of fire.

I had not been overrash although the outlook was so
unpromising at the start; for here, indeed, was novelty.
In past years this water plant was to be met with here
but very sparingly, and now there were hundreds in dense
clusters. The birds that flew over, the fishes that gazed
skyward, and the frogs that skulked among the humbler
weeds alone knew of this bright water garden, and well
had they kept the secret. I wondered not that they protested so vehemently, when by lucky chance I too discovered it.

Heresy, if you please, but flowers alone can not fill for
me a long summer's day. I will not say that in this case
I tired of them; but ere long I was ready for other objects to fill in the wide landscape, and soon they came.
A pair of snowy egrets dropped from the fleecy clouds,
sinking earthward with as soft a flight as might bits of the
clouds themselves. Nearer and nearer they came, until I
could see the fluttering down upon their breasts. Then,
with closed wings, these beautiful creatures touched the
water with their extended feet and stood upon the soft
mud, the embodiment of grace. They came to rest rather
than to feed, and preening a misplaced plume was the extent
of their labors. Nor did they speak. I could not detect
the faintest utterance, although so very near them. Over
a little space of open water, they occasionally walked to and
fro, as if the statuesque attitude they usually assumed became at times a little tiresome. Despite their beauty they
were stupid, and their listlessness robbed them of all interest after a few minutes' gazing at them. I became impatient at last, and suddenly emerging from my retreat,
shouted loudly. With startled cries they instantly took
wing and rose to a great height before deciding upon any
course. I thought that they might return, but they did

not. Nevertheless, I was not to be left alone. I had startled the many small birds that throng the marshes, and these life-long familiars crowded about me. I am not far wrong when I say, the smaller the bird the greater its curiosity.

Among the many that ventured even into the cluster of button-bushes that was my shelter, came a crested titmouse, and I laughed when it sang, after due inspection of the spot, *'t sweet here, 't sweet here!* The bird was right; I had found an enchanted isle.

While the day lasted I was content with these small birds—wrens, thrushes, warblers, titmice, and sparrows. All came and went without let or hinderance, and accepted my presence without complaint, as some had done while I was struggling in the marsh. Some sang sweetly, and others chirped in so contented a strain that their voices were musical by merit of suggestiveness. Association is the needed charm when we watch the birds. The stately egrets were soon forgotten; but who can forget the dooryard songsters that have been favorites for years? I even forgot the treacherous marsh as well as its rare visitors and was again at home. My feathered friends had merely rambled from the garden and lawn with me, and we were sojourning together in a little wilderness—a picnic more enjoyable by far than many I have attended. With such fancies I whiled away the sunny afternoon, and feared that no trace of an adventure would enter into the day's outing; but at last it came.

Certainly, not one of the birds in the bushes was nesting; nor were any accompanied by young birds. Thinking of this, I thought to imitate the cry of a fledgling in distress, to see if the birds near by would be disturbed. Immediately a cat-bird shrieked its alarm cry and came very near to me. It located the sound I had made unerringly and berated me soundly for supposed cruelty. I was harassing a young bird, it thought, and must give it up. The marsh wrens were straightway up in arms, but held aloof; the swamp sparrows twittered excitedly, but bravest of all were two cat-birds. They longed to thrash me soundly, and almost came within my reach. As suddenly as I had started the commotion the birds suppressed it. Since that day I am convinced that sudden thoughts occasionally strike a bird. When most demonstrative, in the abruptest manner, one of the cat-birds took up a position directly in front of me, but was silent. He remained but a second and then, in a changed voice, chattered impressively to all within hearing.

"What fools we have all been!" he seemed to say; "there are no young birds now to worry about"—and straightway the gathered crowd dispersed in almost perfect silence.

I may be in error, but if actions ever correctly interpret an animal's intention, this story of the cat-bird is literally true.

It was with a tinge of regret that I finally retraced my steps, or attempted to do so. I found less supporting growth and deeper mud on my return, but reached the higher meadows in reasonable time. As I took a farewell glance at the reed-hidden isle, locating it in fancy, for it was really hidden, a cloud of redwings settled over it for the night, and filled the air with the matchless charm of their flute-like whistle. So what indeed matters it if the katydids do sing, and summer has but six weeks left to it? These need not prove six weeks of idleness, nor will they lack abundant charm, if happily we know where to look.

In one secluded corner, where the old worm fence was well-nigh hidden by poison ivy, blackberry briers, and a straggling grape-vine, I caught a glimpse of a gray lizard, one doubtless that I had set at liberty when studying them a year ago. I have hopes now that they may again flourish on the home hill-side, as they did long years ago.

I was induced to forego the pleasure of constant tropical rambling during the heated term of August, 1887, and spent my time in watching a host of these lizards, sent me from the pine barrens. The conclusions reached when I studied them in the field, three months before, and during many a long sultry August afternoon, subsequently, I trust will bear repeating.

On the outskirts of the quaint little village of May's Landing, New Jersey, there is seen that rare object an abandoned railroad. Starting near this place, and running eastward for a distance of some six miles, is a single track, laid upon a once substantial road-bed of gravel, and extending through typical Jersey pine barrens. For several years not a car has passed over the rails, which, left to nature, have grown nutty-brown with rust, and often concealed by luxuriant growths of false ipecac, great circular mats of deep purple or pale-green foliage, for such is the freak of the plant to vary thus in color.

When I visited this spot late in May, 1887, the charm of the abandoned railroad was rivaled by the beauties of the surroundings. The glistening, snow-white sands were thickly starred with golden Hudsonia; the creek's banks weighted with densest foliage, brilliant with sarracenia in the height of its glory; and everywhere the more modest grasses gave way to sparkling sun-dews. One knew not where to turn, so crowded were the spot's enticing features, and the rambler was likely to return empty-handed, as is so apt to be the case where attractions are spread out in bewildering profusion. Wondering what novelties might be in store as I passed the outlying traces of the village, I soon found my progress suddenly and effectually stayed—I had reached the tottering, crumbling trestle over Babcock's Creek. Here the gray lizards found a most congenial home, and the peculiar locality offered every reasonable facility for studying them. A long-desired opportunity was at last mine, and birds and botany were no longer thought of.

This pretty creature, known as the gray or pine-tree lizard, is also in many localities called the " brown swift "; and this seems a most appropriate name, as we read the remarks of Holbrook, De Kay, and of Alexander Wilson, on the habits of the creature. For instance, the last named, in his "Ornithology," expresses surprise that a sharp-shinned hawk should have captured one, " as lightning itself seems scarce more fleet than this little reptile." I was not prepared, therefore, to find the " swifts " on the trestle anything but swift. It was by hiding, and not through speed, that they sought to escape, and it proved comparatively easy to capture them with the unaided hand. Often they played bo-peep merely around the timbers, and were readily surprised, so that they ran into one hand as they avoided the other. This proved to be the case, also, when I searched for the lizards in the pine woods, which were as readily captured when up on trees as were those on the trestle.

The village boys adopted ordinarily the simple plan of using a thread-noose placed at the end of a short stick. Dropping the noose gently about the neck of the lizard, they lifted the creature slightly, when its struggles at once tightened the thread and made it a prisoner. It was a favorite pet with the children, and when I asked some of them if it ever bit or snapped at their fingers, they were greatly amused. I lay stress upon this point, because of the rather widely spread opinion that these lizards are venomous. It is one with the equally absurd impression, due to ignorance and belittling prejudice, that all our snakes are harmful; but a curious feature in this case is the fact that the impression of the lizard being venomous obtains in inverse ratio to the abundance of the animal. Where exceedingly rare the lizard is dreaded; while, where abundant, as at May's Landing, it is a favorite pet with the children.

Probably a closer study of animal life would materially reduce the list of species supposed to be harmful by those who see but little and know absolutely nothing about them, and put an effectual check upon those who, taking advantage of the ignorance of their audiences, assert deliberate falsehoods, because more entertaining than the simple truth.

As is well known, the pine-tree lizard is quite sensitive to low temperatures. It does not make its appearance in southern New Jersey earlier than May, nor remain abroad later than September. Of course, this is a general statement, and only approximately true, as all such statements must be. Perhaps there can be found nothing more absurd in scientific literature than the frequent *ex-cathedra* statements—for instance, concerning the movements and range of our birds, as though the latter recognized any other law than that of their own convenience and fancy.

At May's Landing I found the lizards sensitive even to the ordinary variations of temperature of average summer days, observing that whenever it was cloudy, they were far less abundant, and actually sluggish. On the other hand, the extreme degree of heat to which they are willing to expose themselves is not a very high one, judging from the actions of a large number kept in confinement.

Fifteen adult lizards were placed in an inclosure in which every prominent feature of their homes was reproduced. I found that at 120° Fahr., with the atmosphere perfectly still, they invariably sought shelter, clustering in one cooler and dark corner; but at 100° they were exceedingly active, particularly if hungry, and made no effort to avoid the direct rays of the sun.

When exposed to a sudden transition from a very high to a low temperature, they quickly became inert, and, as the warmth was allowed to increase, it was instructive to see the sluggish movements of both the lizards and the imprisoned flies give way to more active ones, which culminated in the restored suppleness of the reptiles being equal to the capture of the swiftly darting insects. Forced exposure, for a period of three hours, to a temperature of 135° caused death in four instances, and brought about a condition akin to æstivation in nine specimens thus exposed. As the pine-tree lizards are always found in localities where there is adequate shelter from excessively high temperature, it is not probable that æstivation ever occurs, as it does occasionally among some of our wild mice; but it is interesting to note that a condition closely allied to it can be artificially produced.

The conclusion reached by both field observation and experiments was, in brief, that when the temperature is such that those forms of insect life upon which they depend become inactive, the lizards withdraw to their shelters and likewise remain quiet if not asleep, this period of inactivity extending over several days, as during the prevalence of a northeast storm, or a protracted "spell" of cool and cloudy weather. Again, experiments with a large number in confinement showed that when kept without food at a low temperature, they live for many days, while a like number starved in a short time when a high temperature was maintained. This lizard, therefore, appears to be one originally belonging to a tropical climate that has gradually become adapted to a temperate and variable one.

The normal coloring of the pine-tree lizard is distinctly protective. Whether this has been gradually acquired or not, it is certain that it now renders the animal quite inconspicuous. Particularly when it is resting upon a rough-barked tree is this true; and one of my first objects in studying the species in its native haunts was to determine how far the markings were changeable and under their owner's control. Many specimens were found to be quite dark—indeed, almost black—while others were so light that the undulating transverse bars upon the back were very distinct and discernible at a considerable distance. This difference, I am quite sure, bore no relation to the surroundings; and the specimens subsequently collected and kept under daily observation for nine weeks practically retained the light or dark coloring they possessed at the time of capture. In confinement many individuals remained of a light color under all circumstances; others, that were dark when received, became light for brief periods, but were very dark fully ninety-five per cent of the time they were under observation.

The long and broad glistening green markings upon each side of the abdomen are equally variable—certainly not a distinction of sex, as suggested by Le Conte and Say—and often absent for weeks in specimens which occasionally exhibited them in all their brilliancy.

In no instance was there that prompt change of hue that we see in the tree-toad, and even more so in the wood-frog. The change in the latter is as abrupt and complete as in certain fishes, and is particularly significant, inasmuch as it is the only frog that needs protective coloring, living as it does in woodland tracts, where it is exposed to an abundance of enemies; and may it not be that, by its power to adapt itself to the general color of the surroundings, it renders itself inconspicuous to the insects upon which it preys? If so, the control over its color becomes doubly advantageous.

Vision in the pine-tree lizard is apparently not very

acute, although the eyes are exceedingly bright, and, when coupled with certain movements of the head, suggest considerable intelligence. It was found very difficult to test their visual powers, although, once captured, these lizards became extremely tame, patient, and obedient, and I could only infer that the sense of sight was none of the best from the fact that when held to a mosquito-frame in a window, upon which house-flies were walking, they missed fully one half of those at which they snapped; and other lizards in confinement, but where every possible freedom of movement was practicable, often made many attempts to capture flies before success crowned their efforts. If, therefore, when at large, they depended principally upon winged insects for subsistence, their lives would indeed be laborious ones; but insects of sluggish movements, ants, and small spiders, are all freely partaken of. A friend who is a very careful observer assures me that of the two insects, house-flies and Croton-bugs, his lizards certainly preferred the latter, but were not particularly expert in capturing them. And now, assuming that the eye-sight of these little reptiles is not highly developed, what of the curious "pineal eye" which they possess? Prof. Macloskie has recently announced in " Science " that it " is so well developed . . . that it may probably seem to warn its owner of the advent of daylight. It is a lenticular, glassy area of the skin of the vertex (about a millimetre in sagittal diameter), surrounded by a yellow border, and having a dark spot in its center. The dark spot is opaque, caused by a mass of pigment internal to the dermis, set on the extremity of a pineal outgrowth from the brain. The clear area around it is caused by the dermis, which is transparent and free from the pigment which covers it internally in other parts. The eye is covered by an escutcheon shaped epidermal shield, more transparent in the center and larger (three by three millimetres) than the normal epidermal scales. The only sign of degeneracy is the central cloudy mass of pigment, like a big cataract."

I was naturally desirous of determining for myself how far it was sensitive to light, but found the investigation beset with difficulties. Chloroformed lizards that were deprived of their eyes, although the amputation was dexterously performed, did not revive sufficiently to make their subsequent movements suggestive; or did sympathetic ophthalmia set in and affect the pineal eye?

I subsequently hit upon a plan, using very thin India-rubber cloth, by which the eyes proper were effectually closed, and the " eye " of the vertex left free. The lizards thus provided with a blinding head-gear were separated from their fellows and placed in a roomy inclosure, made up of several almost dark and very light alternate sections, the temperature being even throughout the lizards' range. The arrangement was, perhaps, too artificial for a satisfactory series of observations, but it became evident at once that the lizards recognized the difference between the dark and light areas, and their prompt return to the latter when removed from them, and again their actions when they returned, all showed the appreciation of a difference, which I know was not one of temperature, but beyond this I could determine nothing; but I recalled, at this juncture, the significant fact that in the woods about May's Landing I noticed many lizards buried in the fine sand and leaf-mold, their eyes closed and covered, but the top of the head and a portion of the back for its whole length exposed. The same was subsequently noted as a position frequently assumed by the lizards in my Wardian cases. If, therefore, the " pineal eye " is sensitive to light, it is still of some use to the creature, as it would certainly respond to a passing shadow, and so warn the animal of the approach of a possible enemy. It certainly would be greatly to the lizard's advantage if it had a perfect eye in the top of its head, especially when it rests upon the trunks of trees, and is exposed to the attacks of predatory birds; but the "pineal eye" is at most but a remote approach to this. On the other hand, it was found that whenever I converged the rays of light with a burning-glass, always so suddenly that no thermal effect was produced, there was caused a movement of uneasiness, a flinching, on the part of the lizard that was extremely suggestive.

The most superficial examination of the external ear of the pine-tree lizard will at once lead one to infer that the animal's hearing is acute; and this is true. When watching the lizards on the trestle over Babcock's Creek, at May's Landing, I was forcibly struck with this fact. Such of them as were basking on the timbers of the bridge were not disturbed when I approached them with moderate care, stepping only on the cross-ties, or between them; but if I struck the rails with my cane they instantly took notice of it and assumed a listening attitude. I subsequently experimented upon this point, and found that when my companion struck the rails a smart blow, even at a distance of fifty yards, the lizards were aware of the peculiar sound, and acted accordingly, even darting out of sight with that swiftness that characterizes their first few steps. I have recently learned from a correspondent that his observations lead him to conclude that the sense of hearing is not very acute, but the character of his experiments to demonstrate this does not seem to me to be such as should carry conviction with it, and I find it is contrary to the general impression of those more or less familiar with this lizard.

It is a most interesting fact, although so very wild when first met with, that once captured, the pine-tree lizards instantly become tame. Indeed, I have had them lie quietly upon my hand, while walking in the woods, and make no effort to escape. There is a bare possibility that the efforts on their part to escape, and fear, when finally captured, may produce a hypnotic condition, or something like it, but this would pass by and leave them wild. This, I think, never occurs. Once in my hand, I have never known a pine-tree lizard to be otherwise than perfectly tame. But, in a large series in confinement, I found that the sense of hearing was constantly brought into play, as shown by their ludicrous actions when flies, shut in a thin paper box, were placed near them. They not only heard but recognized the noise—a very important matter, bearing as it does upon their intelligence. Indeed, in the woods about May's Landing I found that the lizards were perfectly familiar with many sudden sounds and paid no attention whatever to them. Some of these were the sonorous croak of the bull-frog, the quick scream of the blue jay, the rattle of the golden-winged woodpecker, and the coarse cry of the great-crested fly-catcher. These were all unheeded, while my own coughing, the whistling of a single note, or the loud utterance of a word, caused them either to assume a make-ready attitude or to dart away. On the other hand, have these lizards any voice? Their actions *inter se* are strongly suggestive of the affirmative, but, so far as I am able to determine, their utterances are confined to hissing, and this I only heard when I provoked the creatures by the sudden infliction of severe pain. Among a large number, in nine weeks I never heard a voluntary hiss. This, however, is wholly negative evidence, and I am disposed to believe that an animal possesses a voice, if its habits, in their entirety, suggest that it has one. This perhaps unscientific method of reasoning arises, on my part, from the fact of having long suspected that certain fishes and salamanders had voices, before they were detected—my suspicions being based upon the habits, as a whole, of

these creatures. Certain snakes, too, that are now thought
only to hiss, will, I believe, be found to have a limited
range of scarcely audible utterances—so with the pine-tree
lizards. I certainly have no reason to believe they talk,
but possibly they may whisper in each other's ears.

Upon several occasions I sat, unseen by them, for a
long time, very near my pen of lizards, and listened
attentively, hoping to catch some sound that was clearly
a voluntary utterance of a lizard. I only determined that
one's ears, under such circumstances, become highly supersensitive, and a great deal is heard at a time when, in
fact, positive silence prevails. Generally, the lizards were
perfectly quiet, but at times one would move, and then a
general scuffling ensued; but how far the noises were
attributable to their activity I can not say; probably entirely so. The faint, snake-like hiss, that has fairly to be
squeezed out of them, is the range of their vocal utterances, so far as I yet know.

Concerning the breeding habits of this creature, I had
no positive knowledge prior to my visit to the pine-barren
regions of southern New Jersey. I had heard the statement made that the eggs were small, quite numerous,
and deposited on the under side of prostrate logs, and
even in loose wood-piles that were constantly disturbed,
and that the eggs were not concealed or protected in any
way. All this I knew to be false; but where were the
eggs of the pine-tree lizard placed? Questioning observing residents of localities where the species abounded, I
was invariably informed that the eggs were laid in sand,
in pits dug by the lizards, and carefully covered up. They
were only discovered by accident, no trace of their presence being noticeable. Further, that after heavy showers
the eggs were sometimes exposed, and in this way a check
was put upon the increase of the animal's numbers. Of
course, solar heat alone was relied upon to mature the

eggs. Recently, a resident of May's Landing has informed me that the eggs "are said to be laid in bunches," but just what is meant by being "bunched" I am at a loss to understand. They certainly are not attached to each other by any agglutinating substance. At least, the female lizards in my pens laid only dry, free eggs, which they deposited in conical pits, one egg, the lowermost, being in the bottom, then three above it, and four in the third tier. Such was the position in two sets of eggs, while the others were scattered over the sand in bewildering confusion. None of these hatched, the failure to do so, inasmuch as they were fertile, being due, I believe, to the surroundings being too dry. Probably a certain amount of decaying vegetable matter is mingled with the sand when the eggs are laid, and thus a moist heat is produced, which is as necessary as it is in the case of the eggs of the alligators and crocodiles.

The ova laid by my penned lizards were long, narrow, covered with a tough skin, free from calcareous matter, and varied in weight from twenty to twenty-four grains. At May's Landing, I am told, the eggs are usually laid about June 1st, and hatch about July 10th.

While the abandonment of their eggs in this apparently heartless manner leads to the supposition that they are indifferent to their offsprings' welfare, which is true, it is somewhat interesting to notice how very tolerant they are of the petty annoyances to which their own or another's young subject them. My observations on this point were made from a number of young and old confined in a roomy Wardian case, but probably what I there saw holds good among the lizards in their native haunts. I am sure it did among the many living on the old trestle at May's Landing. Often a little lizard, and sometimes two, would perch upon the head and back of an adult, and there be allowed to sit for fully an hour. The sharp claws of these

14

youngsters seemed at times dangerously near the eyes and ears of the patient old one, but it offered no resistance, and, when I forced such burdened lizards to move, it was always with a deliberateness that suggested that they were really averse to disturbing those resting upon them. Again, adults would often rest upon each other, in what appeared to be a most uncomfortable manner for the one beneath, often pressing the head of the latter into the sand and completely blinding it for the time; yet I never saw the slightest evidence of ill-humor, not even when they were being fed. Often it happened that some sleepy fellow would quietly snap up the fly toward which another lizard was cautiously crawling, yet no fight ensued. Anything more trying than this to humanity can not be imagined, yet the lizards took every such occurrence as a matter of course.

In running, as well as when walking about deliberately, which they less often do, the lizard brings all four limbs equally into play, and their gait is much like that of a cat. When progress is suddenly arrested, they usually squat upon their hind limbs only, holding their head well up and elevating the body, as does a cat or dog, by keeping the fore limbs straight. Every attitude is suggestive of intelligence, and I refer particularly to the matter, because the differences in these respects between this lizard and the blue-tailed skink, the only other saurian found in New Jersey, is very marked; the latter, as we shall see, although having less suggestive manners, has, I believe, a greater degree of intelligence.

I have spoken of the rapid and complete submission of the pine-tree lizard when captured. This did not prove true of the great brown skink that I captured among the rocks at Lake Hopatcong. This specimen I placed in a Wardian case, May 20th, and immediately it burrowed in the thick mat of sphagnum at the bottom, and for a week seldom if ever made its appearance. I could only determine that it was alive by searching for it, and invariably was bitten. It then showed a disposition to come from its intersphagnian retreat, but remained wholly suspicious of every sound or object that approached. Concealing myself, I watched it carefully, and found that the shutting of a door, the crowing of a cock near the window, and loud conversation in an adjoining room, always frightened it; while the singing of a canary, and of robins in a tree near by, were not noticed. A quickly passing shadow was particularly feared. Did it associate this with the birds of prey that are the skink's most dangerous enemies? Having disappeared, it never returned by the same burrow, but, cautiously peeping from a hole in an opposite corner of the case, studied the outlook for a long time before reappearing. It showed no disposition to be sociable until June 10th, when it seemed suddenly to gain confidence, but only to a slight degree. June 19th it ate for the first time, and then became somewhat tamer, but still was essentially wild, and seemed perhaps the more so because of the contrast with the pair of lizards that were all the while its companions. July 29th it was transferred to a roomy fernery belonging to a friend, where it found a close resemblance to its lake-side home in all essential features, and immediately it became more active; and now, three months after capture, has become comparatively tame.

The skink, as we have seen, is exceedingly shy, irritable, and resents the slightest interference by biting savagely, but of course is entirely harmless. Nearly every prominent feature of the lizard is represented by an opposite trait in the skink. What appeared to be evidence of more sluggish wits than the former possesses, is the fact that it did not learn to associate my presence with a supply of food, as was true of the others, but the truth is it was its greater fear of man that held it back, and not really a want of cunning.

In many respects the skink recalls the snakes, and its manner of crawling, often without making any use of the posterior limbs, and generally keeping the body greatly bent, adds to the resemblance; and so, despite its shyness and courage when captured, evidences of intellectual strength, the skink seems lower in the scale of intelligence than the pine-tree lizard, but is probably its superior.

CHAPTER IX.

SEPTEMBER.

THE Delaware Indians called September *Kitschitach-quoach gischuch!* and this is said by Heckewalder to signify "the autumn month." This is next to meaningless, and I suggest as nearer the Indians' meaning, and certainly more appropriate, the Moon of the First Frost. I doubt if ever the month passes without some trace of it, and until it comes, the month differs nothing from the one preceding. Every rambler has noticed how song gives place to silence toward the end of August. The monotony of soulless sunshine has proved irksome, and the birds that have not already departed cluster by the dripping springs. The squirrels, until now a timid and day-shunning folk, thread the tall, out-reaching oaks, tapping, in ill-humor, at the still resisting acorns. Impatience is now the moving factor of the animal world, and with it is sulky silence. Furred and feathered life, alike, are heartily tired of summer and await a change—do they know what? He who is given to country rambles has long since learned the secret—it is the first frost.

The first frost does not usher in a new season, but renews the summer. Sleepy, silent August days, half stifled in a worn-out atmosphere, are the really melancholy ones, "the saddest of the year"; but at once, with the first frost, is activity renewed. This earliest intimation of the on-coming winter need not be everywhere. You will find no trace of it upon the upland fields. There are, in low-lying, damp, weed-hidden nooks, a few dainty crystals, that disappear before the sun rises, as though frightened at what they have done. They might well have tarried, for they deserve a blessing.

What then does this first frost accomplish? The pulses of the song-birds quicken, and they resume their singing. Their limp wings are braced, and they scatter over the fields, along the wooded hill-side and close-woven thicket. Not only they, the wearied summer visitors, re-appear among their several spring-time haunts, but down from a frostier north, the advance guard of the winter songsters come—Canadian tree-sparrows, a cheery, twitter-ing host—come, as do many others, to make glad our winters and replace those that, fearing to face the ruder blasts of the north wind, seek shelter in the south. It is strange that the idea is so prevalent that here in New Jersey we have comparatively birdless winters. There are two score species that are, with very few exceptions, mod-erately abundant; many are phenomenally so. Even about the most unpromising spots, a dozen or fifteen species of winter birds may readily be found. Every one of the forty has been listed, and without going into a wilderness too, by more than one observer. The fact is, to see birds at this season, one must not stick closely to the highways, but pass from field to meadow, from woodland to marsh, to do so. Forty species may seem an extrava-gant claim, but it is a simple statement of fact. There are at least forty. Why call it thirty-nine? It has been flatly contradicted. Well, there is an element of our population that, having ears and eyes, yet neither hear nor see, and these are they who, lacking powers of obser-vation, are prone to criticism. It is a good plan to listen to the nut-hatch, while these critics carp, for the bur-den of that bird's song is *crank-crank! crank-crank!*

It boldly sings what politeness forbids us even to whisper.

The first frost has come; dare autumn leaves be mentioned? I have seen a striking picture of an irate editor flooring the twentieth spring poet that had that day called upon him. Should I not take warning? At least, I should not venture far. Whether or not the frost actually ripens the leaves, it can not be gainsaid that the change of color begins at this time or earlier; but often, excepting one or two trees, a year passes with no change save somber brown. Always, however, there are tiny areas of the brightest tints, a change more beautiful than the general reddening of the forest. A branch of a maple turned to dusty gold, a solitary gum tree clothed in scarlet, a winding creeper bronzed to the very tips—such bits as these, rare as gems along the pebbly shore, are commonly held to be the fruits of the first frost, and loved the more because of their rarity.

Those faithful friends of the poets, asters and goldenrods, convenient blooms that have done duty in literature for a solid century, flourish, it is true, before the coming of the frost, but renew their youth in the reinvigorated air. It is not they alone, however, that brighten the dusty highways and deck the winding wood-lanes; at least, not here. The dittany empurples the leaf-strewed forest; with mosses and sweet fern, it carpets the upland woods; and then, with the first frost, comes the chincapin—a pygmy, but still a very prince among our nuts, graciously evolved for impatient autumn-lovers. To gather them is only a foretaste of the nutting season proper, it is true, but a foretaste often with a keener flavor than the feast that follows offers. Chincapins are the last gift of summer—a gift that comes with gladness; solid nuggets of sunshine —not wrapped in dead leaves and sodden with the tears of melancholy November.

What of the cooler meadows and the lotus? It would dampen my ardor certainly if it were cut down; but it is not. Hailing as it does from far warmer lands, we tremble for the tardier blossoms, yet really need not. From afar I can see those gigantic leaves and tall flower-stalks, capped with the roseate bloom of this historic plant. It is as much at home and as hardy as the sweet white lily or the yellow nuphar. And here, in the flooded marshes, we can go nutting again. From the great funnel-shaped torus or seed-pod of the lotus, one can gather sweet fruit, larger and as toothsome as upland chincapins. In the dense shade of this lotus of Eastern lands, I recall that rare native form, once cultivated here by the Indians. Perhaps I am wrong here. My friend the State botanist tells me it is far more probable that the widely separated localities where the native lotus still flourishes are remnants of a wide area over which, long, long ago—perhaps before the great ice age—the plant flourished as now do our native lilies, splatter-docks, and calamus. If, then, it was not a cultivated but a wild plant, it was still highly prized by the Indians. There are abundant historical references to this effect. Recalling these to-day, I can picture a group of Indian women in canoes, or perhaps their vagabond husbands wading in the water, gathering the large seed—a true nut—or reaching into the shallow depths for the newer growth of tubers. From the nut was made a good flour; the tubers, boiled, are equal to potatoes. The Indians did this far back in prehistoric times; some of their descendants do so still; and it would not be strange, could it be shown, that where I to-day gather lotus nuts in the same marsh, the long-forgotten Indians, in centuries past, did the same. Be this as it may be, nutting in the marshes is one of the luxuries following a first frost—for the nonce, I am a happy lotus-eater.

In the woods and over the meadows alike, the air trembles with the cry of innumerable crickets—if not they, then of insects unknown to me. Single shrill trumpeters are hard to find. Trace up never so closely the sound that issues from a certain bush, when at a given distance the noise ceases. You rest a while, and it begins again; you move, it stops; one step more, and it ceases altogether. Scan with all care every leaf, twig, main stem, and very roots of the shrub, if such it was, but you will not find the musician. To crickets we attribute all these late summer sounds not made by birds or frogs, but how far correctly I would that I knew.

It was long after the first hard frost, and even thin ice had formed once or twice, that I happened along the Crosswicks meadow with a friend, and our talk had been of insect sounds. There was a thrill in the air, at the time ascribable to millions of insects, but not a single utterance could we detect. At last, upon the bank of a ditch, a shriller stridulation could be heard, a sound that could be located. Very cautiously, upon hands and knees, my friend approached the spot. For minutes there was profound silence, and then the sound would start up more distinctly than before. With all the caution of a well-trained setter, my friend drew near, and at last, believing he had marked the precise spot, he sprang forward and seized a clod of meadow mud. He had stalked his game successfully. In his hands was a mole-cricket. So I learned that this creature, too, is an autumn as well as a summer songster.

Not the first frost nor the second—no, nor a black frost —seals to silence either the tree-toad or the red frog of the woods. They croak spasmodically at all times and seasons, but give no hint of the utterance's proper interpretation. It may be a croak of thanks for such sweet, life-giving days, or a complaint that the chilly nights have lessened their food supply. If there is any distinction, it is an all-hearing ear that can detect it. To the average rambler they croak, and nothing more. It is the same note now that is heard at short intervals all summer long, and that they utter in early spring when they join in a deafening epithalamium.

But one glory of the time of early frosts has well-nigh departed—but fitfully, at best, do the roostward flying crows pass over. No more are seen the long lines that streaked the eastern sky—a scarcely broken procession, whose front reached the meadows about 2 P. M., and the rear rank was still on the move as the sun went down. This, thirty years ago, was so regular a feature of each autumn and winter day that the old hall clocks of the farmers along the ridge might well have been regulated by it. The crow-roost of recent years, to which these birds flocked at night, was in Pennsylvania, about Rocky Woods and in the Pigeon Swamp. I give these particulars for a purpose, being a Jerseyman.

In the "American Naturalist" for August, 1886, Mr. Samuel W. Rhoades has published an interesting article on these birds and their habits, but at the very outset I am puzzled at certain of his statements. He writes: "Careful observation and inquiry convince me that during winter a radial sweep of one hundred miles, described from the city of Philadelphia and touching the cities of New York, Harrisburg, and Baltimore, will include in the day-time, in its western semicircle, fully two thirds of the crows inhabiting North America, and *at night* an equal proportion of its eastern half. The eastern area of this circle, with the exception of more fertile portions of west and north Jersey, is as notably devoid of them by day as it is infested by them at night. Their most extensive breeding grounds in New Jersey are well-nigh deserted during severe weather.

"The popular local notion that crows all ' go to Jersey to roost' and return to Pennsylvania to forage, while far from correct, has more truth in it than the average Jerseyman will admit," and I add, the average Jerseyman is correct in denying it. For over a century, the crows have roosted on the Pennsylvania side of the river, as all can see for themselves of an autumn afternoon, and if these same people will be astir at dawn, they can see the same crows coming back to Jersey, where they will forage until noon. Fools if they didn't! There is a wonderful difference between the two sides of the river in the matter of temperature, and so follows a difference in plant and animal life. Many a day the winter through, when a crow would starve in Pennsylvania, amid snow and ice, the ground would be not only bare but unfrozen in Jersey. How the impression got abroad, and became so general, that all Jersey was a crow-roost and never a bird flew westward during the afternoon, I can not learn, but it does not hold good in the writer's region.

Mr. Rhoades says: "As yet no evidence is at hand to justify the supposition that the roosting-place which Wilson and Godman have vaguely described as situated 'near Bristol' was in Pennsylvania. It seems more probable that it was located either on Burlington Island or on the mainland near the site of the city of Burlington, in New Jersey."

There is evidence, though, for the spot has been but recently disturbed, and I live on a line with the main flight that, so long as I can remember, crossed over the river and continued westward into Pennsylvania for some three miles. Both this and the Florence Heights roosts were occupied at about the same time; and if, as stated, the latter was deserted forty-five years ago, it was again reoccupied by a small colony—an off-shoot possibly of the overcrowded one in Pennsylvania, four or five miles west of it.

I doubt if ever the crows were given to keeping within such hard and fast lines as has been suggested. At all events, if it is applicable to the sandy pine barrens of south Jersey to say the crows only roost there, it is not true of central Jersey, at and about the head of tide water in the Delaware Valley. I think I have positive evidence that Wilson was right in speaking of a crow-roost near Bristol, Pennsylvania; and I have personal knowledge of the occupancy of such a one for many years—one that is yet occupied, but only by a tithe of the former numbers that frequented it. It is not unlikely that a great change in the birds' habits is being brought about. They appear to be decreasing in numbers, and probably their cunning is leading them to the safer method of scattering over wider areas to roost.

In spite of all the ugly things I have heard of crows— not one in a hundred of them really true—I early learned to love the bird, and their full-toned autumn cries are music to my ears. It is ever with regret I hear of woodland tracts laid bare, and the poor birds' roosting-trees destroyed. More and more the crows are scattered autumn after autumn, and so the close of summer loses one considerable charm. It is painful to think that even the scanty remnants of our forests may soon disappear—that the black frost of greed may ere long irreparably blight the country.

After a pleasant ride over the rolling hills and across many a pretty intervale, I found myself, recently, in a commodious tent, erected in anticipation of my coming, and from this, my present comfortable quarters, I have given myself to strolling wheresoever my fancy led me, for I have been spending in camp nearly the whole month of September. Searching for nothing in particular, I was eager to light upon every novelty of which this favored region, the valley of Brush Creek, in Adams County, Ohio, might boast. And my last ramble was one of greatest interest. Passing over a monotonous stretch of bottom land, now a forest of ripening corn, I came suddenly upon the babbling creek that scarcely concealed the time-worn pebbles of its narrow bed. On either side tower gigantic sycamores and grand old elms, a wealth of autumn flowers clustering about their trunks. For a narrow space, nature had outwitted the grasping farmer, and wildness reigned supreme.

Whatever might be in store, I could not pass hurriedly by the creek that I had found. I tarried long, lulled by the music of its rippling waters that, singing the same sweet song, cheers many an idle hour at home. Nor was I alone. Strange, indeed, if ever so sweet a spot should be deserted. As I strolled slowly down the stream, a lone wood-duck from a grassy cove sped like an arrow into leafy depths. Quails called to their mates, vireos warbled, the titmice gave warning, and cardinal redbirds flashed through the thickets, whistling as they went. My shadow startled many a timid fish—wee minnows that I wonder should have any fear; and anxious crayfish, from the mud-lined dens, hastened to muddier and to deeper caves. My presence was a source of trouble to all the life about me, and thought of this alone was the shadow, sure to be, that dimmed my joy. Wild life seldom stops to argue the question whether you are friend or foe, but forms its own conclusions when at a safe distance.

But the day was fast closing, and I had yet other fields to explore. Threading a tangle of rich autumn bloom, I was stopped by a crumbling wall of jutting rock, deeply scarred and caverned by corroding time. A hundred feet in height, or more, it frowned in the glittering light of the setting sun and denied my further progress.

I was in no humor to be denied. The valley soon

would be shut in by mist, and I was all anxious to escape
the pent creek's gathering damp. I walked boldly to the
cliff and seized whatever projection offered. The pleasure
of the stroll had vanished. Progress now meant toil, if
not danger. Every promising cranny seemed to shrink as
I placed my hand within it; every jutting corner trembled
as I placed my foot upon it. The rock that at first was
perpendicular was now overhanging, and at every inch
that I progressed the valley receded a foot. To scramble
over gravel bluffs at home proved a poor schooling now.
Every tree was just beyond my reach, and the half-way
ledges, promising a refuge and rest, were but snares, need-
ing little more than a hand's weight to send them thundering to the creek below. I am yet alive, and why recall
a perilous and painful past? The summit was reached—
no matter how—and in due time I stood upon a broad
plateau, overlooking miles of wooded valleys and beyond
the reach of those threatening rocks, which, in future, I
shall contemplate, and leave to others to explore. But if
not directly upon rock, I stood upon firm earth. Save a
solitary maple, that for years has stood the lone spot's silent sentinel, no trees sheltered it from storm or sunshine;
and here, on this bleak, unprotected bluff, Art, not Nature, held the upper hand. The transition was indeed
startling.

If it taxes the equanimity of the average person to
come suddenly upon even a harmless snake, what shall be
said of him who, with head and shoulders at last exulting-
ly raised above a beetling cliff, finds himself confronted by
a serpent more than a thousand feet in length, and with its
huge jaws widely agape? Yet this is the fortune of him
who clambered, at one point, from the Brush Creek Valley
to the high ground above. But I speak enigmatically.
The serpent is not and has never been alive. It is not
even, as the reader may have guessed, some great fossil of

a distant geological epoch. It is the Art that here over-shadows every natural feature, to which I have referred—the handiwork of an unknown people, who, finding this region suited to their needs, wrested it from Nature.

The great Serpent Mound of southern Ohio is one of those curious earth-works that for nearly half a century has been a puzzle and delight to American archæologists, and one that has led to much wild speculation. Much of this is truly funny, and none of it more absurd than the dogmatic assertion recently given to the world that it is of Cherokee origin and of no significant antiquity. But before discussing its age and origin, let us consider what it is as it appears to the visitor of to-day. At first glance, one might suppose that the earth had merely been heaped up into a long and gracefully curved line, so as to repre-sent an uncoiling serpent or a snake in motion. It is more than this. Before its construction, the place was leveled, and the serpent, in all probability, outlined with stones and clay, and not only all the material gathered in clearing the ground, but more was brought to the spot. In short, the work was planned before its construction was commenced, and built with care. Its architect was at once an engineer, a naturalist, and an artist; or, if the joint product of a community, then they all showed skill in high departments of human intelligence, such as we look for in vain among historic Indians.

When, by whom, and for what purpose, then, was this Serpent Mound constructed? These are the three ques-tions every visitor will ask—does ask, at this writing—of the eminent archæologist, Prof. F. W. Putnam, who is now on the spot endeavoring to solve this triple problem. I will not, at this time, anticipate any of his conclusions, but consider some of the suggestions he and others have al-ready given to the world.

Concerning the antiquity of the mound-builders and

their works, Prof. M. C. Read, with apparent good grounds for so doing, has remarked that the evidence was well-nigh conclusive that when occupied by this people and these works erected, the site and the surrounding country was a treeless region. He writes: "Their erection with mound-builders' tools, if it involved the clearing of a forest as a preliminary work, is so nearly impossible that we can not imagine it would be ever undertaken. It involved not only the clearing of the lands of the forest, but also the neighboring lands which were to be subjected to tillage. It is with the utmost difficulty, in moist and tropical climates, that men armed with the best of steel tools make a successful battle with the forests. It is much more reasonable to suppose that these works were originally located in a treeless region, and the works evidently of the same age scattered over (this portion of Ohio) indicate that this treeless region was of large extent. . . . The inference would follow that the abandonment of the region marked the time when the slow intrusion of the forests reduced the amount of tillable land below the necessities of the community. When this took place can only be vaguely estimated, but that it was many hundreds of years ago is beyond all question. It required many centuries, as has been frequently proved, for a mixed forest growth to take possession of a country." It is in vain to attempt to express by numbers the age of an earth-work, but a scientific examination of both the structure and its surroundings may demonstrate a relative age that antedates all history.

This has already been accomplished, so far as the Serpent Mound is concerned. It is a veritable relic of remote antiquity.

By whom was the Serpent Mound erected? Here we are confronted by a problem that probably will never be solved to universal satisfaction. It is an unfortunate fact that the great subject of the origin of races is, and is likely to be, in a miserably chaotic state. The craniologist, the philologist, and archæologist agree only to disagree; and the student of general anthropology can not yet, it is quite certain, blend the strong arguments of these specialists, and reach to a plausible conclusion. The stronger the argument of any one phase of anthropological science, the more decidedly contradictory is it of the assertions of the others. It was not a cheering outlook when, at a recent scientific gathering, an eminent anatomist remarked that he " did not care a rap for languages as a means of race identification," to which a philologist replied, " What is so variable as the shape of a skull?"

But the shape of a skull seems to have some bearing on the question of racial origin in connection with the Serpent Mound. The recent exhaustive examination of the broad plateau stretching southeastward from the earth-work has yielded, among others, the very significant fact that two peoples have used the place as one of burial, and that one antedates the other; and it is further very significant that the evidently more recent occupants were historic Indians. After all, the shape of the skull does mean something—is a tangible fact; and the difference between the crania of Indians and of the earlier mound-builders is too persistent to be denied or explained away as a mere coincidence. In the burial place that I have mentioned, the more ancient interments—those, that is, that may be safely referred to the time of the Serpent Mound and its builders—are of a short-headed people, that were of the same stock as the ancient Mexicans. I would not be understood as saying that the mound-builders were Mexicans or *vice versa*, but that they were both offshoots from a brachycephalic race that reached America by a trans-pacific route. This is the view that has been expressed by Prof. Putnam in recent lectures, and his most recent

15

explorations have yielded nothing that conflicts with it. On the contrary, every fact gathered by the most laborious and exhaustive examination of mound after mound goes to establish the view that the people who built them were not the historic Indians, nor even their immediate ancestors. On the other hand, that certain well-known tribes of Indians, notably the Shawnees and Natchez, as an instance, were descended remotely and indirectly from these builders of earth-works, is extremely probable.

The fact that Indians, in very recent times even, built mounds—mere conical shapes of earth placed over their dead—does not warrant us in assuming from such a fact alone that the elaborate structures, such as the Serpent Mound, were also the work of their hands. Had it and many other of the earth-structures in Ohio been erected by them or their immediate ancestors, it is highly improbable that this fact, and that of their significance, should have been completely forgotten; yet not one of them finds place in Indian history.

Its purpose? Whether we admit its origin to be pre-Indian or not, this question will be asked, and it is a curious fact in the experience of the writer that the visitors to the Serpent Mound never wait to hear a reply after putting the question, but follow it with their own views. Probably the average student of archæology would only go so far as to suggest the probability that it had, in the minds of the builders, a religious significance. This view, I have found, meets with little favor from the casual visitor. "Injuns were heathen, and hadn't no religion," was the prompt reply of one.

In the minds of its builders, this great earth-work was doubtless tenanted by a serpent spirit which was thought to faithfully guard the dead who rested near it, if not the living who dwelt in the surrounding region. But that kindly spirit slumbers as profoundly now as do the mighty

coils and gaping jaws that have braved for unknown centuries alike the torrid heat of summer and pitiless raging
of midwinter storms.

This religious or symbolical character of the entire
structure is emphasized, I think, from the fact that a
large oval embankment is situated directly in front of the
serpent's gaping jaws. This added earth-work gives an
even more life-like appearance to the whole, although it
was by no means needed. What, of course, is the significance of the "egg," as this oval structure is popularly
called, can only be conjectured; but indeed there is little
to be done but guess, and never very shrewdly perhaps,
while we wander along the curves or pause to admire the
gracefully coiled tail, or, from the park-land behind it
all, we survey the structure as a whole.

And here let me add that every opportunity is now
offered to him who would study this vestige of antiquity.
It was a happy thought to preserve it for all time from the
destruction that threatened it. Recently it was purchased
by private contributions, and is now, with all the immediately adjacent land, held in trust by the Peabody Museum
of American Archæology of Cambridge, Massachusetts.

I saw the Serpent last when a death-like stillness
brooded over all; when even the cricket's restless rasping
was hushed, and it was fitting at such a time to bid this
mystery of a distant past farewell.

On the 10th of the month I happened to be wandering
along the enormous curves of the Serpent Mound when my
attention was called to a little tuft of grass that for some
reason had been left standing.

The day before the ground for a considerable space
had been closely mowed, and not a trace of the beautiful
autumn bloom that had made the spot a garden of delights had been left standing. Mist-flower, golden-rod,

iron-weed, and asters were all laid low, leaving the lone
tuft of grass a prominent object. On a near approach
I found that it covered but did not conceal a sitting
quail. Stooping down, I put my face within a foot of the
brave bird, and yet she would not move; but never for an
instant did she take her eyes from me. It was evident
that I must actually touch her before she would leave her
nest, and this I abstained from doing.

Day after day I saw her, and she was always equally
courageous. A week later, my companion happened to
pass by, and found that the nest had been abandoned.
The mother bird and her brood had gone, but the nest
was not really empty. Seven pearly egg-shells remained,
and they were well worthy of study. Each had been
opened—not merely broken—alike and in a curious manner. A clean cut had been made nearly around the shell,
but enough remained intact to hold the two portions together. This unsevered portion acted as a hinge, and so
the little quails had merely opened a wide door of their
own making, and through it stepped out of their cramped
quarters of the past two weeks or more into the outer
world. Occasionally I have seen a single egg, or perhaps
two in a nest, the shells of which had been opened in such
a methodical manner, but never before where such marked
similarity characterized the whole series.

I have said that the young birds had "stepped out";
rather they had run, and I can testify to what good purpose they can put their tender feet. Still, for the first
day of their freedom they were somewhat bewildered by
the strange sights about them, and their helplessness
when but a few hours old touched even the heart of the
grizzled archæologist who for weeks had been studying
the mysterious earthen serpent that for centuries has
rested upon the summit of the cliff. He almost wished
himself a naturalist, as in former days, when the callow

creature that he caught and carefully stroked was cuddled in the hollow of his hand, and a spark of old-time enthusiasm thrilled him when the warning cry of the mother bird was heard, to which the captured baby quail feebly responded. But here the unearthing of relics called the archæologist away, and I took up the study of the quail.

That parent birds are cunning all the world knows, and it is commonly added that young birds, the moment they are hatched, know *by instinct* the meaning of their parents' calls. I do not believe it. Baby quails have a good deal to learn in the first two or three days of their lives, and the old birds realize that it falls to them to be the teachers as well as protectors of their offspring. It was very evident, I hold, that the seven little quails at the Serpent Mound did not understand the urgent whistling of their parents when they squatted in the grass. They did not now respond, nor had the antics of the mother bird, when she feigned being wounded, any effect upon them. They occasionally shifted their positions, and as often exposed themselves as sought a better cover. Later, when the field was clear, the parent birds gathered them, after long search, and as systematically as a shepherd traces the wanderings of lost sheep. For at least a day, if not for two, the anxious movements of the old quails were meaningless to their young; but not so a day or two later. Then you could no more have caught the latter than the former. A little experience had gone a great way in educating the brood, but that little was necessary.

I have laid stress upon this trivial occurrence, as I wish to add a word of caution as to the common use of the term "instinct." It is better to explain the habits of an animal by other means, and fall back upon instinct when all else fails. I have followed the fortunes of many a

hundred broods of wild birds, and know with what astonishing rapidity they mature intellectually. In many
cases it is but a matter of two or three days, but it is a
transit from ignorance to knowledge, nevertheless.

I had no glimpse even of these young quails after they
were four days old; yet I knew they were very near me
many times each day. They had learned that mankind
were enemies—not from instinct, but through instruction;
their parents had told them so. This may seem strained
and overfanciful, but after being many weeks afield and
disposed to observe without preconceived notions, I, for
one, always fall back upon this leading thought, that
birds, at least, if not all animal life, are quite well gifted
with sound common sense, and this is their main safe-
guard.

For a month a pair of Bewick's wrens dwelt opposite
my tent, holding our ample wood-pile against all comers.
At sunrise, let the weather be what it might, they were
astir, ready to resent the near approach of any bird, and
for an hour or more each day sang so sweetly that the best
efforts of the crested tit, the summer redbird, or the cardinal seemed poor indeed.

Close at hand was the rude oven of unhewed stones,
about which Katie, the cook, flitted industriously, and
her the suspicious wrens ignored entirely. As breakfast
was being prepared the old wren cheered her with his
song, but I was never to be so favored. Neither my companion nor myself could do aught but listen from our
tents. The moment either appeared, the bird darted to
some safe cranny among the logs. This, as I have said,
was not a chance occurrence, but the established habit of
the wrens. They were not afraid of a woman; they were
afraid of men.

There was of course some reason for this, and I would
that I could report its discovery as mathematically demon-

strated; but how seldom can we do this! I let my fancy run riot for three weeks, and imagined all sorts of extravagant explanations. At last a ray of light seemed to fall upon the mystery. Toward the close of my days in camp I noticed that when the wood-pile was rudely disturbed by the chopper, the wrens appeared and scolded vehemently; and then until the next day all would be quiet, and the morning song lost none of its sweetness because of the ruffled temper of the day before. A week later the ox-team brought a load of drift-wood from the creek, and when this was rudely tossed, stick by stick, upon the pile, again the wrens protested.

Here, then, was an apparent clew. Whatever the wrens suffered was by the hands of men, while the ever-present Katie in no wise interfered with their pleasure. Is it possible that the birds realized the difference between Wallace and his ox-team, or Martin with his axe, and Katie the cook? It certainly appeared so. With my field-glass I watched these wrens one morning, more closely than usual, as soon as they appeared. Early as it was, Katie was already astir, yet the wrens appeared not even to see her. Without hesitation they flew into the open kitchen and caught the chilled flies that had clustered about the pots and dishes. If Katie came too near, they flitted to the other end of the long table and continued their hunt, and when their morning meal was over, the old male sweetly warbled thanks for both.

There can be no question but that they recognized our cook as their friend, perhaps supposed she provided the flies for them. Be this as it may, they were bold to a degree until the professor or I appeared, when they promptly skurried off, to be seen no more that day. I may be wrong, but I believe my explanation is not wholly wild. It is something to watch the same pair of birds for weeks. You get by so doing an insight into their character that a chance meeting will never afford. I came to look upon these cunning wrens as creatures that thought, and I hold, indeed, that we should so look upon all birds.

Away from camp, down in the tangle of the wild Brush Creek bottom, I found many a cunning bird. How cleverly, just as I leveled my field-glass, they all eluded pursuit and disappeared in the caves along the cliff, or, if not there, in the cavernous old dead sycamores! Cardinals, jays, titmice, sparrows, fly-catchers, and wrens, they all knew they were upon dangerous ground, and shunned all living creatures but themselves.

Why dangerous ground? Those rocky ledges, draped with impenetrable growths, were the black-snakes' paradise; the bleached and hollow trees that stood like so many ghastly sentinels along the creek's crooked shores ambushed innumerable hawks and owls. There was scarcely a cave but harbored a mink, a raccoon, or a skunk; while in the dark pools into which the rippling waters ominously disappeared lurked the wily soft-shelled turtles that have a serpent's neck and head, with also their agility and cunning. In such a spot it behooved the harmless and helpless birds to be cunning and careful, for their safety lay only in their quickness of wit. When I saw what hosts of enemies surrounded them I did not wonder at their wildness.

Within a stone's throw of my home in New Jersey these same birds are abundant, but there their foes are few. I can always approach reasonably near to them without difficulty. They quickly learn that here they are comparatively safe. A few months ago I chanced upon a nest of the small green-crested fly-catcher without disturbing the sitting bird. Twice daily after that I visited the nest to see if I could have so remarkable an experience as did a friend with another sitting bird. Before the young

had left the nest I twice stroked the parent bird without
her taking flight. Never, I venture to say, a nesting bird in
the Brush Creek Valley would prove so trustful. Nature
there is more evenly balanced, and every bird that tarries
has a veritable struggle for its existence. Certainly those
that nested in the more open shrubbery (and they were
many) must have been ever on the alert. Indeed, I came
to look upon every empty nest as necessarily the scene of
a tragedy, yet in truth the great majority had escaped
molestation.

But this cunning had its ludicrous phases; at least I
was daily entertained by the quick wits of the kill-deer
plover. During September these birds were phenomenally
abundant. Even throughout the night they passed over
my tent incessantly, often at a great elevation. Aroused
at times by the hooting of the great horned owls, I have
caught the faint *dee-dee* of a wandering plover, falling as
softly as the whisper of a star, and then, as the bird
swooped earthward, the shrill *kill-deer! kill-deer!* rang
out with startling distinctness on the still night air.
They gloried in the glimmer of the harvest-moon as I
never before had known birds to do; but where were they
at high noon? I missed them for a long time, and
learned at last that they were skulking, often in silence,
upon the plowed fields. I often tried to approach, but
found it impracticable. Long before I was within a reasonable distance I was discovered, and away they flew. I
tried stalking, but this proved of no avail; they knew
they were being pursued, and posted sentinels wherever
they were. Think for a moment what an elaborate mental effort this implies! These birds devised an intricate
plan to insure, not individual safety, but that of their little community. Their actions showed that they not only
planned, but jointly planned; and therefore, be it language or something else, they had a means of conveying

their thoughts one to the other. The few kill-deers that
frequent the meadows in early spring at home had never
appeared to advantage as birds of brains; but here, in
southern Ohio, they were pre-eminently so.

I have not exhausted the list of birds I found within
the limits of my daily walks while in camp, but they were
all alike in this one respect—they were quick-witted.
Vultures were abundant, yet, though they often swept by
the trees upon the cliff, not even a timid sparrow lifted a
wing, knowing full well their harmlessness; but if merely
the shadow of a passing hawk fell upon the leaves, the
timid birds that instant sought safety in the dense undergrowth beneath. I had noticed something of this before,
at home, but never until now in so marked a degree.
Here is an instance where discriminating knowledge has
been acquired.

To see a bird poise upon a trembling twig or cut the
clear air with its pulsing wing, to hear it sing of a bright
May morning or warn its callow brood when danger is
near, is to *see* simply, but never to *learn* also, what manner of creature a bird really is. To live among them for
weeks, and to watch them daily and nightly, is to gain at
least an inkling of their true character; and they who do
this are of one accord, I think, that a bird possesses a
goodly store of wit.

And the same is equally true of other forms of life.
My tent had not been pitched more than an hour before I
had occasion to enter it, and to my surprise I found it already tenanted. A grim gray spider had an elaborate
web in one corner, in which a fly was already tangled; a
gray lizard was dozing on the mattress; shining beetles
crept through the cracks of the loose board floor. This
was encouraging. I was assured of many friends under
my canvas to entertain me during rainy days, and so it
proved. Beetles in abundance, but stupid to the last;

spiders, lizards, and snakes, knowing creatures all of them, and endlessly amusing.

Let us consider them in the order named. I was soon compelled to make friends with the spiders, as they straightway became so numerous and fearless that mutual toleration was necessary. Had there been rebellion on either side, the chances were in favor of my discomfiture.

I had no trouble. Not a nook or corner for several days but was occupied by a web, and often I was forced to destroy these to get at some of my photographic or other apparatus. In a few days the spiders learned where I was most apt to be and what objects in the tent were likely to be disturbed, and retired to the ridge-pole, beneath my table, and behind certain boxes that were constantly opened but never moved from their places.

This is a bold if not a rash statement. I have said the spiders " learned." Do spiders learn by experience? Can they be taught? Let us see. From the very necessities of the case spiders must be cunning or they would starve. Their food is not taken by brute force, nor captured by outrunning the pursued insect. As their dependence is so largely if not wholly upon strategy, a high degree of intelligence must be accorded them. Spiders have been known to weight their webs with stones that they might be steadied during a gale of wind, and one at least has been known to completely alter its mode of life because of accident making impracticable the ordinary methods of food-capture. These more wonderful evidences of mental strength are too well attested to be doubted, and I was well prepared to find those spiders that crowded my tent equal to all that I have recorded of them.

As is my wont, I devised various simple experiments to test their cunning, and so whiled away many a lonely hour. Choosing one great gray fellow that had an elaborate web just back of my table, I endeavored to determine if it would recognize me as a purveyor if I assumed that office. At the outset no sooner was my candle lighted and I had taken my seat than the spider would retreat to its innermost sanctum, and not reappear while I was at work. It was afraid of me, and of me only, and not of the candle or its flickering flame. I commenced then by offering a fly impaled upon a delicate splint from Katie's broom. No notice was taken of it so long as my hand was in sight. I kept the fly in position all the evening, resting it between two books, but still in line with my hand, which was in constant motion, for I was busy writing. Directly after I retired the fly was seized and dragged away. Night after night I struck a match to determine this, and always with the same result. It was quick work with the spider, for I relighted my candle several times almost the same moment that I extinguished it, but never caught the spider, and yet the fly had disappeared. It evidently followed my movements very closely—a proof itself of cunning.

During the second week the necessary confidence was gained, and the flies were seized if the splint was several inches long and I did not move my hand. The rest was easy, and every night the splint was shortened until but two inches in length, but I never could induce the spider to take a fly directly from my fingers or allow me to touch it. Then came the concluding evidence of the spider's teachableness. Long before I left camp it would come from its web and take its place before me, when the candle was lighted and I had sat down to write, expecting its nightly ration of two or three flies. These I nearly always provided. During the day the spider did not pay any attention to me, nor would it show itself at night if I moved about restlessly, had company, or made any unusual noise, such as whistling. It had learned to associate my position at the table, directly facing its web, with an available supply of food; and probably of my personality, otherwise, it had no conception. It did not, I think, go so far as to distinguish me from others; but still it can be said that the spider had proved teachable.

Sir John Lubbock, in a recent volume on " Animal Intelligence," does not consider that spiders have good eyesight at all; but certainly my " tent " specimens saw what they were about, or, if not, by what means were they guided to act as I have described? Indeed, one seemed even to see in the dark, but in this case, I think, the exact bearings were taken and it felt its way along—something, by the way, that was truly marvelous, considering the rapidity of the creature's movements.

Another cunning spider in my tent had an enormous web attached to the roof and around the ridge-pole. To it I made daily many offerings of house-flies. It seemed at last to know me and expect them, so I tested the creature's patience, if not its ingenuity. Filling a homœopathic vial with flies, I placed it just beyond the web and suspended it by a thread to the pole. The spider made several attempts to reach them from the nearest point of the web, and, failing in this, made an addition to it, and so secured the vial, but could, of course, go no farther. Daily additional webs were placed about the little bottle until it was almost concealed. The flies were all dead on the third day, and on the morning of the fourth the bottle was lying on the floor of the tent. I do not know, but suspect that the spider pitched it overboard in disgust.

A word more concerning spiders. About noon one clear, warm, quiet September day I chanced to pause at a turnstile before going through, and at that moment caught sight of a curious spider. It appeared to be standing upon its head and fore legs, and was quite motionless. On examination I found that it was spinning almost invisible threads, which mounted directly upward and were lost to view. First one and then another spinneret gave up its thread, and a dozen or more were wafted into space while I stood watching. Then, without any premonition, the spider gave a leap, and with its legs folded up beneath it, passed upward and out of sight.

My old favorites the gray lizards too were ever present. Fly-catchers, like the spiders, they rambled over the tent without hinderance, and afforded no end of amusement. They were never careful of the spiders' rights, and often ran recklessly through an elaborately adjusted web. The spiders never resented this; not because they were afraid, I think, but for the reason that they were powerless. Not one was capable of effectively biting denser tissues than those of insects. None, probably, either in the fields or woods, are venomous. Some may be, but the danger has in all cases been grossly exaggerated, and the common fear of our spiders is not warranted by anything known of these creatures as a class.

One old lizard became exceedingly tame, and was my tent companion for many days. Its fear of mankind vanished on the day of capture, and it was very glad to have me offer it flies, which it took directly from my fingers. I soon learned the reason—it was not expert at catching them. I saw it make many failures, and so I soothed its disappointment frequently by catching them for it. I became, therefore, associated with food in its mind, and so gained its confidence.

One afternoon I entered the tent suddenly and placed a large dead garter-snake upon my table. I did not notice the lizard at the time, but it was watching me, and no sooner had I laid the serpent down than it darted behind my mattress. I was not sure but this was a mere coincidence, and brought it back to the table. The instant I put it down uncontrollable fear possessed it, and its efforts to escape were indescribably frantic. Recapturing it the second time, I placed it in a pen, quickly constructed of books and boards, and slowly introduced the snake, pushing it forward, inch by inch. Immediately the lizard stood nearly upright, and as the snake's head touched it, swelled up until I thought it would burst, and then fell over, limp, shriveled, and apparently dead.

I was puzzled at this, and left the tent in hopes of finding another lizard in the wood-pile. Failing in this, I returned, and was more surprised than ever to find that the lizard had not really died from fright, but had merely swooned from fear. It was now partly itself again, almost colorless or a very pale gray, crouched as far as possible from the snake, and trembling. Did it expect every moment to be seized and devoured? I am at a loss to know; the more so because I have had serpents and these gray swifts, as they are usually called, associated in Wardian cases, and no evidence of fear on the part of either was detected. I can only suggest that my tent lizard had had an ugly experience in which a snake had prominently figured. A valuable point would be gained could this be proved, for then it would be shown that lizards have memory. But those persons who have had them as pets are generally convinced of this; and is not general conviction tantamount to a demonstration? Not always, I admit; but in such a matter as evidence of intelligence in low animal forms it is about all that can be offered.

And here is what I have to offer as evidence that my pet remembered. When I released the creature it slowly crawled away, for it was yet weak, and gradually widened the distance until hidden in a far corner of the tent. Three days later I chanced upon it as it was darting after flies. Its activity showed that it had wholly recovered. Again I brought it to the table, and although neither snake, books, nor boards were there, the lizard was sorely frightened, and made desperate efforts to escape, and this fear of that spot, the table-top, continued during the remainder of my stay in camp.

I had no pet snakes, I am sorry to say, but I made some progress in acquiring the good graces of one small serpent, a half-grown garter-snake, that was brought to me a day or two after my arrival. While I held it in my hands, and for the two days it was in a little box, all efforts to tame it were a flat failure. As it was quite uninteresting, I let it go, and it took refuge under the floor. During the heat of the day this timid snake would bask on the floor while I was out, but scuttled off as soon as I appeared. So I tried my old tactics of gradual approach. First my shadow would fall upon it, then I would move a step or two forward and remain a moment perfectly still, then advance, and so on. Day by day I gained a little, and at last could enter the tent. But this was all. The snake preserved a make-ready attitude, and if I stooped or swung my arms it was gone in an instant. Very different proved a young black-snake that my associate, the archæologist, had nerve enough to bring to me. It would do nothing but bite, and fairly exhausted itself in impotent rage. Although less than a foot in length and but a few weeks old, it was unteachable. Its hatred of mankind had not been developed by experience, but was inherited, and this law of heredity I endeavored to overcome by kindness. But the snake would have none of it, and not even when alone would it accept the food provided. I mention this because an adult black-snake, although fierce and brave when cornered, is something of a coward, after all; and, as I know by experience, it is intelligent and tamable. I have never dared to write the history of one I finally conquered by persistent kindness. But does not this all go to show how intelligent snakes really are? When young, hopelessly unreasonable; when older, willing to listen to reason, and at last be guided by it. Does not this smack of human nature just a little?

So ended my camp experiences in the study of animal intelligence. The results were all the same, whatever forms of life I tested. Cunning, ingenuity, memory, all were evidently features of their minds. I say "minds," for I can think of no other word that meets the case. How, indeed, can one creature outwit another; how can it plan to meet some desired end, new until then to its experience; how can it remember people, places, things— unless it has what we call in ourselves a mind?

CHAPTER X.

OCTOBER.

A WRINKLED quince, a rotting pear, three grapes, and a gnarly apple comprise the list of " goodly fruits " that I gathered, this hazy, dreamy second of October, 1887, from an old garden, of which but the merest traces are remaining. The day was fitted only for retrospective work such as this. The mellow light of the half-hidden sun, the muffled notes of the birds from the fog-wrapped meadows, the steady dropping of decaying leaves, all led to meditation. I called back the spring time of another century.

It was of this garden that Jane Bishop, in May, 1703, wrote : " We have now an abundance of goodly fruit, which father planted some seven years ago ; and it is with joy that I see growing, as we wished, the blossoms that sister and I did gather from the adjoining woods."

Jane Bishop was young then, and cared far more for flowers and the wild world about her than the monotonous tirades against frivolous pleasures to which every First-day she was doomed to listen. Her love of flowers and a spirit of mischief went hand in hand, and she it was who, in October, 1705, deluged a meeting of sedate old Friends, at her father's house, with thousands of scarlet autumn leaves. It was purely an accident, so she said, and of course it was—not. She it was who, on plea of shading the little porch, cunningly chose Virginia creepers, that soon covered the cottage, and made it as brilliant

as any tree of the forest after the first touch of frost.
Never a blossom was found nestling in her hair, so far as
we are told, but they clung to her dress—accidentally, of
course.   Mild reproof proved irksome at last, and her
troubles ended by marrying out of meeting.

Let this suffice of her, this Quaker fairy, as she was
called, save casual reference; and what now of the remnant of her father's garden?   Perhaps not a tree or vine
that I found was one of those planted one hundred and
ninety years ago; but the pear may have been.   That
pear tree is beyond description.   Once it was a stately
growth, perhaps nearly two feet in diameter; now a mere
fragment of a hollow trunk is left, from which projects a
single stunted branch, and from this I gathered a single,
rotting pear.   The little that remained of it at all edible
was evidence that in its day the Bishops had excellent
fruit.   I ate that morsel with closed eyes, and sat by the
fireside of the Bishops in early colonial days.   Is this not
happiness enough for a hazy, dreamy October day?

Three grapes!   Small, seedy, and sour, yet what of
that?   Whether or no John Bishop planted the vine—for
it was not a native grape—some one had, and I saw the
Quaker fairy gathering fruit as I plucked the three wrinkled berries.   Their bitterness brought tears to my eyes,
but with what juice they had I drank a deep draught of
that cunning wine which Jane Bishop well knew how to
make.   For home-made wine was then as much a necessity as vinegar, and far more wholesome.   And while I
struggled with the mat of weeds, hoping to trace out the
narrow path edged with the white stones " dear cousin
William gave me," as she has left on record, I found the
neck of a small glass decanter.   It was well buried in the
soil that here has certainly never been disturbed since the
old garden was abandoned. How vividly the old side-
board, a remnant of which I cherish, floated into space,

and the living-room of the old stone house replaced the garden site, while I stood amid the weeds, holding a bit of broken glass!

The quince proved better as a nosegay than as fruit to eat. It was hard beyond safe mastication, but the fragrance was delicious. How sadly changed the fruit of that tree during the long years of its abandonment! Plump as the finest apple of them all, as deep a yellow as the orange itself, with what care the fruit was once gathered and prepared for winter use! A dainty that set well with venison, bear-steak, and pheasants; for the Bishops loved good living then, nor accounted a well-appointed feast one of life's vanities. Quince jelly was their boast, and it was with pride, however they might have denied it, that they saw the jelly stand alone as they emptied the cracked cups that held it. Sugar was a luxury then, and this secret of their jelly-making died with the thrifty Quakers of early colonial times.

And that apple! it certainly came from a comparatively young tree; for there be none that have weathered the storms of well-nigh two centuries. I say comparatively young; the tree had been large, and was now but the merest ghost of its former self; perhaps it was a century ago that the seed was planted; dropped from a core thrown down by one of the fair Jane Bishop's children, it may be. The tree stood too near the "pebble-edged" path, I think, to have been intentionally planted.

Apple orchards were one of the features of Indian farming about here, and the juice of the fruit was no novelty to the earliest English settlers. Thrifty old Mahlon Stacy wrote from near here, in 1680: "I have seen orchards laden with fruit to admiration, their very limbs torn to pieces with the weight, and most delicious to the taste, and lovely to behold. I have seen an apple tree from a pippin-kernel yield a barrel of curious cyder." He who could write this thought well of his stomach, and how was the cider " curious," one wonders? Was it so tickling to his palate that he felt " curious " ? Well, let us hope not; but such a thing was not so dreadful then as now.

How diligently I searched for traces of those wild flowers that Jane and her sister gathered " from the adjoining woods " ! It was only one hundred and eighty-five years ago that they were here, and a bit of that old forest still remains. Every flower that I found now—asters and golden-rods only—I fancied spring blossoms, and direct descendants of those she mentioned. It was child's play, I know; a game of making believe—but what of that? If one would indulge in retrospection of a dreamy, hazy October day, he must not stick too closely to the naked fact. I had wandered along the hill, at first without a purpose; then to locate the old garden, if I could; this done, had I not earned the right to play I was of an earlier time—an inhabitant of this degenerated locality in its happy, long-gone, early colonial days?

Kick as vigorously as he may, if one does not dress conformably to the custom of his station he must pay a social penalty of no light severity. It is different when beyond town limits; but here let me disclaim all intention of advocating carelessness. He who assumes to be wholly independent of custom in such matters gains absolutely nothing, and risks a good deal.

What may be worn in the country comes under the headings—worn in the field, and in the house. A successful outing becomes practicable when the subject of clothing is farthest from our thoughts, yet if at all inappropriate it will enforce itself upon your attention continually. Stuffs that adhering matters will not injure, cut to fit you accurately, cover the whole ground; with such a suiting go stout boots. Clad thus, when in the field, one is in full dress; but when the day's jaunt is over, if we return to the house instead of camping out, every stitch of such a suit is a dead weight, and boots are little better than a ball and chain.

It is nothing but affectation to carry the ways of the woods and marshes to the house. In early colonial days, when cloth was scarce, it may have been necessary, but not so now. The most enthusiastic rambler has no excuse for bringing wet boots to the library andirons. In gown and slippers he can prove the most delightful of companions, but as a mud-bespattered mortal, indoors, is little less than a nuisance.

Such thoughts came well-nigh spoiling a recent outing, and not until I had had my growl could I attempt the narration of groping in a fog.

It is a common practice to pronounce a rainy day a dismal one, and to suppose all the world is of your way of thinking. This is quite untrue, and the question of clothing settled, a walk in a rain is really delightful. It is quite practicable now, for weather-proof stuffs are readily obtained that defy the rambler's arch enemy, rheumatism.

Very recently a fog, a Scotch mist, and the ragged edge of a northeast storm came arm in arm up the river, and picnicked on the meadows. From the upland fields nothing could be seen of the low-lying tract but the tops of the tallest trees. So dense a fog I had never seen before. Previous to its arrival birds and insects had been unusually abundant; now nothing was to be seen or heard. This roused my curiosity, and I tested water-proof clothing at the same time as I took a well-worn path to the pasture meadow. When I left the last tree at the foot of the hill I was completely at sea, so far as my point of orientation was concerned. I might as well have been on the bottom of the ocean. Instead of being caught

10.28.'13

up I was held down in a cloud. Space, save the little grass-plot at my feet, was shut out. Think of standing nowhere on a bit of sod!

Such were the fog-wrapped meadows yesterday. Guessing the direction, I struck out, but never knew where I was until some familiar object solemnly ushered itself into my meager range of vision. The silence was absolute at first. Even the adhering drops that I brushed from the taller grass and bushes rolled noiselessly to the ground. The sound of my own footsteps was muffled and borne earthward before it reached me. Passing on, the density of the vapor was somewhat less pronounced, and faint sounds came from many directions, but none was distinguishable. Finally I saw a song-sparrow scarcely an arm's length away. It made no attempt to fly, but dropping from the bush hopped off into fog-wrapped space. Reaching the marshes, I found the little rail birds happy. They cackled more loudly and incessantly than ever before, but I saw none. Skirting the marsh, for I now had a clew to my whereabouts, I passed to my neighbor's pasture, when a curious sound, one wholly new to me, was heard. To learn its origin became an interesting problem, and I strove to proceed in the apparent direction of the sound's course. This was no easy matter, and whether I was going east or west soon became a question I could not answer; but the strange noise never ceased, and I kept on. Suddenly a familiar clump of bushes was dimly outlined before me, and I knew that I was near the railroad. Not a safe place certainly, but I followed the track without walking upon it. The low cat-like cry as of an animal in distress, so the strange sound now seemed, was still heard, and appeared to come from the direction in which I was going. I was delighted at my success, and felt sure of being on the eve of a discovery. What that feeling is the rambler well knows. Then the sound ceased, and I was baffled and angry. Should I go on? I asked myself a dozen times, and while in doubt it re-commenced. I hurried forward, and a huge black mass stood up before me. What could it be? I stared and listened, then stepped forward, and the mass took shape. I was facing a locomotive on a side track. The wheezy escaping of steam was the strange sound that had lured me over fog-bound meadows.

As the sun rose yesterday there came with it a dainty film of cloud, that by noon had thickened and shut out the sky; later, a faint murmur only the trained ear could catch filled the dark pine trees' lofty tops, telling a secret to the favored few. So I gathered firewood to the music of peeping hylas and whistling white-throats, knowing full well the storm was on its way. The sun set, without a sign, three hours ago, and the steady trickle and drip from the trees and the low eaves of the cottage tell their own story—October's northeast storm has come at last.

I know not what others may be doing, cooped in the burned air of their furnace-heated houses; but what so fitting on such nights as these as facing the andirons? The fire is not really needed for its warmth, but is wel-come as the inspirer of pleasant fancy. It is too se-ductive for the student, for the hours prove as light-footed as the flickering flames; but for idle whim or retrospection, a crackling blaze upon the andirons has no equal.

Safe from the storm without, I still think of the happy creatures I met while gathering wood. Where are they now? They need a shelter quite as much as man. If they had yesterday an inkling of what was coming they heeded it not, and until afternoon to-day the squirrels barked, the birds sang, the hylas peeped, the green frogs croaked. Even the south-bound warblers were not mute, and many a one chirped so cheerily it reached the border-land of song.

The squirrels, the tree-toads, and the frogs are well provided for; but what of the many birds abroad to-night? The last one that I saw was a grass-finch that flew up from the deep ruts in the lane and darted into the high weeds. As they shun the trees and do not dig caves, where do they go? It is raining so hard now the grass and weeds will be soaked; yet at daybreak, if the storm be over, they will be abroad, chirping a little, and active as crickets.

I remember one fearful February day, cold as Greenland and blowing a gale, when many birds took refuge in the overhanging banks of a ravine; I knew that cardinal redbirds will seek the shelter of a hollow tree, and bluebirds gather where the densest cedars grow; but still the great problem is yet to be solved of where and how birds find shelter from the storms. Sparrows and thrushes remain abroad until the storm is really here, and reappear so promptly at its close that it is hard to believe they suddenly speed away to the outer edge of its path, and so escape its severity. To find dead or disabled birds after a wild night is not usual, but happens frequently enough to convince one that the great bulk of every species have suitable shelter in mind to which they can resort when necessary. I have long hoped to come across such places, and searched diligently, but not with much success. Some of the ways of birds are still a mystery, but I am not disposed to believe they are past finding out.

The wind is rising. The angry blast that tugs at the fastened shutter screams shrilly in its rage, and at last finds entrance through some petty cranny that I knew nothing of. With what fiendish delight it pounces upon my shoulders, and sends a chill to the very marrow! It matters not that the fire burns with renewed vigor; there is little comfort in a blistered face while your shoulders ache with cold. How I long for the high-backed settle that graced the kitchen fire-place forty years ago! Then you could snap your fingers at the wind though it blew a hurricane; now you are largely at the east wind's mercy.

Find the pin-hole through which the monster rushes before resuming work or play. Shut it out, or, though you were soaring afar off in the realms of fancy, you will be brought back ingloriously to the level of plain prose. When finally I had guarded my fort against another such assault of the wind fiends, I placed the remaining stick upon the andirons—a gnarly, hollow, twisted knot of oak—and settled to an hour of retrospection; but the men and women of colonial times were not called up, as I had hoped. Instead, a redbacked salamander trotted from that last stick, and in blank astonishment stared at the fire and then darted toward me. The fender checked it, and it became frantic. I gave it full liberty as promptly as I could, and now it is cowering in a far corner. When fumbling among the books piled there I shall one day find its shriveled skin, but I need not search for it now that its history may be written.

Spiders, centipedes, beetles, and such small deer have often crawled from the rough wood that I gather along the hill-side, and once a mouse crept from a stump I dragged from the meadows after a freshet; but never before a salamander. If this was a common occurrence in days of yore, no wonder that these creatures should have been held in horror by the good folks of colonial times, especially if their only knowledge of them came in such a way, which is scarcely possible. At any rate, this horror at length took shape in the belief that salamanders were bred in the fire, and another phase of it was that too long continued fires upon the hearth would cause the house to overrun with them. Of course, too, they were thought be to be venomous. The ignorance and superstition of two centuries ago was something marvelous, and it is scarcely less strange that until to-day even ignorance of our commonest forms of life is the rule rather than the exception.

Whatever the origin of salamandrine myths, they were more than myth to our ancestors; and how my grandfather would laugh as he told the following, which doubtless has been told in many a hundred families in the land:

A long and bitterly cold night was succeeded by the coldest day of the winter. After much hesitation, rheumatic Uncle Natty Olden, a man with not the sweetest temper in the world, arose, and hurried to the forbidding-looking hearth to see how the coals had kept through the night. They had not kept well. From the cold gray ashes a few were raked, and with numb fingers he gathered them together, and endeavored to start a blaze with the light kindling he had prepared the night before. But the fates were against him, and the snow that drifted down the chimney had dampened them. Crouching on all fours, he blew upon the coals, rearranged the splinters, blew again, and interlarded all with ominous grumblings. He had known happier moments. At last, a flickering flame shot up, and then another and another, and a cheerful blaze was about to reward his labors. At that moment there came a thundering knock at the door, and the prompt "Who's there?" brought reply from Jemmy Cumberford. Knowing the voice, Uncle Natty unbarred the door, and Jemmy stalked into the dimly lighted kitchen and stood for a moment before the fire; then seizing the piggin on the bench, he dashed the water it contained upon the hearth, extinguishing every trace of blaze, and said to Uncle Natty, "Your fire's so old it'll breed salamanders."

The row that morning between these men the reader can imagine. For myself, I love old furniture, old ways, and to revel in thoughts of old times, but am duly thankful lucifer matches were invented when they were.

There have been several nipping frosts already, and now the cold gray sky threatens rain. Under the oaks there is naught but gloomy silence—

> " The very birds are mute,
> Or, if they sing, 'tis with so dull a cheer
> The leaves look pale, dreading the winter's near."

And well they may, for soon the shortening days will bring a northern blast that shall strip bare the trees; the winding woodpath will be hidden, and the moss-grown roots—great wooden serpents, harshly kinked and curled —will be lost; the scattered birds'-nests in the leafless thicket stand out in melancholy array, a deserted village. A new world is open now to the rambler; but let him take heed lest his thoughts be of what has been and not of what is. It is a too common error.

There are many compensations for the want of leaves. The showy dogwood that this year blossomed before the snow-banks of the great March storm had melted, offers berries of the brightest crimson in their place. The fruit-laden alder glows as a cloud of fire; but turning from these last brilliant gifts of the dying year, let us take up a humbler theme. I love to gather acorns. I learned to love them many a year ago, when, deftly transforming them into cups and saucers, I dealt out tea to others, fun-loving as myself. Such retrospection is too sad to be courted now, but every acorn that I gather summons a picture that but slowly fades.

A half-dozen or more species of <u>oaks</u> that either cluster on the hill-side or are scattered over the meadows provide acorns of as many patterns, but all are, of course, distinctively that fruit. One can not mistake the acorn for any other nut, as he might the leaves of the tree that bore it. Those of one species are like the chestnut's foliage; another's is like that of the willow. Of the various shapes, colors, and sizes, I prefer the pretty marbled fruit of the chestnut oak, which is usually as richly colored as the asters and golden-rods upon which it falls. Why I gather them, often until my pockets overflow, I can not tell; but as I look upon them they appear such goodly nuts that none should go to waste; and yet, of all tree-products, none seem so neglected—so without a purpose, here, at home. Unlike the chincapin or hazel-nut, they can not be eaten; at least, I have yet to find a person who owns to eating them; and not one in thousands, if it sprouts, becomes even a sapling; not one in a million reaches to the dignity of an oak tree.

Are acorns bitter or sweet according to the soil upon which they grow? I am surprised to find any of them asserted to be edible, in Gray's Manual. Here they are disgustingly bitter; or are we overnice, because of having such an abundance of sweeter nuts? I have called them a "neglected" nut, and so they really seem. Nor mice nor squirrels care for them while other food lasts. I have found untouched hoards of acorns that squirrels had gathered, but left because the shell-barks also stored had proved sufficient. And yet I have seen squirrels bury them with care, as though foreseeing their needs, and planting an oak for their indefinitely great grandchildren. I do not suppose a squirrel proposes to disinter the nuts it hides singly in the ground and use them as food. A mammal with such an extraordinary memory would soon cease to be a mere mammal by reason of it. It is, perhaps, as hard to believe that it plants the acorn that a tree may grow. Why it does it is a problem yet to be solved. It may have no connection with the hoarding of many nuts in the hollow of a tree, the purpose of which is unmistakable. Is it a survival of a habit established in an earlier geological epoch?

Birds are said to eat them, but this is a rare occurrence here, I am sure. The blue jay is said to hoard them for winter use. I have never seen any evidence of this, but have known these birds to feed upon beechnuts and chincapins. These latter nuts, however, do not appear ever to be stored away, in this neighborhood, by the jays. Life higher in the scale than the larvæ of insects, it would seem, practically ignores the acorn. It appears, therefore, to be a fruit born under a lucky star, but is it? Plant one and be you ever so careful the chances are slim that you will possess an oak. As a twig with two leaves it is full of promise; but there, alas! the matter ends. The upstart weeds of April crowd them to the wall. An infant oak shrinks to fatal obscurity beneath the shadow of a bramble. But should Fortune smile upon the timid growth and saplinghood be reached, then practically all danger is passed, and a perfect oak is promised to the succeeding century. Until at least one hundred years old the tree is incomplete, however symmetrical its branches or stately its general mien. The solid, gnarly limb; the wide-spreading crown, in outline almost a globe; the deeply wrinkled bark; the twisted roots above the sod and mossy nooks between them; these are not features of a growing tree, but of the completed growth.

It is an ideal forest where these trees are grouped, and pleasure enough for a day's ramble to meet with even one such tree. Oak forests are features of the past, and when we come to deal with dry statistics the number of really fine old oaks scattered over the country is painfully small.

Happy is he who can lead his friend to a dozen in a day's walk. Let me not be misunderstood. I do not refer to oak trees merely, but to matured oaks—trees from one to four or five centuries old. At present I know of but one, to which I have already referred, and it is perfect.

Two hundred years ago it was vigorous and large, and was spared for the goodly shade it gave, when, in 1690, the Crosswicks meeting-house was built. Five generations of my kin have gathered beneath its wide-spreading branches, and whenever I chance to pass that way I long to know the wealth of secrets locked in its speechless heart. In the traditions of half a score of families that I could name this old oak prominently figures. It has been the silent witness of mild tragedy and harmless comedy from generation to generation. Eye has met eye, and hand clasped hand beneath this tree, that so doing sealed the happiness of many an anxious heart. Under the Crosswicks oak to-day the past and present mingle. Time hath wrought few changes save in those who come and go. Were the Friends who worshiped here two centuries ago to return to earth, they would know the meeting-house they built, and this noble oak beside it.

There are several pin-oaks in the home meadows of which I never tire. Three that shade a dozen rods of a pretty brook are giants of their race, and gathered near are all the glories of October. To explore these trees is to learn much of the wild life of the neighborhood, for squirrels, oppossums, and occasionally a coon, harbor in the hollows of their trunks or find security in the wilderness of their close-set limbs; mice safely tunnel among the tangled roots; birds nest in the tree in summer, as well as rest in it throughout the year. From its topmost twig the sentinel crow announces the danger, if any, to its weed-hidden followers in the marsh; and a red-letter day is that when an eagle deigns to spend a few hours on the meadows, making the largest of those pin-oaks his resting place. His presence is only submitted to under very audible protest by the resident birds. Particularly if it be spring or early summer, the crows and king-birds are not only very outspoken, but follow the words with blows. I have seen a thoroughly organized band of crows attack an eagle and cause him to retire. The dauntless king-bird does not hesitate to rise above and pounce down upon the eagle's back so long as the latter remains compara-tively near the ground, but the fearless fly-catcher can not follow when the eagle soars to any great elevation.

Throughout October, unless storm-beaten, the leaves and acorns drop but slowly, and there is often dense shade beneath these pin-oaks during November's half-mythical Indian summer. As yet, there is no change; leaves and fruit are still stem-bound, although the month is near its close. But elsewhere, a mighty change has been effected, and the richness of color scattered along the hill-side is something marvelous. When the meadows, in Septem-ber, were purple with Vernonia and the brookside golden with Helenium, the limit of gorgeous display was sup-posed to have been reached, but how it pales before Octo-ber's tinted leaves! If the meadows were grand in Sep-tember the adjoining hill-side is fairly dazzling now. The little forest has caught the trick of the sunset, and glows at the season's setting with all the glory of the evening's western sky.

But the wind is rising. The robins chatter, the king-lets scold, and many a warbler hurries from the oaks as if it feared the shower of leaves and acorns that fills the air. In such a shower, I am all eagerness to stand and catch at the listless leaves that seem never ready to quite touch the ground. The acorns that fall at such a time are really few in number. I do not remember ever being struck by one, although to lie under the tree, face upward, and watch the fluttering leaves, is a favorite pastime. It is the sharp clatter upon the heaped up leaves, or dull thud as they strike the yielding moss, that gives a contrary impression; and generally, although so often forewarned, I look to see the ground covered; when, in fact, sharp eyes are needed to find the few that fell.

It may not have occurred to ramblers generally, but to lie upon one's back and study a tree-top, and particularly an old oak while in this position, has many advantages. If not so markedly so in October as in June, still the average tree-top is a busy place, though you might not expect it, judged by the ordinary methods of observation. If you simply stand beneath the branches of a tree or climb into them, you are too apt to be looked upon as an intruder. If you lie down and watch the play—often a tragedy—with a good glass, you will certainly be rewarded; and, not least of all, you can take your departure without some one or more of your muscles being painful from too long use. If the tree-top life deigns to consider you at all when you are flat upon your back, it will count you merely as a harmless freak of Nature.

Often have I been fairly startled by the boldness of migrating warblers that came to the lowermost twigs and then scanned me closely as though I too might prove good feeding-ground. I have expected, more than once, that the birds would alight upon me, but as yet they have only come very near to doing so.

I have often been asked which of our wild birds is the tamest. All seem tame enough to me, but the two which have appeared the most indifferent to my presence are the brown tree-creeper and the black and white tree-creeping warbler. Only recently, while gathering acorns under the big pin-oaks, I had them come within reach of my

17

cane; and in fact they usually do so; but when to watch
other birds I have been lying beneath the tree where its
limbs nearly touch the ground, they have come as near as
possible, without leaving the tree's trunk, around which
they ran.   Often I have tried to catch with my hands the
brown tree-creeper, but it always kept just out of reach.
Unless I was too demonstrative, it would seldom fly.   The
creeping warbler is not quite so tame, yet I have many
times marveled at its fearlessness; particularly during cool
October days, when it seemed more intent upon food-
gathering than its personal safety.

A circumstance, itself of little moment, held me, not
long since, until a one-act comedy was performed.   My
readers will agree that one spectator was enough.   For
some time I had been gazing skyward from the ground
beneath an oak.   Its widespread, labyrinthine top was
silent for a time, and if I did not fall quite asleep, I at
least had but a confused idea of my whereabouts, and the
dropping of an acorn, falling very near my head, did not
arouse me; but soon another and another came in quick
succession, and I was at last aware of being in the line of
some busy squirrel, or jay, perhaps, overhead.   I could not
see the acorn-plucking creature, and somewhat curious
about it, awaited developments with my eyes widely open.
Presently a flock of noisy robins came from behind me,
and alighting in the oak I forgot the dropping acorns as
I listened to them.   Then I heard, but could not see, a
flock of redwings that came from over the creek and
rested in the same old oak.   Their voices with those of
the robins filled the air with music, and I was charmed as
I watched and listened, lying flat upon my back—but suddenly all were silent, and then, like a flash of light, redwings and robins together beat a precipitate retreat with
a pigeon-hawk in pursuit, darting earthward and outward
over the meadow and directly over me.

So far, a tragedy rather; but there is yet more to tell. I was directly in the track of these frightened birds, and to the cathartic effects of fear I am ready to testify.

For the moment I thought it more, but it was, in fact, but a trivial matter, although I do not care to have it repeated; and now, while I write, I am ready again, weather permitting, to lie under the oaks, or to wander beneath their outreaching branches and fill my pockets with acorns.

October 14 1892

Oct 2, 1892

Oct 16 1892

Oct 9-1944. arrw Santa Barbara, Cal.

CHAPTER XI.

NOVEMBER.

THE change of the landscape's prevailing tint from green to brown is not a cheerful one. Look wheresoever one may, he is pretty sure, in November, to drift into a brown study, and this is seldom exhilarating.

"Whither shall I wander?" has been the initial question of each available day, and now, a goodly portion of the month having passed, I find my note-books recording, to describe it somewhat figuratively, the fact that my home has been the wheel's hub and my daily routes a series of closely set spokes. The dreary, lifeless, and repellent features of many a ramble had better be passed by in silence. Winter's skirmishers, the white frosts, have strewed many a field with dead flowers, and who cares to crush their bleached skeletons at every step? But deflecting a little from the preceding day's course, I have sometimes avoided these sad reminders of the defeated summer and chanced upon sheltered nooks from which the besieging frosts have retired discomfited. One such, strange as it may seem, was a wide reach of level meadow dotted with old trees. The day was essentially forbidding. A gray sky, a fog-patched atmosphere, and a fitful, chilly breeze that smote my cheek whichever way I turned, were discouraging at the outset, but abundant recompense awaited me, for the meadow was yet beautiful, green as in May, and rang with the voices of a thousand forms of life.

The meadow-mice held high carnival in their grass-hidden runways; the birds of the season, best equipped of all creatures for finding where summer still lingers, had congregated here. Snakes still tarried, although the nights are cool, and insect-life crowded alike the trees, shrubbery, and sod, singing and humming without appreciable rest, and above all I heard from the tangled marsh afar off a regretful frog twanging his unstrung harp.

Small areas of such cheerful meadow are not uncommon, and during November and all through the winter they are a source, or wonder. A sense of mystery rests over them. An acre, or perhaps ten or more of living green, surrounded by hundreds of lifeless brown, impresses every one who sees it. At least, I have escaped those who could pass it by unheeded. Abercromby, in his volume on weather, remarks: "From the fact that frost depends on radiation, we can readily explain why cold is so local. Radiation is very sensitive; the least breath of wind or any local shelter may interfere with the free play of radiation, and so we find two places only a few miles apart, one of which records 10° or 15° lower than the other."

In a somewhat similar, if not precisely the same way, the home meadows differ *inter se.* I have not gone to the trouble of hanging thermometers at different points, and tabulated the readings of a given hour, but the natural effect of a difference of 10° or 15° is often noticed between two meadow tracts, separated, perhaps, by only so slight a barrier as a willow hedge. But this alone can not account for all the differences we find, and to the warming influence of a wind-guard must be added the condition of the soil, the amount of decomposition of vegetable matter, and the elevation above tide-water. Then again, many a green meadow remains so throughout the winter, because hardy plants have replaced less vigorous ones, and we

have many growths that retain their chlorophyl unaltered,
even though subjected to actual freezing.

I have had reference only to such tracts as could be
walked over in safety; but the same difference in a more
marked degree is noticeable in the low-lying wet meadows
which are often scarcely more than a quaking mass of
weeds and water, often many feet in depth. Summer
lingers among these tracts in direct proportion to the
abundance of bottom springs. I have been long familiar
with some forty acres of such quaking meadow, or, more
properly, marsh. Three years ago it was divided by a
gravel bank, of considerable width, that rests upon the
hard-pan, and prevents the commingling of the water on
the two sides. One half of the tract remains as it has
always been; the other is permanently submerged to such
a depth that the characteristic vegetation of the marsh
has been killed. It is most instructive to walk during
the winter along the embankment. Summer lingers in
the marsh; even when the drowned meadow is firmly
frozen. The severest weather has little effect upon the
unaltered tract, and never has its "Seven Spring Corner"
been glazed with ice. As a consequence, animal life is
little affected where the warm spring water keeps the
meadow green; and here it is that, in the matter of their
habits, the many forms of animals living in this marshy
tract contradict the statements of those who think of winter as reducing the active life of summer to comparative
inactivity, or as its actual destroyer. The destructive effects of severe cold hold largely good, of course, of the upland ponds, and is true, now, of the "lake," as my neighbor
calls his submerged meadow, but it is not applicable to the
unaltered marsh that adjoins it. If the startling differences sometimes to be seen between adjoining fields, and
more frequently between contiguous tracts of meadow, had
been more generally noticed by out-of-door students of an-

imal life, dogmatic statements to the effect that, once winter arrives, life flees the spot or retires to hibernacula, would not so frequently mar the pages of our natural histories.

To return to the green meadow with its towering trees, that had not yet acknowledged the sovereignty of winter, I had first to marvel at the abundance of the birds. Their voices filled the air, yet I could not find them. Save a brown creeper or a blue nut-hatch, not a feather showed in any tree nor in the tangle that now hid the treacherous barbed-wire fence through which I had had to struggle. As I progressed in my too eager search, I finally came, very abruptly, upon the congregated songsters, an enormous flock of cowpen birds. These are small, steel-blue blackbirds, with a dozen common names and one hideous scientific one. As single individuals, they excite little interest, and their best efforts at singing fall far short of success; but when a thousand or more are gathered together, their united voices closely verge upon melody, although never so thrilling as is a chorus of ten thousand redwings.

Desirous of watching these birds close at hand, as they ran over the ground, reminding me of an excited colony of ants, I approached far more cautiously than I had been doing, and kept my hands behind me. My curiosity increasing, I attempted to approach within a dozen steps of them, and so, as usual, overstepped the mark. The birds nearest me arose, each with a warning chirp, and in a moment the broad landscape before me was shut from view. Broader and higher grew this solid wall of birds, and when its base line was lifted from the ground, the curious spectacle of a retreating hill confronted me; for I can liken this moving mass unto nothing else. Suddenly caught by a passing breeze, more quickly than it had veiled the landscape, the flock became a thin sheet, of which I could see but a ragged, fluttering edge. Then, caught by the wind, each bird was tilted toward me for an instant, the light played upon its back, and a broad sheet of silver floated across the meadow, settling slowly on the leaf-strewed sod and lost to view, although not twenty rods away.

Piqued by my failure to approach as closely as I wished, I made a second attempt, creeping this time upon my hands and knees for nearly one hundred yards. But this again was illy planned. I could see the birds at times, it was true, but only caught the most aggravating glimpses, and learned nothing, except that the same extraordinary restlessness possessed them that I had previously noticed. Tiring soon of my futile efforts to learn even the cause of this, I arose without any caution and stood in full view, not five paces distant. Not a bird noticed me! If they saw me at all, I was mistaken for a bush; but I gained one point—I saw that they were feeding upon insects. Running forward and shouting at the same moment, the whole thousand or more took flight as one bird, drifting before the wind like the autumn leaves that mingled with them, over and beyond the adjoining marshes.

The departing cowpen birds did not leave me deserted; but the contrast for a time suggested solitude. The merry clatter of their many voices still rang in my ears, but was gone in a moment, when I heard the sharp "peep" of Pickering's hyla. Perhaps no autumn sound is so generally misinterpreted as this. Few people in this region seem to know that so small a tree-toad exists, and most of those who do, attribute its shrill call, particularly when heard in November, to a bird. It is not a strange mistake. The familiar tree-toad of summer has long since been silent, or practically so; and then we never associate him with November and the leafless tree-tops. At best, he lives among the lower branches, and I, for one, have never found them at any great distance from the ground. Among the old apple trees in the lane, all that I have ever seen have been nearer the ground than the trees' tops; but, on the other hand, the dainty little yellow tree-toad —Pickering's hyla of the naturalists—is seldom content with so humble a perch, and when in summer they quit their aquatic and mud life for an arboreal one, they often wander to the very highest available resting-places in the trees. I once found one at the very top of a tulip tree, at least sixty feet from the ground. " Peeping " shrilly at such an elevation, it is little wonder that the sound should be thought to be the whistling of a bird.

As so often happens at the close of a dreary autumn day, the sun shone then with peculiar splendor. For a few minutes the meadows were gilded with a mellow light that brought out even distant objects with startling distinctness. Animal life at once responded to the welcome change. Rabbits darted from their forms, squirrels scampered through the trees, and mice stood up above their runways, as though in doubt about their safety. Many birds, whose presence I had not suspected, began to sing, and the crows, that had been silently seeking their roosts, abruptly broke ranks and clamored at the strange advent of a sunny day. Moping herons rose from the rank growths of the weedy marshes, sailed in the gilded air above me, crossed and recrossed the meadow and returned —their sole object apparently in so doing, the pleasure of a sun-bath. And beyond, where the creek shone like molten metal, water-snakes, roused to active life again, left behind them tortuous streaks of brilliant light; while everywhere, above, beneath, and on every side, rang out the shrill chirp of the restless cricket. Here, in this still green meadow, summer reigned. Asters, golden-rod, violets even, and scattered dandelions acted well their part. I had but to keep the leafless trees from view, and it was June again.

The landscape from any comprehensive point of view still shows a wealth of foliage, although it is the first week of November, 1887, and until very recently it was necessary to search for colored leaves. Here, about the home meadows, the painting of the woods is an uncertain occurrence. The frosts of October dulled the freshness of the leaves as a whole, but many held their summer hue for weeks after, and others will do so to the very last, and finally turn brown, wither, and fall in wonderfully quick succession, the whole change occurring within two or three days.

There are always, it is true, maples, liquidambars, and Virginia creepers that show a varied range of red and yellow—just as in August the tupelo turns crimson—but these make up but a small part of the woods.

To-day I have been rambling in a ravine where trickle the waters of a hundred springs, gathering "autumnal leaves that strow the brook," and I culled them while standing among green ferns, fresh-leaved privet, and in the shade of white oaks. The latter will retain their foliage, although crisp and brown, until the coming March winds blow. Indeed, I have seen them cling to the branches until apparently pushed off by the swelling leaf-buds of the new year. The privet will be green until January at least, and sometimes until later; but the ferns are quite contradictory. Last winter I found them fresh as a May morning along the roadside, and in an exposed position, yet in what appeared to be more sheltered spots the same species in October had withered and disappeared.

It is really an open question whether or not the frost kills the leaves of our forest trees, or is the cause of their changing color; and there are grounds for thinking that the two occurrences are merely synchronous, and have from this fact been considered as cause and effect. We

all know that prior to any trace of frost some forest trees
lose the green tint of their leaves, and assume quite brilliant colors; and, too, a single branch may change, while
the other limbs of the tree remain unchanged; again, in a
cluster of trees of the same species one or more may
change, but not the others—this occurring either before
or after a frost or a succession of them.

Fortunately, premature frosts, as we may call such as
occur earlier than September 20, are of such rare occurrence that their effects can not be satisfactorily studied.
It has often been asserted that when such frosts did occur
the foliage quickly responded by changing its color. In
but one instance have I been able to test the truth of this,
and I found that the trees apparently affected were in
every case those that change early in September, quite
irrespective of the temperature. Like the Virginia
creeper and the tupelo, there are several trees and some
small shrubs that undergo this change of color as the summer draws to a close, but such growths when scattered in
a wood are not apt to be noticed. Autumn leaves are
not generally known as a phenomenon of summer, so
are not looked for; but they are a sturdy fact, nevertheless.

So uncertain and contradictory seemed the whole
matter that I have for several summers followed the trees'
course from early spring until autumn, in hopes of learn-
ing something concerning the supposed relationship of
frost and the coloring of leaves; the following may bear
significantly upon the question.

The condition of the growth of the leaves in spring
appears to have much to do with the progress of the
autumnal change. As an instance of this I may mention that three enormous beeches near my home were in
full foliage, May 1, 1886, and the rich yellow-green of the
growing leaves had wholly disappeared. During the first

week in June, the branches of one of these trees having
an eastern exposure, produced a copious second growth of
leaves. In October following, when the foliage generally
had dropped, this second growth still held its place, and
did not fall until the middle of November. It came a
month later and tarried that much longer. The same
phenomenon I have often noticed in connection with the
many oaks that abound here, and notably the broad-
leaved or post-oak.

Frost, it is well known, is quite irregular in its distribution. It needs but a slight variation in condition to
ward it off when all about the ground is covered as with
snow; but it seems scarcely possible that a tree standing
alone in an open field should be affected upon one side
and not on the other, and that the branches that bear a
second growth of leaves should always be those that escape
being chilled during the first few frosty nights. The
leaf, it would appear, like the fruit, has a given time for
growth and ripening, if we may call its coloring by that
name; and if the tree is in full vigor, the occurrence of
frosty weather does not more than hasten the process, if
it does that. I do not believe that it is the primary
cause. This is an old view, and as applicable to southern
New Jersey, I subscribe to it.

During the spring of the current year I noticed that
trees of the same species varied exceedingly in the time
of coming into leaf—a difference that may be explained,
I suppose, by the variation in the temperature of the soil;
and at this time, November, these same trees may be divided into three classes: leafless, with colored foliage,
and those with curled but still green leaves. The trees
came into leaf last April in the order named; those now
bare being the earliest to bud; those still in the leaf, the
latest. In particular I recall two shell-bark hickories
growing not two hundred yards apart, and one no more

protected than the other. These varied last spring by just two weeks in the growth of the foliage; and differed by the same length of time in October; one being golden while the other was still green, and when leafless the other was yet clothed in maroon-tinted leaves of great beauty. The fruit of the two ripened at the same time.

The effect of a drought, whether early or late, is also to be considered. While I am not aware that any protracted period of dry weather prevented the leaf-bud from maturing, it is true that the size of the leaf is affected with many trees, and the differences in this respect between a dry April and one that has had an abundance of rain, is a matter of from one eighth to one fourth in the size of the leaves. This is particularly noticeable among oaks and chestnuts, unless they are grown in permanently wet situations, as near springs or in low meadows.

We see, too, the effect of an early drought during the following autumn, for the leaves fall earlier in the season if they were checked in April by want of moisture; but a long drought, as is now so common in August or September, does not affect the leaves injuriously—as they freshen when rain does come—or to any noticeable extent so far as their falling is concerned. We had a test case in 1886, when there occurred a protracted late summer drought, yet the leaves remained upon the trees longer than usual—a fact not to be ascribed to absence of frost, but to the vigor they received from a superabundance of rain in April and early May, a vigor in nowise checked by the low temperature of August 29, when frost formed in damp situations. And well I remember the parched and dusty summer of 1874. From May until September scarcely a drop of rain fell. In August the leaves began to fall, and the woods were bare by October 1. There were no colored leaves in the forest save of such trees as become brightly hued late in the summer; and these were dull and withered.

But autumn leaves have another than their natural history—like autumn sunshine they have merits that concern the rambler, who cares not a fig for their botanical significance—what may be called their sentimental history. Concerning this it behooves me not to speak. Many have essayed to record autumn's full suggestiveness, and succeeded admirably. For myself, I never wade through the dead leaves that litter the paths in the woods without thinking of the past. Their rustling, like the monotonous creak of the mole cricket, is, I know not why, associated with days so far happier than the present that I am sobered by the sounds. To-day I rested full length on a bed of autumn leaves, but happily had no gloomy thoughts. The birds were abundant, and they, too, appear to love to 'send them flying hither and yon. Thrushes and sprightly chewinks that the few frosts have not frightened, scratched among them to their hearts' delight, and chirped so merrily one might call it song. And the chipmunks scurried over the leaf-hidden ground, and then stopping suddenly, barked at one another, until the little wood resounded with their squeaky voices. The crested tit and Carolina wrens sang lustily, the jays scolded, and many native sparrows sang as though it were May, and not November. There was nothing gloomy in that little wood, and I started homeward at peace with my own thoughts—started almost joyously, but the leaves creaked ominously as I trod them under foot. That sound suggested nothing but the dead past.

But yesterday it seemed that I wandered beneath these same leaves, thankful for the pleasant shade they cast. What though the air was filled with that dreamy haze that makes an Indian summer of the day? Save in these woods Nature seemed daintly dusted with old gold; very beautiful, but with not a trace of springtide activity. And as I walked the air was full of falling leaves. Slowly they floated earthward, as though struggling against fate. Who, indeed, could be merry in a shower of autumn leaves?

> The mellow mist that wraps the hills,
>   And floods the blighted meadows,
> The river's winding valley fills;
>   Fled are the forest shadows.
> A melancholy ending, this,
>   Of summer's wealth of vigor;
> A veritable Judas' kiss,
>   .Forerunning winter's rigor.
>
> While last these sad November days,
>   The leafy rain that clatters
> About the bosky nooks and ways,
>   Wherein the squirrel chatters,
> Calls back the withered hopes that seemed
>   Life's gold in days departed,
> And endless summer, ours, we dreamed,
>   But age, how wintry hearted!

And what perfect days do we often have, even so late as in the last week of November! The white fog, like snow-banks, shuts out the horizon only, making a fitting background for the forest that rims the river's valley. So the rambler had a little world to himself, and though, save the dark-blue sky, there was little color but brown, that little with its scarlet, winterberry and rich red bittersweet were the more beautiful. But why strive to prove brown Nature dreary? The birds were happy—take a hint from them. Nor was it only the many birds that charmed. Among the still clinging, crisply crackling leaves there was piping gayly a hidden hyla.

I have had much to say, in times past, of the activity of our frogs during the late autumn and winter, and here

would only add a word more about Pickering's hyla, as it
is usually called. I endeavored, during last winter, to determine just how far it was affected by extreme cold, and
was quite unsuccessful. One incident, however, bears
upon the matter. During a sleety, snowy, northeast
storm in December I heard one peeping in a tall birch tree,
and searched long for it. It appeared to be among the
lower branches, but of this I could not be sure. It is pre-
eminently a wood-note that is difficult to locate.

At last, chilled from long clinging to the icy branches,
I sprang to the ground, and in so doing brushed the hyla
with me to the heaped leaves in the wood-road. This I
discovered, for twice as it crouched among them I heard
its shrill peep, and then caught sight of it as with one
desperate leap it vanished.

If here, where

> " sultry summer overstays
> When autumn chills the plain,"

but did not that winter's day, the hylas can find heart to
peep, I am ready to hear them at any time, let the mercury range where it will.

Just before a sudden blast from the north with its
attendant iciness closed the month, there was a soft south
wind that warmed not only the air but the water, and
brought all of our batrachian life to the fore. Great bull-
frogs, spotted croakers, green rattlers, pygmy peepers—
silent now—and daintiest of all, Pickering's tree-toad,
which peeped continually. Then, among the wind-swept
leaves that clogged the brook were salamanders of all sizes—
brown, spotted, red, yellow, and striped. But the little
tree-toad, now calling through the woods and always the
most difficult to discover, I despaired of finding, but fortune favored me, and I saw a single one as it gave a mighty
leap and came to rest upon an oak leaf across the ditch.

Grasping my companion's hand, I leaned over as far as possible and covered the creature with my hand, nor ventured to so much as even peep at my prisoner until I reached the house. While my right hand was thus converted into a frog-pen, I saw a single Savannah cricket or spring peeper, and this, too, I caught. How aggravating to have seen a third *desideratum* with both hands in limbo! But I didn't.

The two little frog-like creatures are in a glass case before me as I write, and a word concerning them before returning to the leafless woods. One is a tree-toad, and has little circular pads on the ends of its toes, by the aid of which it holds on even to the glass. The other has pointed toes, but with some effort, and by always remaining in wet spots, it too can hold on to smooth surfaces marvelously well. The former is the autumn songster; the other is the earliest of springtide vocalists. The tree-toad is of an unchangeable pale-buff color, the other is green-bronze dashed with old gold, black, and white, and furthermore can change its colors from very dark to extremely pale tints. Both are active, and their prominent bright eyes suggest a deal of wisdom, which even long-continued observation fails to detect. Yet they must think! As I watch them now it is impossible to foretell their actions. They prepare for subsequent movements in so deliberate a manner one can not help thinking they decide in advance upon much that they do. The manner in which the tree-toad followed a house-fly showed a modicum of common sense. Again, there was always a "make-ready, take aim," posing before either gave a leap that was readily interpreted. Yet no amount of experience is sufficient to teach a frog the nature of a pane of glass. And at times, as if by accident, they lodge in some comfortable nook, and remain motionless for many minutes. What then, I wonder, is the nature of their thoughts?

18

The birds that thronged the thickets to-day were eminently suggestive. Most of them were from the north,
and here to spend the winter. Were any of them the
same individuals that were here a year ago? Perhaps this
is not so absurd a question as it may at first seem. Let
me ask, have or have not birds a love of locality as have
some mammals? If such a feeling exists among resident
species, why, indeed, may it not among those that migrate?
And, too, of those birds that come to us in the spring from
the south, are there not some that visit the same spot year
after year. It is a widespread impression, and probably
based upon fact. The whole subject is one of great interest, and has its bearing upon the subject of the permanent
mating of many species.

In the woods to-day were dozens of white-throated
sparrows, and their pleasing whistle banished every trace
of the gloom that silent, leafless thickets always have.
Their presence brought up the subject of local attach-
ments, and I discussed with myself some points of the
question as I wandered along the hill-side.

If certain birds that spend the summers with us come
year after year to the same spot, then there is no reason
why the same should not be true of birds that come from
the north to spend the winter. The fact that the former
nest here, and so have stronger reasons for attachment to
a given locality, is, it is true, an argument wanting in
the other case, but this want does not relegate the matter
to the limbo of improbability.

Let us consider some of the common spring birds, as
the familiar house-wren and the cat-bird, for instance.
In the early spring of 1859 a little box was placed in a
tempting position for the benefit of the wrens. In May
of that year the box was occupied by a pair of these birds,
and during the subsequent twenty-seven years the box has
been tenanted regularly from May 1 until September.

Always two, and sometimes three broods have been raised. It is evident that the pair which first occupied the box can not be proved to have subsequently nested in the same quarters, but there is, I maintain, so great a degree of probability that they did, that it is of value in determining that other phase of bird life—permanent mating. The question hinges largely upon whether we can or not recognize individual birds by their actions. This claim has, as a matter of course, been ridiculed by some, and doubted by almost every one; and yet I am by no means convinced that it is a fallacy. My friend Mr. Thomas Proctor, of Brooklyn, has published some very pertinent remarks upon the subject, from which I quote as follows:

"A gentleman with whom I am acquainted has a fondness for cage-birds amounting almost to a passion. The European linnet (*Fringilla linota*) is his favorite, and in the course of years he has kept as pets several hundreds of them. He has assured me that individual traits in this species are as apparent to him as such traits are to him in human beings. In those birds, he says, such traits are manifest in form, motion, manner, expression of face, in voice, and even in moral characteristics. When standing at the outside of the closed door of the room in which he keeps his pets, he will be able to recognize the voice of any particular one of his fifteen or so linnets by its distinctive quality, usually at the first chirp or note given, and when in the room with them, he can recognize any particular one of them by characteristics shown in manner of motion, and most generally at the first hop of the bird from one perch to another. 'And there is an individuality,' he contends, 'shown in a bird's mere attitude in resting.' . . .

"In my experience with cage-birds, distinctive individual traits are more readily to be perceived in the European goldfinch than in any other species; and I think that I can safely say that I should readily be able to recognize any particular bird of that species which had been kept by me as a pet for a period of six months, in case of its subsequent absence from me, in other hands, for a period of two years, unseen by me in the mean while."

And while I will not be as positive about the migratory wild birds that nest near my house summer after summer, I will say that I have recognized the same pairs of some, from year to year, my guide being their individuality. To do so needs no other art than to become acquainted with the birds, by patiently watching them day after day, and finally getting their confidence. House-wrens, for instance, are never mute. The moment they alight, even after a long migratory flight, they commence singing. On one point concerning their arrival in spring I am very positive —they do not straggle into the river valley, and wander aimlessly about for some time before they take possession of the boxes. Yesterday there was no wren along the hill-side—at dawn to-day they are in full song, and perched upon or very near the box that was last year their home. There was no hunting for a nesting site, no feverish courtship, no coaxing of a coy female to inspect the box, no discussion of the availability of the site, no quarreling among a half-dozen, more or less, for possession. Yesterday the spot was as deserted as at Christmas; to-day, not the male wren alone, but he and his mate are at home.

If the wrens that each summer occupied this one box were not mated when they started from their winter quarters, then their courtship occurred while on their northward journey, for I can not believe that, arriving in the night, this pair of wrens agreed not to disagree for a season, some time betwixt midnight and dawn. The sum and substance of the matter is, the actions of the birds can best be interpreted by supposing they are permanently mated, and knew where they were going in advance of their migratorial journey. It may be what a willing critic calls a " surprising hypothesis," but I believe it, nevertheless. Three decades of familiarity with the birds of a country dooryard may not be sufficient to determine such a matter, but it makes one very positive about it, nevertheless, and captious contradiction goes for nothing.

The same promptness to visit, examine, and linger about last summer's nesting tree is characteristic of the Baltimore oriole; and to say, as has been said, that the sexes never arrive at the same time is rot, pure and simple. Even if it were true, it would not conflict with the " hypothesis " of being mated for longer than a season.

Let us turn now to the consideration of cat-birds. Having thought for several summers that possibly it was the same pair that nestled in a clump of blackberry canes near by, I carefully watched them, a year ago, to determine their feeding-grounds, if so be it they had any particular range during the arduous weeks when they had young to feed. I could only determine that the garden was more frequently visited than the hill-side or meadows, and so placed food in easy reach and plain sight. This was soon discovered and continually visited. Gradually I removed the board upon which were placed the fruit and insects farther and farther from the nest, and finally placed it beneath a large gooseberry bush at the other end of the garden. After the young were grown they and the old birds continued to rely upon it for their food supply, which I kept up pretty regularly until the end of August.

The following April cat-birds reappeared, and the first that I saw were industriously hunting in and about the gooseberry bush, a spot not at all likely to be visited by these birds under ordinary circumstances. In May I re-commenced the supplies of food, and the old nesting site was reoccupied, although then a much more exposed position than it was during the preceding summer. Here was an association of two localities in the minds of the birds, and an error of judgment, of course, in supposing the food supply at one point depending on the nest being at another. It is important to note here as usual that there was not at first a single bird but a pair, and they were so intimately associated as to lead any one to suppose that they were mated on arrival.

The same character of evidence has been noted of many species, and the whole subject in its different aspects, of love of locality, permanent mating, and preference of winter visitants for certain spots to which they possibly return season after season, loses much of its vagueness and improbability when birds are studied in one locality year after year for many years.

Impressions of this kind acquired by field studies can not be readily described in minute detail, but one point, however, can be insisted upon dogmatically—when a pair of birds are studied for a season, long before the time of their departure at the close of summer they will be very different birds to the observer from all others of their kind. It is not difficult to distinguish their individuality.

Everybody, it would seem, speaks of Indian summer with that glibness that should arise from positive knowledge, but far oftener it is the outcome of positive ignorance.

Multitudinous as are the references to the subject, there are but few elaborate essays treating solely of it. Indeed, it is but very recently that I have found a few of these. On the other hand the various references to the short-lived season are by no means harmonious statements. The impressions of a dozen authors that I have collated, as to its time, place, and circumstance, are quite as hazy as the brief "summer" itself certainly is.

By most people it is claimed to be peculiar to November, and warm, hazy, *dolce far niente* days in October or December are simply so much good luck, but not typical Indian summer. This extreme view is not commonly held, although the correct one; and by people generally December days of the proper sort are allowed to pass. As there is no established authority on the subject, the laity are happy in being allowed to think as they please—a very dangerous liberty, by the way, as is proved by the fact that this same leaderless laity are quite at sea as to what Indian summer really is; all of which matters nothing to them, and they talk about it as freely as of the round of the seasons.

The term "Indian summer" was applied to the occasional brief spell of pleasant weather in November about two centuries ago the writers having New England in mind, and probably to this day the "summer" of late autumn is more regular in its occurrence there than it is or has ever been in New Jersey. But why call it "Indian" at all? It can scarcely be considered a happy chosen name, even if the following is to be accepted as the explanation:

"In the early periods of our history, when the Indian enemies lurked in the forests and burst out from their ambuscades on the planter, the first settlers enjoyed little security, except in the winter, when the severity of the season prevented the incursions of the savages. The coming of winter was hailed as the commencement of peace by the early inhabitants of the country; they sallied out from the little forts and block-houses, in which they had been hemmed up, with the joyful feelings of prisoners escaping from confinement, and busily gathered in their harvests. To our ancestors the snows of winter were more pleasant than the flowers of spring, as they brought the cessation of the horrors of war. But it often happened that the mild day of November afforded the red men another opportunity of visiting the settlements with those desolating blows, which burst like the lightning from the cloud, leaving the record of their effects in the blaze that followed the stroke. The activity of the red men during these periods gave, as is supposed, the name of ' Indian summer' to those bright days, when autumn bestows its last parting favors."

From Hubbard's " Memorials of a Half Century " I clip the following, as descriptive of the true Indian summer and its peculiarities: " Early New England writers," he states, " speak of this serene portion of autumn as peculiar to America, hence the name they gave it. But we look in vain for any recognition of it in pages not more than half a century old. It seems to have departed from the land of the Puritans with the vanished forests, and doubtless these had much to do with its former prevalence. The French of Canada, called the season ' St. Martin's summer.' . . .

" Yet the Indian summer is no myth. It often breaks upon us from the very midst of storm, frost, and snow, true to the tradition that there must first be a ' squaw winter' before we can have an ' Indian' summer. . . .

" Pleasant as our autumns usually are, . . . not more than one in three or four presents any period of successive days which take on the character of well-defined Indian summer. Intervals between such years may vary from one to ten. . . . Of the fifty years from 1835 to 1885, ten are marked on my calendar as having each a full week of well-defined Indian summer, viz., 1837, '39, '44, '48, '53, '59, '68, '73, '75, and '84; two as having eleven to fifteen days, viz., 1840 and '50; two as having thirty days, 1865 and '74, and one, forty-two days, 1849. . . .

"1865, a cold, changeable, and dry year, but closing with an autumn exceedingly pleasant and warm; the whole month of November being balmy and delightful, though with comparatively little haze, which characterizes true Indian summer."

The above describes the autumn weather of the southern shore of Lake Michigan, at and about Chicago. Let us now consider this portion of the year at home.

In Peirce's little volume on the weather of Philadelphia and vicinity, for fifty-seven consecutive years, the author mentions Indian summer but three times; so the pleasant weather of fifty-four years may be assumed not to have reached the standard required. As I understand it, the true "summer" week must occur in November, and a very marked hazy condition of the atmosphere is an absolutely essential feature. And here let me ask, was this peculiarity a regular feature, or approximately so, of late autumn in Indian times? Had the generally densely forested condition of the country aught to do with it? This is not improbable, and one evidence of it still holds. Among the mountains, where there are still tracts of woodland, although a meager second or third growth, there often occurs a typical Indian summer when such weather is wanting in the comparatively treeless tracts of the lower, level country. But, after all, why the Indians are coupled with it, remains a mystery. The term implies that the aborigines did not appreciate the summer proper, which is not true. They were partial to it, and recognized all its merits. May they called the beginning of summer, June was summer proper, and July was known by a long name, the meaning of which is quite suggestive— "when the bees are busiest." There is no evidence that they ignored three months of fruitful weather for an uncertain week in autumn that perfected nothing. It acquired no place in their religion, and if it was weather to their liking they failed to do more than say as much among themselves; but it suggested nothing, nor were prayers offered for its continuance.

In our own weather-lore, strangely enough, the season, or "spell," does not figure prominently. It is given in "Signal Service Notes," No. IX, Weather Proverbs, that, "If we don't get our Indian summer in October or November, we will get it in winter." How jolly a thought for the rambler, but alas! as is so often the case with glib sayings, there is not a vestige of truth in it. How it collapses when confronted by statistics!

Be then the history of Indian summer what it may, all know it when it really appears, as is evidenced by the readiness to herald a spurious article; and the contemplative rambler plans his outings to cover all the ground.

And wherein lies the charm of this short season? Undoubtedly the yellow haze that softens the horizon and gives the world a dreamy look has all to do with it. The character of this haze is an open question. It is said to be animal life so minute as to escape microscopical examination—hypothetical creatures that make up in numbers what they lack in size, and at one time shake the atmosphere and obscure the sun. By many it is thought to be of vegetable origin; and by a great many, in a pompous manner, it is said to be "haze, and any fool knows what that is." This, the remark of a prominent citizen who is not suspected by his neighbors to be the greatest fool of them all. And of such is many a town made up—and kept down.

I glory in being one of the fools that do not know what haze is. The few Indian summers that I have known have put me in possession of but one or two insignificant facts concerning it. In the first place, it is never just where you happen to be; it is everywhere else, except directly overhead, and disappears as promptly as you change your own position. Again, it is delightfully restless, outwriggling any child in church, so I am told. No dancer has such nimble legs. From sunrise to sunset it waltzes with the distant tree-tops, while the trees near where I am standing remain, like myself, a quiet spectator. But when I run across the pasture meadow, the trees have changed places—those that were dancing are now sedate spectators.

But no one should stand during Indian summer, although it is not a season of activity. I compromised the matter by taking my boat and rowing down Crosswicks Creek from the draw-bridge to the Delaware—four miles or more of a most crooked course; here, between wide meadows but a foot or two above high tide, and there, at the foot of a wooded bluff, where the current is swifter and ripples over shallows studded with pebbles, mussels, and, strange to say, even to this day, stone implements fashioned by prehistoric men. The vicissitudes of centuries, one would think, should have buried them before this. But the floods divide their favors, and where they cover here, they expose elsewhere. For how long must this valley have been inhabited, so thickly studded is the meadow mud with weapons of rude workmanship! Yet not here does the story of man's occupancy of America open. There is an earlier and even more striking chapter.

The suggestion that absolutely primitive man ever existed in America has been and still is vehemently denied; but it is cheering to know that gradually his presence in an earlier geological epoch is being admitted. Why so cautiously admitted, though, is not quite clear. Still it is something gained to have him in the probability stage, in a new school-book.

As I round the wooded bends and weedy corners, I
conjure up this ancient man, and people the near-by hills
with him and his, picturing to myself what time the first
Indian summer dimmed the near distance with its golden
mists. Not strictly speaking an "Indian" summer then,
but the mellowing of an ice-age autumn. This, when the
river was a mightier stream, and the first tide of the creek
was yet to flow.

And later, when the black mud that now makes these
wide, weedy meadows was being slowly laid down, yet
another folk were here, and after them the Indian.
There is something mysterious in the human mind that
it rebels the instant that man's antiquity is broached. The
mammoth and mastodon, the moose, reindeer, and extinct great beaver, they are all well known, and none
doubt their place in the earth's geological history; there
are the same evidences of men, earlier in time than the
Indian, mingled with the animals I have named, yet the
statement makes men still shrug their shoulders. The
just law that sauce for the goose should be sauce for the
gander, fails for once. Bones of mammals are as old as
the deposits that contain them; but bones of men must be
intrusive objects. Why, must be, has never been explained.
Superstition has such a grip upon the world, it may yet
die in ignorance.

But let us to a more pleasant subject, where rancorous
discussion can not creep in. The dreamy days of this
short season do not have a depressing effect upon animal
life. I startle the wary wild duck as I round a jutting
bush-clad point, and its clear alarm cry goes bounding up
the valley until lost in the open meadows. The foraging
musk-rats cross the creek before me, bearing calamus
roots upon, if not above, the surface of the water; but
more delightful than all else to see or hear now, are the
close-gathered redwings that fill the whole valley with

their united voices. It matters not to them whether it
be spring or autumn, summer or winter; there is melody
in their hearts at all seasons, and they mean that the
world shall know it.

The flowers of summer, even the everywhere present
golden-rods of September, are not missed at such a time.
A single happy bird will make glad the dreariest landscape; and before Indian summer came, the meadows
and creek-side were filled with a cheerful, chirping host
that will spend the winter with us. I never want for a
companion when I come to the creek. It is the great
highway of an endless host, and to be one with them, if
not of them, is a treat fit for the gods.

However full the day, the thought that this sweet
"summer" is so short will constantly intrude. Not a
cloud flecks the sky but we wonder what of the morrow?
Not a breeze stirs the branches and rattles the withered
but still clinging leaves but we scan the northern skies
for a herald of winter. As quickly as the Indian summer
came, so she departs. The storm-king takes up the
scepter, and a new order is established.

The Delaware Indians called the eleventh month *Wini-
gischuch*, or Snow Moon, and our records show that the
first snow-fall is usually before December 1st. Hence the
common saying that the date of the first rabbit-tracking
snow in November indicates the number of snow-storms
of the winter; and trustworthy meteorological records
show that snow and ice are more a feature of the eleventh
month than is a week of beautiful, warm, and hazy
weather. Nevertheless, November is neither a winter nor
a wintry month.

A jumping mouse that I have had for weeks has become so stupid since the mild days of last month that I
have generously passed it over to a friend. A word is in

season, therefore, when these creatures are out of season concerning not only this one in particular, but others of its kind. My field notes and indoor studies are as follows:

March 13, 1887, was a delightful day. There was sufficient warmth to cause one to forget that winter had still the upper hand. Peewees were abundant, and those about the old draw-bridge over Crosswicks Creek sang suggestively. Frogs croaked hopefully—something like " no more frost! no more frost!" was the burden of their unceasing chorus; but I may add, parenthetically, that there was more frost, and for the benefit of those who have expressed a doubt, even snow in April.

With two enthusiastic "outers" for companions, an exploration of a curious mound in the meadows was undertaken, we three being archæologists for the nonce. The little hill proved to be Dame Nature's work, and no long resting bones of Lenni Lenâpè were brought to light. But we did not come away empty-handed. The first shovelful of dirt removed exposed a hibernating jumping mouse. It was a cold, stiff, globular mass, looking wonderfully like a huge hairy caterpillar, closely curled. One of my companions wrapped it in his handkerchief, and placed the bundle in the capacious side pocket of his overcoat. From time to time the package was examined, and in less than an hour his mouseship was quite active and required extra precautions to prevent his escape. Some hours later, when placed in fairly comfortable quarters, he showed no disposition to return to a torpid condition. It was evident that anticipating summer had no ill-effects upon the creature's health.

This mouse lived for several months, and finally became quite tame, but never changed its nocturnal to diurnal habits.

To-day, November 21, has proved thoroughly delightful for outdoor occupations. Too cool, perhaps—Indian summer on ice; but not disagreeable to take. Late in the afternoon, a cozily nesting jumping mouse was exhumed from a high knoll on one of the upland fields. The animal was in a globular nest of closely interwoven grass, and this was about six inches from the surface.

As in all cases that have come to my knowledge, the position was such that under ordinary circumstances the nest would remain dry, although at such an inconsiderable depth. But the creatures do not always make a wise choice in this all-important matter, as we have already seen, for the freshets sometimes wash the earth away from their retreats, and the occupants are drowned, often without previously being roused to consciousness.

In the locality examined to-day, the ordinary autumn saturation of the soil would, of itself, not penetrate the thick mat of grass that filled the burrow, and the ground freezing early in the winter would thereby further protect the nest from protracted rainfalls and the soaking arising from the melting of snow. So far as I have been able to determine, open winters, with alternating freezing and thawing and rain instead of snow, are more destructive to these mammals than steady cold, however intense or prolonged. Indeed, the latter condition can never prove hurtful, so long as the hibernacula remain undisturbed. Hence the greater abundance of the species farther north (?).

This curious kangaroo-like creature is certainly not favorably constructed for elaborate burrowing. The fore feet are weak, and the fore limbs too short, or so it seems; and yet the winter quarters of the specimen found to-day were neatly arranged, and the more interesting from the fact that it is not very clear how the hibernating chamber had been constructed. There was no evidence, such as loose dirt or a hole in the surface of the ground. Had the presence of the animal been suspected, I do not think there existed the slightest clew to its precise whereabouts. The excavation, as judged by the undisturbed portion, was nearly globular, and about five inches in diameter. The cavity was filled with fine, flexible grasses, except the very center, wherein was curled the torpid jumping mouse. As with the earth-chamber, so the grasses lining it were without the slightest trace of an entrance to the center. Apparently, after the mouse had curled itself up, it had kept one paw, at least, free and shut the door and barred it on the inside. Then, tucking this paw under its chin, the world was to go easy with it until next spring-tide.

My captured and now contented mouse was thrown from its nest to the surface of a load of sand, and fortunately rested on the load instead of beneath it. The creature's unceremonious eviction did it no harm, and when first seen, at the end of a very short journey, it was subjected to a toss to the hard ground, upon which it fell with some force. A moment later, it was handed to me. From the time of its exposure until I received it, not more than ten minutes, if so much, had elapsed. When I laid it upon the palm of my hand, it was, to all appearances, a fuzzy stone—a hard, cold, oval pebble, such as one might pick up anywhere. Neither ears, limbs, nor tail were visible, the former being pressed closely against the breast and abdomen, while the tail was lost to sight in the fur of the back and head, to which it clung as closely as poison ivy to the oak.

With it still in the position mentioned, I sat by a stove for fifty minutes, intent upon watching the effect of a high temperature, trusting the transition would not prove too sudden and so fatal. It was no light task toward the last, but I persevered in spite of discomfort. For twenty minutes there was no change beyond that of temperature, the mouse no longer feeling like ice, and, I think, the tail relaxed slightly. About two minutes later, there was a well-marked, convulsive movement at the neck, the head rising a short distance from the breast and then resting against it again. This occurred at intervals of about forty seconds, for four or five minutes, and then ceased. In the mean while the tail uncurled, but did not move when placed in different positions.

For about three minutes the mouse seemed dead. I could not detect its breathing, and when gently prodded it did not flinch. Then suddenly the fore feet commenced twitching at about one minute intervals. Five minutes later, the hinder limbs likewise twitched, and a tremor siezed the whole body. The movements collectively strongly suggested that this tedious process of returning to consciousness was decidedly painful; which, of course, it can not be. The general trembling and twitching grew gradually more violent, but less rapid, and finally developed into long-drawn inspirations, or what appeared to be such, and suggested more strongly than ever severe pain.

At the elapse of forty minutes from the time of commencing my observations, control of the limbs was acquired and the mouse stood up; regaining its position whenever pushed over on its side or turned upon its back. It now appeared to be asleep merely, the violent respiration or spasmodic thoracic movements that disturbed the whole body having ceased. Fully ten minutes later the eyes opened, but such a sheepish, sleepy look it had! Still it kept them open and was evidently trying to collect its thoughts, a task that required some time for it to accomplish.

I infer, from the movements of the animal, that it was absolutely unconscious during the time the body was steadily responding to the influence of the warm atmosphere surrounding it.

19

Since the above was written, I have had my jumping mouse in cozy quarters for sufficient time to have learned a good deal about its other habits, but have not done so. Except upon rare occasions, it has proved undemonstrative and uninteresting to a degree. One difficulty in the study of its habits is not readily overcome, that of the creature being active only at night. And yet, while strictly nocturnal, the creature never appears dazed, even when suddenly plunged into the brightest sunlight. The eyes are small and bead-like, and have not the suggestiveness of weak vision and star-lit nights that do the large blinking eyes of the flying squirrel and white-footed mouse; and yet the creature is always inactive during the day. Judging solely from certain movements and the result of simple experiment, it is probable, at least, that the creature's other senses are exceedingly acute—more so than with the true mice—and that this supplies the deficiency, if such exist, of weak vision. In more than one sense, I have had to work in the dark, to determine this, if, indeed, it is determined.

Twice my specimen has been on the alert when I opened the cage to supply food and water, and with astonishing quickness made one desperate leap and vanished. To recapture it was difficult; and it was during these two occasions that I learned the quite unsuspected fact that its scansorial ability is sufficient to stand it well in need. If a surface was moderately rough, the fact that it was perpendicular did not bar its progress. Hence, while scrutinizing the carpet, as though looking for a pin, his mouseship was on top of a table, contemplating my senseless search. Nevertheless, I had opportunities on both occasions to observe its gait upon level surfaces, and found it to be quite the same as that of an ordinary house-mouse. It only leaped when I attempted to place my hand over it. In other words, when pursued, it ran, and only leaped when about to be overtaken.

And in all these weeks my mouse has never squeaked. Even when his tail is pinched, it has muttered to itself, if at all; and during the gloaming, and often until well in the night, I have sat in darkness by its cage, hearing its movements and dimly discerning them, but not a sound has it uttered. Yet I can not think that it is a mute individual; and I know that in the field, of a warm summer night, they can and do squeak, and sometimes soften this short utterance until you might almost say they sang.

Probably, had I found my specimen in May instead of November, when fresh from a long winter's nap, instead of being suddenly aroused at the commencement of it, I should have had something more interesting to report concerning it; for such as I have seen within a year or two, in the field, have shown themselves to be exceedingly intelligent; particularly in their usually successful efforts to elude their enemies, which are so abundant that it is a marvel the species has been able to maintain its ground; although, of course, its nocturnal habits are somewhat in its favor; as is also the fact that for some five months of each year it is safely tucked away from the jaws and claws of its most persistent foes. Yet, notwithstanding all this, the species, in this vicinity at least, is not nearly so common as the beautiful white-footed mouse, the Hesperomys, daintiest of all our mammals.

A year has now passed since this second section was written, and I have again something more to say of the little fellow. Some years ago, I expressed a doubt as to the possibility of this mammal leaping as far as stated by Dr. Godman, "from five to six feet at every spring." I have learned since then that the white-footed mouse can do this, and here we have a mammal whose construc-

tion does not suggest as marked leaping powers. I recently chased one over the smooth rocks of Brush Creek, in
southern Ohio, where I could mark and measure its tracks
as it sped over the mud-coated stones. Its leaps varied
from two to three feet, and once, bounding over a shallow
pool, the distance cleared was a few inches more than a
yard.

Brayton, in his report on the mammals of Ohio, says
of the jumping mouse, the "kangaroo-like structure enables this little animal to take enormous leaps, of even
eight to ten feet when alarmed," and I have found this
true of the species in New Jersey. Early one morning,
during the summer just gone, I noticed in a clover stubble a great commotion, in which a hen that had her
chicks with her was the only visible participant. Sus-
pecting that a weasel might have attacked her brood, I
approached without due caution—something a naturalist
should never do—and was startled when quite near to
see a small mammal give a sudden bound into the air and
reach the ground again at a surprising distance. I knew
of no other creature possessing like jactatorial power, and
pronounced it a jumping mouse. A very hard chase, directly afterward, proved that I was correct. To make an
accurate measurement of this creature's initial leap was
not practicable, but certain mullein stalks from which it
started and at which it landed led me to believe that the
distance was little if anything less than nine feet.

Of course such jumping is unusual, but I noticed that
while I pursued the same mouse, it several times gave surprising leaps, after running in a zigzag course for some
distance. It appeared to be able to leap only when it
reached some spot peculiarly adapted to the act—a lay of
the land, as it were, that took the place of a spring-board.
I say, it "appeared so"; but in all such matters one can
not safely express an opinion unless based upon a series of

observations and experiments. These are necessarily difficult, good luck rather than good management making them practicable. On one point, however, all observers will undoubtedly agree—that no other of our mammals possesses leaping powers equal to those of the pretty jumping mouse.

Nov 10, 1899.
Nov 7- 1892
Voight's

CHAPTER XII.

DECEMBER.

THE round of the seasons three or four centuries ago was less frequently interrupted, probably, than now by overstaying summer. The Delaware Indians, as has been mentioned, expected at least one snow-fall in November. This year, 1888, we have had next to none even in December. It was continually "in the air," so my neighbors averred, but if so, it remained where it was; but at last, the long threatening clouds assembled in full force. A dim and dusty atmosphere shut out the horizon. The gloomy pine trees' pointed tops trembled, though there was no wind, and a muffled moan filled the long avenues of leafless oaks. Not a bird chirped; aye, not one hopped from its perch, as I passed them by, snow birds and tree sparrows, as if even they too, although visitors from the north, awaited with fear the coming of the storm. Soon, with no *avant-courier* to warn, singly, through the locked branches of the thickset trees, sifted the icy snow-flakes. No patter was heard, as of April rain on last year's leaves. They each came silently, glinting a moment in the fading light and straightway disappeared. Then, as the clouds darkened, they fell in greater haste, whirling against and at last enshrouding alike tree, bush, brier, and withered wind-rowed leaves.

The first snow had come, and to-morrow field, meadow, and hill-sides will be new countries to explore. And so it proved. Throughout the night the storm continued, and at sunrise I thought how happily the Indians had named the year's last month, *M'chakhocque gischuch*, the moon when the trees bend with snow.

That we have less snow than formerly can not be questioned; that we shall have next to none when our forests are all gone, goes without saying; but, happily, it yet occasionally invades even the sheltered meadows, and I, for one, am duly thankful. It is a fact that it matters not how intense the cold may be, nature is never at rest, nor wild life banished; merely every object is more strictly conditioned. Even an arctic winter teems with suggestiveness, and a mild one is too often but a summer in undress.

Field, meadow, and hill-side, alike snow-clad; let us ramble over them. Even were the country literally covered with the snow, a day's outing would not prove fruitless, for there are ever the birds that soar above it—crows in the upper air, larks in the tree-tops, and sparrows in the hedge-rows; then, too, the snow itself is often alive with pretty creatures akin to fleas, marvels of activity and grace as they flee from your advancing shadow. Still, the average rambler is not an Eskimo; his ancestry is tropical rather, and winter is loved only as a novelty. Hence, how the countenance brightens during a winter walk when one comes to a bare spot of earth! How tenderly he kneels to examine and perhaps to pluck some little faded flower—a bit of chick-weed or withered dandelion! But I did more than this; tired with picking my way over half a mile of stubble, starting the mice from their runways and flushing grass-finches from their favorite hollows, I came, at the public road, upon a narrow strip of naked earth. So, at least, it was in common parlance; but what a beggarly idea of nature one must have to call it naked!

At the upper margin of the loose, red earth, that nearest the unsheltered field above, the frost had lifted sand-grains and even pebbles from their beds, and wrought many a winding cave, crystal grotto, and ravine ; but beautiful as they were, they smacked of winter, and I turned my back upon them; for scarcely more than a pace distant, this same red earth was carpeted with pink-fruited lichen, and holding yet against the season's rigor was a forest of sweet-fern. Here rested summer and winter face to face, if not hand in hand. Summer, plucky to the last, and not to be ousted—winter, impotent to harm, despite its bluster.

Such little spots are not uncommon, and interest the more for that so many, like this road-side slope, have a northern outlook, and the temperature, of course, falls very low at times. To-day, when all is gloomily arctic in the fields hard by, here is no hint save that of a genial summer sun, for the sweet-fern although bronzed and brittle has not yet wilted. Recalling the birds and mice that I had found on my way hither, the conditions at the road-side contradicted the general impression as to wild life in winter. It does not always seek the more sheltered places; for, notwithstanding the northern exposure, this was a sheltered spot; else why such vigorous growths? Lichens, it is true, are unaffected by ordinary winter weather, but besides this, there were other growths that remained green and fresh as ever a plant in June—saxifrage, prince's pine, and Mitchella with its crimson berries.

But animal life: there should have been an abundance of it, I thought, coursing over such a cheerful scene, but I could find spiders only, and very few of them. Hurrying over the ground, they looked quite formidable, and were doubtless indignant at my interference, but far too timid to resent it.

Leaving this brilliant winter garden, I passed down the road, and where the slope was higher and equally exposed to every breath of the north wind, I found the ferns still green. This excites no surprise at favored spots on the home hill-side, where the sun looks down at noon and every breeze but that from the south is held at bay. But here on the road-side every condition is reversed, and where one would naturally look for the earliest effects of frost none are to be found. This can be explained in part by recalling the conditions holding good in summer. Having a northern exposure, it lost none of its moisture through exposure to the direct sunlight, and while plant life on the opposite side of the road was withered and sere throughout the dry weeks of August and September, here it was fresh and green as in early June. There was no check to its growth from early spring until late autumn, and so it had vigor enough to withstand the ordeal of a winter's cold. This is the apparent reason, but, alas! apparent reasons are not always the correct ones.

Climbing to the top of the bank, the snow-clad field is again before me, and with a feeling akin to dread I start across it. The bright sunshine is blinding; the fitful breeze is all too keen for comfort; but even here there is plant life that bids both the wind and snow defiance. Trailing Mitchella, laden with crimson berries, brightens the little circle of sod beneath a lone cedar, where no plow appears ever to have invaded. A bit of mossy, gray-green sod there has as aged a look as the old tree itself, and this we know has weathered the storms of two centuries —an all-suggestive bit of sod, upon which one might fancy still remained the imprint of an Indian moccasin; a bit of sod that should have been studded with arrowheads, and here, indeed, I found a fragment of one. With the whole world laid bare in midsummer, what matters a mere speck of weedy ground? Nothing then, perhaps—

but now how we treasure the little space that the cedar
has shielded! It is useless to attempt the spot's description; a serious task to enumerate all that might be
gathered. With a spray of the partridge berries to remember it, I pass on, wondering why the season's first
snow is not more suggestive. My mind runs continually
upon what it hides and not what upon it is. The treasures
beneath it I am continually seeking, and give scarce a
thought to their covering. Even now, as a quail whirls
up before me, bouncing from the little cluster of rag-
weed, the snow-dust in the noonday sun—a pink and
gilded cloud—is less admired than the speedy but graceful flight of the bird. The corn-rows can still be traced,
and, although many a one is beautifully arched with snow,
I lose sight of them directly as the grass-finch threads the
glittering maze before me, recalling what time this same
bird ran in the deep ruts of the dusty lane all summer
long, keeping just out of danger as the carriage hurried by.

The field I am crossing ends at the bluff overlooking
the low-lying meadows, and here, as at the road-side, the
transition is startling. What strange power has made
way with the snow? The leaves are again bare, and,
where they have not enviously concealed the hardier
growths, green plants cover much of the ground. One
has but to pass down the hill-side a few paces to realize
what winter sunshine may be, give it half a chance. The
tops of the tall trees are waving in a wind that never
reaches the ground; and no obstacle intervenes, except
the clouds, to shut out the noonday sun. It is rarely the
case but that what snow gathers during the night is here
melted before night comes again; and when the great
storms, such as were more common a century ago than now,
deeply covered even this sunny, southern slope, it was the
first ground to reappear when the skies were again clear.
And so, even now, in December, although

" Icicles hang by the wall,
    And Dick the shepherd blows his nail,
    And Tom bears logs into the hall,
        And milk comes frozen home in pail,"

I can collect green growths under the old oaks, and
make me a nosegay of saxifrage, columbine, pale cory-
dalus, feverfew, fleshy stalks of narcissus, and dainty
spring beauty. Leaves, nothing but leaves, remember;
but these have grown in importance since the flowers fell,
and will increase therein after the first snow has been
long forgotten, and until the impatient buds bursting
their bonds smile upon the lingering drifts of the winter's
last snow-storm.

But winter is not always so behindhand; not so two
years ago when the storm-driven snow-flakes beat angrily
upon the windows, as if daring me to face their fury;
while from the trees came threats of dire import, as their
bare branches lashed the whitened air. A long-planned
outing seemed indefinitely postponed; but New England's
December weather proved as uncertain as is that of New
Jersey, and as quickly as the wind and snow appeared, so
they passed by.

As they scurried together over the distant hills, leaving bright sunshine in their track, my companion and I
started for a walk, hoping, between the acts of a capricious winter day, to see the oaks at Waverley.

It was fitting that I should see the spot where these
trees stood for the first time in winter; for it was that
great winter of many thousand years ago, the Glacial
Epoch, that gave to the place its present contour.

Crossing an undulating meadow that was a novelty to
me in that our home lowlands have no projecting rocks,
we reached one of those strange and not yet wholly accounted for earth-works of the long vanished ice-sheet
known to geologists as a kame; and upon its side, with

others, stands the largest of the oaks that cluster here, a majestic growth of mighty girth—" the noblest Roman of them all." For how long it has withstood the winter storms and summer heats of New England's fickle climate it were in vain to conjecture; yet, guided by what is known of oaks the world over, it is safe to say that this one had burst its acorn-shell before Columbus sighted the Western Continent. And for him who loves an outing, it is something to stand beneath the outreaching branches of a tree that has doubtless sheltered many an Indian, and may have, deeply imbedded within it, the illy aimed arrowheads of the stone-age hunter.

Leaving the old oak for a time, we passed along the curious heap of earth and stones upon which it stands. I can recall nothing that offers a similar outlook at home to that which presents itself when walking on the crest of the kame, except, perhaps, the high railroad bank that skirts the Delaware River meadows. Before reaching its termination, I thought of the great Serpent Mound in Ohio; but this ice-age mound is straight, not tortuous, and suggested rather a legless lizard that had gorged itself with loose stones until its skin had burst.

On either side of the kame was an undulating meadow, rough and wrinkled with outcropping rocks as the skin of a warty toad. Near by flows Beaver Brook, which I was compelled to cross, and learned then and there how sadly at fault were my level-country legs. There is a world of comfort in feeling that your footing is sure. The tussocks in the home meadows never fail me, but I had no faith in those gloomy, ice-bespattered rocks. They seemed to take the world quite coolly, with sparkling waters at their feet, and armed *cap-a-pie* with icicles, but I could not. Rocks and rapids, I maintain, are pretty features of a road-side, but poor substitutes, particularly in winter, for the highway itself. How my companion crossed the brook I never knew; I crept cautiously, and with fair success reached grassy ground again.

A grand old elm, now much decayed, graces the meadow here, and called up at once some of these splendid trees near home. Although so very large, it is not im- probable that this tree at Waverley is much younger than some of the oaks near which it stands. I know of many of great size that have not yet rounded out a century, and one in my own yard that not quite sixty years ago was planted by my grandfather—the tree being then little more than a switch—now measures over three feet in diameter a yard or more above the ground, and at the root it covers half a square rod, at least. Few would suspect it to be so young a tree.

Why, when such trees as are perfect specimens of their kind stand near public roads, can they not be held —well, semi-sacred, at least? Should not their owners be induced to let them stand? Indeed, could a community do better with a portion of the public funds than to purchase all such trees for the common good? Particularly is it true of a level country that the only bit of nature held in common is the sky. I would that here and there a perfect tree could be added to the list. I have known enormous oaks to be felled because they shaded too much ground and only grass could be made to grow beneath them. It is sad to think that trees, respected even by the Indians, should have no value now. The forest must inevitably disappear, but do our necessities require that no monuments to it shall remain?

My companion,

> "Climbing the loose-piled wall that hems
> The road along the mill-pond's brink,"

led the way to the ruins of an ancient mill and old mill-dam that is still intact, and fairly darted down a stony

stairway such as a chamois might admire. My thoughts
were all in one channel while I followed ; but the charm
of the falling waters compensated for the discomforts of
such superlatively rough walking.   The lichened rocks,
ancient masonry, scattered shrubbery, troubled waters, and
the fretted frost-work, each beautiful in itself, lent a charm
to the whole, and but a few birds were needed to complete
the picture. These were wanting, and a single nest of the
red-eyed vireo was the only evidence that birds were ever
here; and yet I am assured that the whole valley is alive
with warblers during the early summer.   The mill-
dams harbor so much winter life at home, even birds, that
its absence here struck me the more forcibly.   It seemed
incredible that no winter wren was spider-hunting in the
wide gaps between those loose piled stones.   But, this
late December day, I could not expect to find that

> " From 'neath the arching barberry stems,
>   My footstep scares the sly chewink ; "

yet in southern New Jersey this is no uncommon occurrence, for the chewink is a hardy bird, and haunts the
sunny nooks of the hill-side from early to late, and sometimes tarries the year through.

   The barberry bushes, still holding their ruddy fruit,
were the more attractive because as yet we have none on
our mill-pond banks; and, on the other hand, I failed, at
first sight, to recognize the privet growing here.   At
home this shrub is almost an evergreen, and fruits but
sparingly, while the branches of the bushes along Beaver
Brook were weighted with coal-black berries, recalling the
ebon clusters of our glaucous smilax.

   So staid and steady, save when stirred by freshets, is
the flow of the spring brooks in the Jersey lowlands that
a roaring torrent tossing over rocks, even when on a
humble scale, works a potent spell, and I would gladly

have tarried here until the close of day. It is strange, though, that mere mechanical activity should be so fascinating. I have sat for hours by a meadow brook at home, seeing nothing but the rippling waters, oblivious even to the mosquito's ominous hum. Here, at the mill-pond, are forever the same immovable rocks, and the waters that lash them sing forever the same song. It matters little, whether we come in June or December, a bit whiter or greener as the case may be, yet we stand and gaze by the hour, and, lulled by the rushing waters, are often lost in thought. But there are torrents of ever rushing life of far mightier import than mere troubled waters, and why, it may well be asked, do they so seldom attract us? Though cold and forbidding the day, as I clambered, almost helplessly, down what my companion called the " steps," I found in a crevice of the mist-dampened rocks a small black spider that resisted all my efforts to entrap him. Think of the current of his thoughts as they rushed through his brain! for spiders, be they great or small, are as actively intelligent as any ant or bee.

Doubtless, until within a few weeks the icy waters have sheltered madcap life as impetuous in its way as the plunging currents that encompassed it, but it were in vain to seek for it at such a time as this. No fishes flash in the shallows now; no salamanders lurk beneath the flat stones, and beyond, down the stream, where hardy weeds have worked their way through the crowded rocks, no overbrave frog lingers to contemplate the round of the seasons. All have fled to hidden quarters beyond the reach of some forbidding feature of the winter here, but what that feature is, who knows? I can now, far better than heretofore, realize how many are the differences between localities but three or four hundred miles apart, and how widely the same creatures vary in habit, whether in Massachusetts or New Jersey; a fact that merits constant repetition until its full significance is felt.

Except the ceaseless sound of the falling waters, nothing broke the silence of the little valley. What music would we then have had, had a flock of tree-sparrows settled in the scattered shrubs! What melody, if, perched upon the top of a lone cedar, the cardinal had whistled his winter roundelay! How I longed for the bluebirds and the crested tit, and placed, in my fancy, a Carolina wren upon the rocks; where its song would blend with the roar of the rushing waters about it. Could the winter songs that gladden my home hill-side but be brought to this wild spot and paradise would be almost regained.

It was with unwilling steps that I turned from the flashing water-fall. That unchecked flow leaping over and through the loose wall soothed me, as does the moaning of pine trees or the murmur of the sea; and who, while happy, cares to brave an uncertain world? The distant hill-top, bathed in warm light, was so beautiful from afar that one might readily doubt if its merits would increase by nearer acquaintance.

Following, as best I could, my sure-footed companion, we crossed the valley and walked rapidly over steadily rising ground. Rapidly? He did, but time and again I stopped to catch my breath and allow my heart to become less active. But such halting progress has its merit. At one corner by an old stone wall I flushed a partridge. The whirr of its wings was indeed music. We had been out for hours and this was the first bird that I had seen or heard. Then, noiselessly, and high overhead, a sparrow winged its way toward the woods. I listened for at least a chirp, but the bird was too intent upon reaching some distant goal. As I passed up the cleared field that extends to the summit of Helmet Hill, I confidently expected some visitor from Canada, some hardy sparrow from the Arctic Circle, to flit across my path, but I saw not even a stray feather floating in the wind. However beautiful a country may be, and the outlook here is grand, I must confess to a feeling of disappointment if there be no birds. However artistic in design, or complete in all its appointments, it may be, a deserted dwelling has for me but little attraction. Its beauty is in proportion to the evidence of the happiness of its occupants, and Helmet Hill in winter sadly needs what it lacked when I was there—birds, birds, birds!

From the hill's rounded and half-wooded top we looked westward awhile toward Mount Wachusett, whose outline was but dimly discerned, and then, glad to escape a cutting wind, turned our faces homeward, and far more quickly than we went up, descended and reached that curious kame again upon which stand several of the Waverley oaks. Here we again halted. The sunset itself was enough to hold us; but this afternoon the atmosphere was of unusual clearness, and against the sunset's ruddy hues the gnarly branches and interwoven twigs of the old oaks stood out in bold relief, presenting the trees under a new, beautiful, and somewhat novel aspect. Leafless trees seen against the gray winter sky are familiar to many, and all acknowledge their beauty; the same trees sharply limned upon a rich red sunset are a memorable sight. The minutest twigs were as clearly defined as the largest branches; while the great rounded stumps of the oaks' amputated limbs flecked the western sky as bits of the blackest storm-cloud might. I was fortunate in seeing these noble trees at the close of day wrapped in such a warm and mellow light. Giants of their race, they stood in quiet repose, conscious of their might; ready alike to battle in their own defense with the fiercest of midwinter storms, or offer shelter, in due

20

season, from the hottest of midsummer suns, to him who
loves their shade.

They built no houses in happy colonial days in which
the chimney was an inconspicuous feature, hidden in the
end wall, and very likely to prove a death-trap, through
the carelessness or cupidity of the contractor. On the
contrary, there was erected an enormous chimney, and
a cozy house was built surrounding it. " Blow, wind!
Come, wrack!" it mattered not; the chimney stood up
for the house, and never allowed even a hurricane to
harry it.

Besides the fire-places—of which more anon—these
chimneys had other features of merit. The sustaining
arch in the cellar, in one case at least, had yearly stored
therein the choice barrels of cider that were not intended
for vinegar—there was no chance for change save for the
better as a beverage. And the weather-stained bricks
above the roof—they too are worthy of consideration. An
uncouth box-shaped mass, it is true, but beautiful of a
keen winter day, when, after a long tramp, one marks the
curling smoke. However grotesquely it shapes itself in
the upper air—whether it runs to hieroglyph or rune, it
matters not. For the chilled rambler it has but one
meaning—comfort.

A vacant hearth is as repellent as a coffin. It is not
strange that in summer they are screened by fire-boards,
and these again by high-backed chairs. Stately chairs that
overtopped the surbase, and torturing to humanity to-
day, were shunned, I doubt not, in the good old times.
At least, I have never had a friend to remain long in one
of my great-grandmother's chairs. Occasionally a victim
drops into one, but only to squirm; then he arises and
stares at the innocent-looking structure. I have never
heard any remarks, but the countenance, at such times,

speaks volumes. Yet who could throw away his great-grandmother's parlor chairs?

But it is winter now, and the hearth is not vacant. About it, in proper place, are the andirons, shovel, tongs, bellows, face-screens, and, never to be ignored, quaint silhouettes above the tall wooden mantel with its narrow shelf. Add to these a generous supply of hickory blazing on the hearth, and he who could not be happy when a winter storm rages deserves discomfort to his dying day.

The dignified pillars of the bright brass andirons stand to-night like sentinels between me and the fire, and I would that they were able to cope with those who will raid upon the heaped up hickory in spite of every form of protest.

Neither shovel nor tongs are essential to the maintenance of a wood fire, although the latter are convenient; but I have been tempted to spoil the hearth's appearance and remove them, because of the meddlesome disposition of every adult visitor. I have yet to see the man who was content to let an open fire remain as he finds it. It seems to matter not how cold he may be, he must rearrange the sticks, before spreading his hands to receive the wholesome heat of hickory coals.

I am told that Ben South, keeper of the cross-roads tavern, a century ago, determined that his bar-room fire should remain unmolested for at least one day, and to effect this he removed every bit of fire-side furniture. He was unsuccessful. Every customer asked for the tongs before asking for his toddy, and nine in ten kicked the logs— the tenth burned his fingers, shaking the andirons, and threatened to withdraw his custom. " Such a fire as that was too unsociable for him," was his remark. Ben gave up, and so do I. I know what is coming when my city friends drop in. The smile, the rubbing of the hands,

and the suggestive ah! all forewarn me of an attack upon
my fire.   If an angel from heaven were to place the hickory in order and every flickering flame was the perfection
of grace, it would avail nothing.   There would be instant
interference from the first mortal who happened in.   Of
course, I wish each one of my friends to consider himself
the exception that proves the rule; at the same time, I
would have all my readers, who know me not, understand
that there are no exceptions.

The pretty, fan-like screens for the face that I have
mentioned have ever interested me more than all else
about the hearth.   It requires some effort to realize that
your great-grandmother was once a girl, but it is true, and
what might not these neatly decorated bits of board, which
shielded her pretty but not painted face—what might
they not tell us, could they but speak!   How steadily have
bright eyes gazed upon them that dared not look up;
how stealthily have they glanced aside, meeting other eyes,
yet shielded from all the company.   Can it be possible
that in a quiet way there was a mild form of flirtation
even among the early Quakers?   These screens hint at it;
and we do know that they were always widely awake to
all the world's real worth—witty, fond of literature, nor
accounted it vanity to see themselves in print.   It is eminently appropriate to take up the volumes of the " Evening
Fireside," published eighty years ago, and read the pithy
prose and dainty verses of many a young Friend.   Indeed,
at least one of the contributors to this earliest of literary
weeklies has sat before my fire and held these screens,
listening, as I do now, to the moaning of the wind in the
chimney, singing then as now, as her poetry shows, a
melancholy song of long ago.   But how different her
" long ago " from mine!   I think of the time when this
country was young, as long ago; and my great-grandmother then was recalling the stories she had heard of her

parents' home in England; stories, it is hard to understand why, that have not been handed down.

It needs the fire's red glare and sickly candle-light to animate the inky silhouettes upon the wall. They are best stared at in such a light and when a storm rages. The coziness of an open fire leads to contemplation, and a step further, to retrospection. Fancy plays tricks with us on a wild night, when the north wind leaps from the tall pines and screams like a demon as it swoops down the chimney, scattering the ash-hidden sparks that gather again in force and rush headlong after the howling fiend, as it seeks the outer world again. We are ready for wild fancies then; and when the wind returns, as if repenting of its rashness, mild of mood and sighing dolefully, I hear my ancestors uniting in a prayer to reassemble before these andirons once again. Then the silhouettes take livelier shape, and one after another slowly float before me. What were their whims, or were they always as sober as their portraits? They are puzzles now; for the women have head-gear no Quaker ever wore, and the men strange overhanging locks of hair that would have endangered their status in meeting had they ever worn them.

But we must not forget the fuel, nor its history. I would not give a fig for straight-grained wood that promptly turns to ashes without protest. Give me, rather, knotty and gnarly sticks that boldly fight for their crookedness, and, at last, become coals that fiercely glare at you in impotent rage. Better than all is some old stump that has lain long upon the ground and perhaps been tunneled by mice and beetles, and long the fortress of the grim, gray spiders of the woods. These stumps do not find their way to the wood-pile, and are too scattered to be gathered by cartloads. Hence the necessity of systematic chunk-hunting—a most delightful sport.

Many a curious adventure have I had, and, too, some
narrow escapes. Once, from the brow of a steep slope, I
attempted to dislodge a cedar stump. Long I tugged at
it and made slow but, as I thought, sure progress. Suddenly it gave way, and with a mixed but otherwise inde-
scribable sensation I rolled with it to the ditch below.
The stump won the race, and I collected my senses while
sitting upon it. Bruised as I was, I shouldered it, and
that night nursed myself by the genial warmth it gave,
as the substantial back-log of my open fire. Next to the
gathering of a night's supply of wood when in camp, for
solid satisfaction, is chunk-hunting; and I have no patience with a heartless critic at my elbow who suggests
that the pastime illustrates a peculiar phase of human
nature. "If," she says, "the chunk-hunter is asked to
carry twenty pounds to a neighbor's house, he is helpless
at once; but forty pounds have been carried twice as far,
and no hint of fatigue escaped the hunter as he marched
in triumph to the fire-place." It is prudent not to reply.

It was on the eve of a storm when I gathered the
chunk now upon the andirons—a half of a persimmon
stump. It is garnished with windfalls from the oaks and
beeches, and all goes well. This bit of a persimmon tree
has a history, too; as I dragged it from the mat of leaves
and sand that had been accumulating for several years, I
unearthed a colony of mole-crickets. Perhaps the association was accidental, but there were certainly a hundred of
them, huddled in a little space. They did not stridulate
when disturbed, and scarcely squirmed, but all appeared
to be alive. These are among the creatures, I have
learned, that fill the air at night with an unceasing dis-
syllabic thrill, from early in August until after frost. I
find them credited with singing in spring and early summer, a statement that does not hold good of the species

found to-day. The last song of this cricket heard this year was October 18th, and my companion caught it in the act. There was not the same vim in its stridulation that marks a hot night in August, but it was unmistakably the same sound; and with it was heard a full chorus of croaking green frogs, for these, unlike their spotted cousins, croak even during the winter months.

It was on the eve of a storm when I gathered the wood; it was raining when I settled by my fire. The crickets that I had thoughtlessly left exposed, perhaps to die, disturbed my thoughts. I hoped their sluggish senses might so far revive that they could burrow out of harm's way. Then, for a time a burrowing cricket myself, I wandered among the roots of the hill-side trees; wandered until long past midnight, a victim of my own cruelty; and then, in very truth, found myself, a chilled mortal, with cold ashes, face to face.

The lotus and the lily are no more. Through the clear ice upon the meadow pools I can see but shriveled ghosts of noble plants that bore, the summer through, the queenliest of flowers. The royal lotus, once the pride of Egypt, tall, stately, and commanding; the modest lily, unassuming, but sure to receive its full share of recognition. Now, at Christmas-tide, these flowers are but vivid memories at the best, and the wide wild meadows, save where streakily shaded by the leafless trees, are evenly coated with dreary, death-like brown, nature's funereal tint.

It is not strange that the crackle of dead grass and rustling of decaying leaves should jar upon the rambler's ears; they are sounds that would drive him houseward, were it not that from afar come the welcome cawing of the crow, the cracked-flute calling of the prowling jay, the twitter of tree-sparrows, and fife-like exultation of the crested tit. These are sounds to revive the depressed and breathe a new soul into his declining faith. So it was, at least, when I last turned meadowward, bent upon a ramble, caring not where nor how long, merely hopeful of finding some green spot.

It is true the cedars and the pine trees are green, and, where the hill-foot springs are bubbling, ferns still hold their freshness, but it is a weariness to the flesh to sit all day in a tree-top, even when, by so doing, you keep company with the birds; and then one can not enter the little territory of a single spring. While he gathers summer in his arms, Jack Frost is tugging at his heels. Between green growths and the snow-bank you can not lay your cane without encroaching upon both. Is there no greater green-clad spot than a hill-foot spring?

The birds' songs cease, as I pass from the hill-side, on my quest for color, but ears and eyes must be separately humored in midwinter, and I turn to the glowing winterberry and climbing bittersweet with pleasure, where they make an almost vain effort to restore the summer freshness of vine-tangled fences, and then pass on to an uncertain glow of green in the heart of a smilax wilderness; but attempting to pass through it proves the verdancy to be more a feature of yourself than of it.

The thin vaulted ice roofs that protect the ditches' banks shut in long strips of green that need a sharp eye to detect; and here crouch hardy spotted frogs, patiently waiting for spring or the January thaw, and never so stiffened with cold but that they can leap into the depths when my shadow warns them. They sprawl into the gray mud that a moment before was but the smooth floor for the liquid crystal that sparkled above it—now the current is a troubled flow of smoky quartz. There is ever a bit of summer lingering by the brook-side, but ever too small a bit to satisfy.

But afar, beyond my neighbor's pasture and over Pœtquissings Creek, I see a film of smoke that hovers in the still air above a treacherous meadow. The tract is as level as a table-top, rankly sodded as a well-tended lawn, but lacks firmness below. William Penn might have written his "Sandy foundations, shaken," while walking there; but he never came, I know, although his manor-house and brewery are almost within sight.

What the "smoke" might be I conjectured as I bent my steps that way; and at last my hoped-for green Christmas was veritably before me. Brown trees, brown moss, brown hedges, and brown grass; even the ice was dusty; the country everywhere was dripping with dreariness but at this one spot. The supposed smoke was really mist, mellowed by the sunlight, and beneath it was a rank, tropically rank green forest, which for birds and butterflies harbored fish, frogs, and salamanders.

As a small picture usually looks well within a walnut frame, so the deep brown of the frost-bitten world proved a suitable surrounding here; and the picture was covered, that no rude wind should mar it, with water, now so smooth and clear, except where the upward current reached the surface, that no image was distorted, or any object, however small, obscured.

As a tired, homeless wanderer in a city seeks to find rest and warmth by peering into the windows of some Crœsus's house, so I forgot that it was winter where I stood, seeing only the perpetual summer of my neighbor's great meadow spring. To merely witness the life and beauty there made me forget that I had long since lost hold of my own youthful vigor, and must soon return to a dreary world, perhaps both cold and hungry. For a time these weaknesses were likewise forgotten; and this, I take it, is next akin to annihilating them. Before me was as near the fabled youth-renewing spring as I have hopes of finding, and it is a discovery I would be well pleased to make.

He who regrets not his lost youth may make an excellent angel, but has proved his manhood to have been defective.

And now let us consider the main features of this noble spring. It is never frozen. The vast volume of water, rushing upward from a silvery sand-pit, twenty feet below the meadow's surface, varies but a degree or two the year round. With this great depth is proportionate width, and a pond fifty feet in diameter is not insignificant in these monotonous meadows; while as a spring it is worthy of notice, even where nature is on a grander scale than here.

But why call it green? Colorless water and white sand; let the sunlight play what tricks it my, it will never make them green. True, but with them grow, in rank profusion, beautiful water starwort, a water spearwort, and that dainty aquatic growth, Nitella; and of late, a splendid water moss that threatens to crowd out the other growths; while hard by the common water-weed covers the bottom of the spring's overflow, making a beautiful background for the brighter and lighter colored starwort. Do you wonder why I call it green at this time and place? That is, surely, the predominating color.

And that such favored nooks are beloved of water animals is not strange. With what a stony glare the pike looks up at me, as I stand by, motionless; but trusts nothing if I move my arms. Then he is afar off on the other side, as I see by the quivering of the rank water weeds that would puzzle any other creature to penetrate. As he goes, the dainty newts peep from their leafy quarters, stretch themselves in the open water, and are gone; while ever and anon the brilliant leopard-frog rises up to the surface, sniffs at the outer air, and seeks repose again in the sandy depths.

There is no moment of the year when this spring

basin is more full of vigorous, active life than now, when it has greener growths, or creatures more alive to their own little world; yet we are wont to think of winter as a dead season; or, if not dead, sleeping.

And I recall now a holiday visit years ago, when the snow covered all the ground, and a biting north wind screamed through the naked branches of the oaks near by. It was the same spring then. Long I lingered by its side, forgetful of all else, and, as the day closed, suddenly a flood of sunlight swept over the meadows. The windows of my neighbor's house were all aflame. Color, color everywhere, as I glanced for the last time into the crystalline depths before me, over the wide meadows about me, over the cloud-flecked horizon beyond the distant hills. A melting rainbow showered the whole world; but for me, it was then, and ever will be, here, a green Christmas.

INDEX.

THE END.

EXPERIMENTAL SCIENCE SERIES.

LIGHT. A Series of Simple, Entertaining, and Interesting Experiments in the Phenomena of Light, for Students of every Age. By ALFRED MARSHALL MAYER, Professor of Physics in the Stevens Institute of Technology, etc., and CHARLES BARNARD. Illustrated. 12mo, cloth. $1.00.

"Professor Mayer has invented a series of experiments in Light which are described by Mr. Barnard. Nothing is more necessary for sound teaching than experiments made by the pupil, and this book, by considering the difficulty of costly apparatus, has rendered an important service to teacher and student alike. It deals with the sources of light, reflection, refraction, and decomposition of light. The experiments are extremely simple and well suited to young people." — *Westminster Review.*

"A singularly excellent little hand-book for the use of teachers, parents, and children. The book is admirable both in design and execution. The experiments for which it provides are so simple that an intelligent boy or girl can easily make them, and so beautiful and interesting that even the youngest children must enjoy the exhibition. The experiments here described are abundantly worth all that they cost in money and time in any family where there are boys and girls to be entertained." — *New York Evening Post.*

"The experiments are for the most part new, and have the merit of combining precision in the methods with extreme simplicity and elegance of design. The aim of the authors has been to make their readers 'experimenters, strict reasoners, and exact observers,' and for the attainment of this end the book is admirably adapted. Its value is further enhanced by the numerous carefully-drawn cuts, which add greatly to its beauty." — *The American Journal of Science and Art.*

SOUND. A Series of Simple, Entertaining, and Inexpensive Experiments in the Phenomena of Sound, for Students of every Age. By ALFRED MARSHALL MAYER. Illustrated. 12mo, cloth. $1.00.

"It would be difficult to find a better example of a series which is excellent throughout. This little work is accurate in detail, popular in style, and lucid in arrangement. Every statement is accompanied with ample illustrations. We can heartily recommend it, either as an introduction to the subject or as a satisfactory manual for those who have no time for perusing a larger work. It contains an excellent description, with diagrams, of Faber's Talking Machine and of Edison's Talking Phonograph, which can not fail to be interesting to any reader who takes an interest in the marvelous progress of natural science." — *British Quarterly.*

"It would really be difficult to exaggerate the merit, in the sense of consummate adaptation to its modest end, of this little treatise on 'Sound.' It teaches the youthful student how to make experiments for himself, without the help of a trained operator, and at very little expense. These hand-books of Professor Mayer should be in the hands of every teacher of the young." — *New York Sun.*

"The present work is an admirably clear and interesting collection of experiments, described with just the right amount of abstract information and no more, and placed in progressive order." — *Boston Courier.*

ORIGINS OF THE ENGLISH PEOPLE AND OF THE ENGLISH LANGUAGE. COMPILED FROM THE BEST AND LATEST AUTHORITIES. By JEAN ROEMER, LL. D., Professor of the French Language and Literature and Vice-President of the College of the City of New York. With Chart and Lithographic Fac-similes of Anglo-Saxon and Early French Writings. 1 vol., 8vo, pages xxiii + 658, cloth. Price, $3.50.

This work is essentially an introduction to the study of early English literature. Founded on the latest works of specialists, who have explored the many branches of the subject, it traces the sources of Modern English among the various races of men—Celts, Romans, Saxons, Danes, and Normans—who, at various epochs, have found their way into the British Isles; and, by inquiring into the origin and national characteristics of these races, their customs, wants, and forms of religion, their social and political differences, their relative progress in the arts of civilized life, it enables the student to draw his own conclusions as to the various influences tending to a corresponding fusion of their various idioms and dialects, resulting in the formation of that great and wonderful language which, from a mere jargon, as it was at first, has grown into the national speech of England.

THE INTERNATIONAL EDUCATION SERIES. Edited by W. T. HARRIS, LL. D.

THE PHILOSOPHY OF EDUCATION. By JOHANN KARL FRIEDRICH ROSENKRANZ. 12mo, cloth. Price, $1.50.

A HISTORY OF EDUCATION. By Professor F. V. N. PAINTER, of Roanoke College, Virginia. 12mo, cloth. Price, $1.50.

THE RISE AND EARLY CONSTITUTION OF UNIVERSITIES. With a Survey of Mediæval Education. By S. S. LAURIE, LL. D. 12mo, cloth. Price, $1.50.

THE VENTILATION AND WARMING OF SCHOOL BUILDINGS. By GILBERT B. MORRISON. 12mo, cloth. Price, 75 cents.

ELEMENTARY PSYCHOLOGY AND EDUCATION. By Dr. J. BALDWIN. 12mo, cloth. Price, $1.50.

THE EDUCATION OF MAN. By FRIEDRICH FROEBEL. Translated from the German and Annotated by W. N. HAILMANN, A. M., Superintendent of Public Schools at La Porte, Indiana. 12mo, cloth. Price, $1.50.

(Other volumes to follow.)

THE COLLEGE AND THE CHURCH: THE "HOW I WAS EDUCATED" PAPERS, AND THE DENOMINATIONAL "CONFESSIONS," from "The Forum Magazine." Crown 8vo, cloth, gilt top. Price, $1.50.

The two series of articles, "How I was Educated" and "Confessions," attracted great attention as they appeared in "The Forum," and are now published in one volume in obedience to numerous requests. The "Confessions" are printed anonymously, but the "How I was Educated" papers are signed, the authors being some of the most distinguished of American scholars.

New York: D. APPLETON & CO., 1, 3, & 5 Bond Street.

New York: D. APPLETON & CO., 1, 3, & 5 Bond Street.

THE HUMAN SPECIES. By A. De Quatrefages, Professor of Anthropology in the Museum of Natural History, Paris. 12mo. Cloth, $2.00.

The work treats of the unity, origin, antiquity, and original localization of the human species, peopling of the globe, acclimatization, primitive man, formation of the human races, fossil human races, present human races, and the physical and psychological characters of mankind.

STUDENT'S TEXT-BOOK OF COLOR; or, MODERN CHROMATICS. With Applications to Art and Industry. With 130 Original Illustrations, and Frontispiece in Colors. By Ogden N. Rood, Professor of Physics in Columbia College. 12mo. Cloth. $2.00.

"In this interesting book Professor Rood, who as a distinguished Professor of Physics in Columbia College, United States, must be accepted as a competent authority on the branch of science of which he treats, deals briefly and succinctly with what may be termed the scientific *rationale* of his subject. But the chief value of his work is to be attributed to the fact that he is himself an accomplished artist as well as an authoritative expounder of science."—*Edinburgh Review, October*, 1879, *in an article on "The Philosophy of Color."*

EDUCATION AS A SCIENCE. By Alexander Bain, LL. D. 12mo. Cloth, $1.75.

"This work must be pronounced the most remarkable discussion of educational problems which has been published in our day. We do not hesitate to bespeak for it the widest circulation and the most earnest attention. It should be in the hands of every school-teacher and friend of education throughout the land."—*New York Sun.*

A HISTORY OF THE GROWTH OF THE STEAM-ENGINE. By Robert H. Thurston, A. M., C. E., Professor of Mechanical Engineering in the Stevens Institute of Technology, Hoboken, N. J., etc. With 163 Illustrations, including 15 Portraits. 12mo. Cloth, $2.50.

"Professor Thurston almost exhausts his subject; details of mechanism are followed by interesting biographies of the more important inventors. If, as is contended, the steam-engine is the most important physical agent in civilizing the world, its history is a desideratum, and the readers of the present work will agree that it could have a no more amusing and intelligent historian than our author."—*Boston Gazette.*

STUDIES IN SPECTRUM ANALYSIS. By J. Norman Lockyer, F. R. S., Correspondent of the Institute of France, etc. With 60 Illustrations. 12mo. Cloth, $2.50.

"The study of spectrum analysis is one fraught with a peculiar fascination, and some of the author's experiments are exceedingly picturesque in their results. They are so lucidly described, too, that the reader keeps on, from page to page, never flagging in interest in the matter before him, nor putting down the book until the last page is reached."—*New York Evening Express.*

New York: D. APPLETON & CO., 1, 3, & 5 Bond Street.

ORIGIN OF CULTIVATED PLANTS. By Alphonse de Candolle. 12mo. Cloth, $2.00.

"The copious and learned work of Alphonse de Candolle on the 'Origin of Cultivated Plants' appears in a translation as volume forty-eight of 'The International Scientific Series.' Any extended review of this book would be out of place here, for it is crammed with interesting and curious facts. At the beginning of the century the origin of most of our cultivated species was unknown. It now requires more than four hundred closely printed pages to sum up what is known or conjectured of this matter. Among his conclusions M. de Candolle makes this interesting statement: 'In the history of cultivated plants I have noticed no trace of communication between the peoples of the Old and New Worlds before the discovery of America by Columbus.' Not only is this book readable, but it is of great value for reference."—*New York Herald*.

"Not another man in the world could have written the book, and considering both its intrinsic merits and the eminence of its author, it must long remain the foremost authority in this curious branch of science. Of the 247 plants here enumerated, 199 are from the Old World, 45 are American, and 3 unknown. Of these only 67 are of modern cultivation. Curiously, however, the United States, notwithstanding its extent and fertility, makes only the pitiful showing of gourds and the Jerusalem artichoke."—*Boston Literary World*.

FALLACIES: A View of Logic from the Practical Side. By Alfred Sidgwick, B. A. Oxon. 12mo. Cloth, $1.75.

"Even among educated men logic is apt to be regarded as a dry study, and to be neglected in favor of rhetoric; it is easier to deal with tropes, metaphors, and words, than with ideas and arguments—to talk than to reason. Logic is a study; it requires time and attention, but it can be made interesting, even to general readers, as this work by Mr. Sidgwick upon that part of it included in the name of 'Fallacies' shows. Logic is a science, and in this volume we are taught the practical side of it. The author discusses the meaning and aims, the subject-matter and process of proof, unreal assertions, the burden of proof, *non-sequiturs*, guess-work, argument by example and sign, the *reductio ad absurdum*, and other branches of his subject ably and fully, and has given us a work of real value. It is furnished with a valuable appendix, and a good index, and we should be glad to see it in the hands of thinking men who wish to understand how to reason out the truth, or to detect the fallacy of an argument."—*The Churchman*.

THE ORGANS OF SPEECH, and their Application in the Formation of Articulate Sounds. By Georg Hermann von Meyer, Professor of Anatomy at the University of Zürich. With numerous Illustrations. 12mo. Cloth, $1.75.

"This volume comprises the author's researches in the anatomy of the vocal organs, with special reference to the point of view and needs of the philologist and the trainer of the voice. It seeks to explain the origin of articulate sounds, and to outline a system in which all elements of all languages may be co-ordinated in their proper place. The work has obviously a special value for students in the science of the transmutations of language, for etymologists, elocutionists, and musicians."—*New York Home Journal*.

"The author's plan has been to give a sketch of all possible articulate sounds, and to trace upon that basis their relations and capacity for combination."—*Philadelphia North American*.

New York: D. APPLETON & CO., 1, 3, & 5 Bond Street.

DARWINISM STATED BY DARWIN HIMSELF: Characteristic Passages from the Writings of Charles Darwin. Selected and arranged by Professor NATHAN SHEPPARD. 12mo, cloth, 360 pages, $1.50.

"A compact and clear statement of the doctrines collectively known as Darwinism. By consulting this single volume it is now possible to know exactly what Darwin taught without sifting the contents of a dozen books. Mr. Nathan Sheppard has edited the work with good judgment."—*New York Journal of Commerce.*

"Mr. Sheppard must be credited with exemplifying the spirit of impartial truth-seeking which inspired Darwin himself. From these condensed results of the hard labor of selection, excision, and arrangement applied to more than a dozen volumes, it is impossible to draw any inference respecting the philosophical opinions of the compiler. With the exception of a brief preface there is not a word of comment, nor is there the faintest indication of an attempt to infuse into Darwin's text a meaning not patent there, by unwarranted sub-titles or headlines, by shrewd omission, unfair emphasis, or artful collocation. Mr. Sheppard has nowhere swerved from his purpose of showing in a clear, connected, and very compendious form, not what Darwin may have meant or has been charged with meaning, but what he actually said."—*The Sun.*

MENTAL EVOLUTION IN ANIMALS. By GEORGE J. ROMANES, author of "Animal Intelligence." With a Posthumous Essay on Instinct, by CHARLES DARWIN. 12mo, cloth, $2.00.

"Mr. Romanes has followed up his careful enumeration of the facts of 'Animal Intelligence,' contributed to the 'International Scientific Series,' with a work dealing with the successive stages at which the various mental phenomena appear in the scale of life. The present installment displays the same evidence of industry in collecting facts and caution in co-ordinating them by theory as the former."—*The Athenæum.*

"The author confines himself to the psychology of the subject. Not only are his own views Darwinian, but he has incorporated in his work considerable citations from Darwin's unpublished manuscripts, and he has appended a posthumous essay on Instinct by Mr. Darwin."—*Boston Journal.*

"A curious but richly suggestive volume."—*New York Herald.*

PRACTICAL ESSAYS. By ALEXANDER BAIN, LL. D., author of "Mind and Body," "Education as a Science," etc. 12mo, cloth, $1.50.

"The present volume is in part a reprint of articles contributed to reviews. The principal bond of union among them is their practical character. . . . That there is a certain amount of novelty in the various suggestions here embodied, will be admitted on the most cursory perusal."—*From the Preface.*

THE ESSENTIALS OF ANATOMY, PHYSIOLOGY, AND HYGIENE. By ROGER S. TRACY, M. D., Health Inspector of the New York Board of Health; author of "Hand-Book of Sanitary Information for Householders," etc. (Forming a volume of Appletons' Science Text-Books.) 12mo, cloth, $1.25.

"Dr. Tracy states in his preface that his aim has been 'to compress within the narrowest space such a clear and intelligible account of the structures, activities, and care of the human system as is essential for the purposes of general education.' And he has so far succeeded as to make his manual one of the most popularly interesting and useful text-books of its kind. . . . The book is excellently arranged, the illustrations are admirable."—*Boston Daily Advertiser.*

THE GEOLOGICAL HISTORY OF PLANTS. By Sir J.
WILLIAM DAWSON, F. R. S. Vol. 61 of The International Scientific
Series. With Illustrations. 12mo. Cloth, $1.75.

"The object of this work is to give, in a connected form, a summary of the
development of the vegetable kingdom in geological time. To the geologist and
botanist the subject is one of importance with reference to their special pursuits,
and one on which it has not been easy to find any convenient manual of information."—*From the Preface.*

**THE GEOGRAPHICAL AND GEOLOGICAL DISTRIBU-
TION OF ANIMALS.** By ANGELO HEILPRIN, Professor of Invertebrate Paleontology at the Academy of Natural Sciences, Philadelphia, etc. Vol. 57 of The International Scientific Series. One
vol., 12mo, 435 pages, $2.00.

"In the preparation of the following pages the author has had two objects in
view: that of presenting to his readers such of the more significant facts connected with the past and present distribution of animal life as might lead to a
proper conception of the relations of existing faunas ; and, secondly, that of
furnishing to the student a work of general reference, wherein the more salient
features of the geography and geology of animal forms could be sought after
and readily found."—*From the Preface.*

ANIMAL MAGNETISM. From the French of ALFRED BINET and
CHARLES FÉRÉ. Vol. 59 of The International Scientific Series. 12mo.
Cloth, $1.50.

"The authors, after giving a brief, clear, and instructive history of animal
magnetism from its remotest known origin down through Mesmer and the Aca-
demic period to the present day, record their personal investigations among the
hysterical, nervous, and generally supersensitive female patients in the great
Paris hospital, La Salpêtrière, of which M. Féré is the assistant physician."—
Journal of Commerce.

**WEATHER: A POPULAR EXPOSITION OF THE NATURE OF
WEATHER CHANGES FROM DAY TO DAY.** By the Hon. RALPH
ABERCROMBY, Fellow of the Royal Meteorological Society, London.
Vol. 58 of The International Scientific Series. 12mo. Cloth, $1.75.

"Mr. Abercromby has for some years made the weather of Great Britain a
special study, and has recently extended his experience by making a meteorological tour around the world. As a fruit of this preparation, he gives us a book that
is to be commended for its simple, deliberate style, freedom from technicality and
unnecessary theorizing, rational description, classification, and explanation of
atmospheric phenomena, and rich store of illustration from the weather-maps of
many parts of the world."—*The Nation.*

New York: D. APPLETON & CO., 1, 3, & 5 Bond Street.

DISCUSSIONS ON CLIMATE AND COSMOLOGY. By JAMES CROLL, LL. D., F. R. S. With Chart. 12mo. Cloth, $2.00.

CONTENTS: Misapprehensions regarding the Physical Theory of Secular Changes of Climate.—The Ice of Greenland and the Antarctic Continent not due to Elevation of the Land.—Mr. Alfred R. Wallace's Modification of the Physical Theory of Secular Changes of Climate.—The Physical Cause of Mild Polar Climates.—Interglacial Periods and Distribution of Flora and Fauna in Arctic Regions.—Temperature of Space and its Bearing on Terrestrial Physics.—Probable Origin and Age of the Sun's Heat, etc., etc.

CLIMATE AND TIME IN THEIR GEOLOGICAL RE-LATIONS: A THEORY OF SECULAR CHANGES OF THE EARTH'S CLIMATE. By JAMES CROLL, of H. M. Geological Survey of Scotland. With Maps and Illustrations. 12mo. Cloth, $2.50.

"I have studiously avoided introducing anything of a hypothetical character. All the conclusions are based on known facts or admitted physical principles. In short, the aim of the work is to prove that secular changes of climate follow, as a necessary effect, from admitted physical agencies, and that these changes, in as far as the past climatic condition of the globe is concerned, fully meet the demand of the geologist."—*From the Preface.*

OTHER WORLDS THAN OURS: THE PLURALITY OF WORLDS, STUDIED UNDER THE LIGHT OF RECENT SCIENTIFIC RESEARCHES. By RICHARD ANTHONY PROCTOR. With Illustrations, some colored. 12mo. Cloth, $2.50.

LIGHT SCIENCE FOR LEISURE HOURS. A Series of Familiar Essays on Scientific Subjects, Natural Phenomena, etc. By RICHARD ANTHONY PROCTOR. 12mo. Cloth, $1.75.

THE MOON: HER MOTIONS, ASPECT, SCENERY, AND PHYSICAL CONDITIONS. With Three Lunar Photographs, and many Plates, Charts, etc. By RICHARD ANTHONY PROCTOR. 8vo. Cloth, $3.50.

THE EXPANSE OF HEAVEN. A Series of Essays on the Wonders of the Firmament. By RICHARD ANTHONY PROCTOR. 12mo. Cloth, $2.00.

OUR PLACE AMONG INFINITIES. A Series of Essays contrasting our Little Abode in Space and Time with the Infinities around us. To which are added Essays on the Jewish Sabbath and Astrology. By RICHARD ANTHONY PROCTOR. 12mo. Cloth, $1.75.

CPSIA information can be obtained
at www.ICGtesting.com
Printed in the USA
BVOW06*1805051217
502002BV00009B/72/P

9 781297 893155